Work, leisure and well-being

John T. Haworth

with guest chapters by Seppo E. Iso-Ahola, John R. Kelly, Stanley Parker, Ken Roberts and Robert A. Stebbins

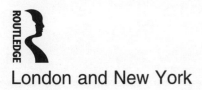
London and New York

First published 1997
by Routledge
11 New Fetter Lane, London EC4P 4EE

Simultaneously published in the USA and Canada
by Routledge
29 West 35th Street, New York, NY 10001

© 1997 John T. Haworth; guest chapters © the contributors

Typeset in Times by LaserScript, Mitcham, Surrey
Printed and bound in Great Britain by
Redwood Books, Trowbridge, Wiltshire

British Library Cataloguing in Publication Data
A catalogue record for this book is available from the British Library

Library of Congress Cataloging in Publication Data
A catalogue record for this book has been requested

ISBN 0–415–01703–3 (hbk)
ISBN 0–415–14862–6 (pbk)

Work, leisure and well-being

The fascinating, changing and important concern with work, leisure and life
is increasingly an issue for the twenty-first century. Interest in the area stems
both from a traditional concern with how society is structured and functions, and
from a concern with quality of life and for the type of society we wish to
become. The experience of work is changing and is more and more uncertain,
and a critical appraisal of factors underpinning work, leisure and well-being is
vital if we are to avoid the threat of social polarization.

Work, Leisure and Well-being reviews the current literature and presents the
findings of the latest research to provide a serious and interesting study of the
most important areas of adult life. It also includes several guest chapters by
world-renowned scholars who consider areas such as the future possibilities for
work and leisure; work and leisure in young people's lives; activity in retirement;
the importance of leisure for health; and the characteristics, costs and rewards of
serious leisure.

Work, Leisure and Well-being will be of interest to students of psychology,
sociology, social anthropology, social policy and leisure studies. It is also
important reading for policy-makers and professionals in the leisure industry and
for everyone concerned about current society and its future.

John T. Haworth is a Lecturer in Psychology at Manchester University and a
founder member of the Leisure Studies Association. His previous books are
Work and Leisure (1975), *Community Involvement and Leisure* (1979) and
Psychological Research (1996). He has also published extensively in academic
journals.

Contents

Illustrations

Contributors

John T. Haworth is Lecturer in Psychology at the University of Manchester. He has a BSc from St Andrews University, an MLitt in visual arts from Lancaster University and a PhD in psychology from Manchester University. His research interests include mental health, work and leisure, the psychology of creativity and the embodied mind. He has published extensively in international journals and presented papers at conferences worldwide. He has edited three books: *Work and Leisure: An Interdisciplinary Perspective* (1975); *Community Involvement and Leisure* (1979); and *Psychological Research: Innovative Methods and Strategies* (1996). He was co-founder of the Leisure Studies Association; founder editor of the international journal *Leisure Studies* and has been associate editor of *Leisure Research*. He has been a member of several government agency research commissions on leisure; has served as Visiting Professor at the World Leisure and Recreation Association International Centre of Excellence, CHN, Holland; and has been the Fulbright Scholar at the University of Michigan, USA.

Seppo E. Iso-Ahola, PhD, Professor of Social Psychology at the College of Health and Human Performance, University of Maryland, is the author of four books and over seventy research articles in scientific journals and chapters in edited books. He served as an editor of the *Journal of Leisure Research* (1983–6) and received the Charles Brightbill Award (1987), the Allan V. Sapora Research Award (1993) from the University of Illinois and the prestigious Theodore and Franklin Roosevelt Award for Excellence in Recreation and Park Research (1987). He has served as Distinguished Visiting Professor in various universities in Australia, Canada and Holland.

John R. Kelly is Professor Emeritus of Leisure Studies, Human Development and Aging Studies at the University of Illinois in Urbana-Champaign, USA. He has published nine books and over 100 chapters and articles on the sociology of leisure, the life course and gerontology. His focus has been on the relationships of work, family/community and leisure from an interpretive perspective.

Stanley Parker, PhD, is a sociologist who has researched and lectured on work, leisure and retirement in Europe, North America and Australia. A founder member of the Leisure Studies Association, and first managing editor of the journal *Leisure Studies*, he has authored several books, numerous journal articles and conference papers.

Ken Roberts is Professor of Sociology at the University of Liverpool. He has a worldwide reputation for his research into young people and leisure. From 1991 to 1996 he chaired the World Leisure and Recreation Association's Research Commission. He is the author or co-author of *Youth and Leisure* (1983), *Leisure and Lifestyle* (1989) and *Careers and Identities* (1992). At present he is directing research into the impact on the lives of young people of the changes that are occurring in seven former communist countries.

Robert A. Stebbins received his PhD in 1964 from the University of Minnesota. He is Professor of Sociology at the University of Calgary and was formerly Head of Department. He served as President of the Social Science Federation of Canada in 1991–2, after having served as President of the Canadian Sociology and Anthropology Association in 1988–9. His research interests include humour, work, leisure, the work and leisure dimensions of deviance and the leisure basis of francophone communities outside Quebec. He has published numerous journal articles and book chapters as well as twenty books. Most of his work in leisure studies has centred on 'serious leisure' (a term he coined in 1982), as expressed in research dating from 1973 on amateurs, hobbyists and career volunteers. Work in these areas completed before 1992 is summarized and theoretically elaborated in *Amateurs, Professionals and Serious Leisure* (1992). He is presently writing an adult education guide to serious leisure entitled *After Work: The Search for an Optimal Leisure Lifestyle*. Professor Stebbins is also a member of the Academy of Leisure Sciences.

Preface

A critical appraisal of factors underpinning experience, understanding and well-being is vital if we are to avoid the threat of social polarisation and instead utilise potential opportunities. The book includes several guest chapters by world-renowned scholars. Stanley Parker examines the work–leisure relationship and discusses future possibilities for work and leisure. Ken Roberts and Jack Kelly examine crucial life transitions. Roberts discusses work and leisure in young people's lives. Kelly examines activity in retirement. Seppo Iso-Ahola discusses the importance of leisure for health, and Robert Stebbins examines the characteristics, costs and rewards of serious leisure. The introduction to the book summarises these contributions and the main thrust of the chapters by the author, which emphasise the social and temporal nature of human endeavour and the importance of enjoyment for sustaining individual well-being and valued social practices. Other chapters by the author examine studies of factors influencing well-being in work and leisure, and review a model of mental health central to research in this area.

Chapter 1

Introduction

WORK AND LEISURE

In modern times there has been a considerable interest in work and leisure and the changing relationship between them. This stems in part from a concern with how society is structured and functions, and with the implications of change for policy. It also stems from a concern with quality of life and well-being, and for the type of society we may wish to become. We all have an interest in work and leisure, but our experience in these areas is complex. If, for example, we were asked to say what constitutes work and leisure we would find it difficult to come up with satisfactory definitions. One person's work is another person's leisure.

The perceptions and meanings which individuals ascribe to a situation influence understanding and interpretation, and in turn help to shape the situations themselves. Social interactions are affected by background expectancies and shared meanings as well as by the nature of the situation. Yet, as noted in Haworth and Smith (1975, p. 2), and applicable today, 'perhaps it is because of the complexity, the difference of opinion, the difficulties of investigation, as well as the important ramifications for theory and policy and for the type of society we wish to aim for, that the subject is so fascinating, challenging and important'.

Classical theories

'Classical' sociological theories of the relationship between work and leisure include the hypothesis of Wilensky (1960) that work attitudes and practices can 'spill over' or generalize into leisure time and that alternatively an individual can 'compensate' in leisure for work practices. A further 'classical' theory proposed by Dubin (1956) considers that the two areas of life are 'segmentalized' and lived out independently, with a particular area of significant social experience constituting a 'central life interest'. A related debate addresses the extent of 'fusion' and 'polarity' in work and leisure (Reisman and Blomberg, 1957), examining the extent to which they are becoming similar to each other, and the degree to which individuals divide their lives into work and leisure (polarity) or see them as an integrated whole (fusion). To the extent that work and leisure have been seen as segmentalized, with leisure enhancing quality of life, and even compensating in part for unsatisfactory jobs, society has been viewed as becoming leisure centred.

Reviewing studies on work and leisure and the implications for policy, Parker (1972, 1976, 1983) concludes that we are not a leisure-centred society. He argues cogently for improving the quality of both work and leisure. In an analysis of empirical and theoretical studies of the relationship between work and leisure, Parker (1976) notes that advocates of the view that work and leisure are becoming fused or integrated, and those who see work and leisure as becoming polarized and lived out separately, should realize that their evidence concerns subcultural and occupational-cum-cultural levels rather than whole societal trends and that there is some truth in both positions. He also notes that the ideologies associated with work and leisure, such that we are becoming a leisure-centred society, have not always been consistent with the facts about how much 'free' time people have and how they spend it.

The conclusion reached by Parker emphasizing the diversity of experience, and supporting different relationships in work and leisure, is also stressed by the psychologist Kabonof (1980). In reviewing evidence of the theories of Wilensky on spillover and compensation and Dubin on segmentalism, he concludes that while each has received some empirical support none has received unequivocal support, and that much of the research is constrained by conceptual and methodological problems. He recommends that future research should study different work and leisure patterns and the processes underlying these patterns, rather than trying to identify universal trends or typologies. However, the specific insights afforded by the 'classical' sociological formulations into certain situations are recognized. In a study of professional, administrative, clerical and blue-collar workers, Kabonof (1982) found no differences in leisure satisfaction between the four groups, which he took to be in line with a segmentation hypothesis of work–leisure relations. His results also showed some evidence for spillover in that skill utilization in leisure was important for the groups where this was deemed to be important in work, and some evidence for compensation in that autonomy was important in leisure where it was deemed to be low in work, this being the case for blue-collar workers. Kabonof and O'Brien (1986), studying the relationship between stress at work and leisure attributes and activities, distinguish between different forms of compensation. Supplementary compensation is considered to be where stress and frustration produced by undemanding, routine jobs help to energize people's non-work behaviour and direct it towards leisure activities that supplement restricted opportunities for self-expression at work. Reactive compensation suggests that where stress is an outcome of overload or over-utilization, as is more likely in high-level jobs, there will be a tendency to prefer passive recuperative activities in reaction to excessive work demands. Their research found that for managers stress was associated with passive recuperative leisure (reactive compensation), but for professionals stress was associated with both recuperative and active-compensatory leisure. Among clerical and blue-collar workers there was no simple association between stress and leisure, possibly because different forms of relationships were occurring. Kabonof and O'Brien concluded that occupational differences in the sources and effects of stress, and differences in coping patterns, still need to be explained.

In contrast to the study of the effects of stress at work, Lane (1995) argues for the potential importance of quality of work for both quality of leisure and quality of life on the dimensions of subjective well-being and human development. He considers that the culture of work, in contrast to leisure, is purposive, constrained by cognitive standards, characterized by cooperative and goal-orientated relations, and that work is inclusive and achievement oriented. He cites research by Kohn and Schooler (1983) indicating that where work has substantive complexity there is an improvement in mental flexibility and self-esteem. Lane argues that challenging work spills over to promote challenging and rewarding leisure. However, he says that where leisure challenges are similar to work challenges, the choice between work and leisure is a matter of indifference.

The continuing search for trends

Tyrrell (1995) notes that research in the UK indicates that the available free time of full-time male workers declined by 4 per cent between 1985 and 1993, and that for females working full time the decline has been just over 10 per cent. In America Juliet Schor (1995) reports that the average American works the equivalent of an extra month each year compared to 1969. In turn, however, it is argued that the increase in work time for those in employment is at the expense of an increase in unemployment. Rifkin (1995) considers that we are in the early stages of a long-term shift from 'mass labour' to highly skilled 'elite labour' accompanied by increasing automation in the production and delivery of services. He claims that 'for the United States alone, this means that in the years ahead more than 90 million jobs in the labour force of 124 million are potentially vulnerable for replacement by machines'. He notes that 'Many economists and elected officials continue to hope that the service sector and white collar work will be able to absorb the millions of unemployed factory workers in search of a job', but adds 'Their hopes are likely to be dashed' (p. 17). Rifkin advocates a shift towards a 30-hour work week, and a 'social income' financed from a value-added tax on high-tech goods and services to pay unemployed people to train and work in the voluntary sector. This non-profit-making 'third sector' as he terms it, is, he believes, 'playing an increasingly important social role in nations around the world. People are creating new institutions at both the local and national levels to provide for needs that are not being met by either the market place or public sector' (p. 19).

The search for trends and influences in work and leisure has recognized that these are not necessarily global or definitive. Parker (1987) noted that there is much evidence to suggest that people in advanced industrial societies live under the tyranny of the clock and that in Linder's phrase, the 'harried leisure class' is growing. With little or no decrease in time needed for work and self-maintenance, and with an increase in the time needed to maintain goods, there is less time for leisure. The attitudes which seek to save time in work and non-work obligations are then seen to spill over into an attempt to save time in leisure, thus affecting the quality of leisure. Parker cites the claim made by Godbey (1975) that in the USA 'what has increased is "anti-leisure": activity which is undertaken compulsively, as a means to an end, from a perception of necessity, with a high degree of externally imposed constraints, with considerable anxiety, with a high degree of time consciousness and a minimum of personal autonomy'. Parker (1976, p. 36) commented, 'This is not, of course, a picture of life characteristic of the majority of the population in the United States today, far less in Britain. But it applies to a significant and growing minority, and the dynamic of industrial capitalism is such that it is likely to spread in the future'.

There are some indications that this is happening. The *Demos Quarterly* (Issue 5, 1995), devoted to 'The Time Squeeze', notes that right across society there is a sense of time being squeezed and points to the growing imbalance between overwork for some and zero work for others, increased time taken to get to work, to care for and transport children and even to shop. In an article on 'Well-being and time', in this issue of *Demos*, Mulgan and Wilkinson (1995) cite survey research in Britain which indicates that over 70 per cent of people working over 40 hours per week wanted to work less. They also claim that studies of time use show that most work and leisure is not used well, whether the goal is happiness or personal development. They argue for the importance of considering both the distribution and quality of time, and believe that the twenty-first century will be all about time and how to use it to achieve well-being.

In the same issue of *Demos*, Juliet Schor reports results of a nationwide Gallup poll in America in which one-third of respondents said they would choose the option of fewer hours for themselves and their spouse, even at the price of a 20 per cent reduction in household income. Schor notes, however, that expectations creep up with income and that much of our spending is habitual, making it difficult to break the work–spend–work cycle. Cross (1995) also points to the new arena of consumer spending – holidays – which serves expanding psychological aspirations.

In this volume, Seppo Iso-Ahola (Chapter 9) indicates that in societies where the puritan work ethic is glorified, as in the USA, this can result in leisure becoming a slave for work, to be used for recuperation from work, and that individuals glorifying work tend to devalue leisure and can find difficulties in reconciling work, family and leisure life. He argues that long hours of work and a work–spend–work mentality can result in the trivialization and opposition of leisure to work, which can promote escapism in leisure, leading to a passive lifestyle, boredom and poor physical and mental health.

Another important trend receiving increasing attention is the flexibilization of work. Pahl (1996, pp. 330–2), in discussing the challenges of unemployment in the mid-1990s, indicates that many people in employment are working in fear of becoming unemployed, and that the relationships between unemployment, flexibilization of employment and social cohesion have not been adequately explored. He points out that unemployment is no longer restricted to those at the bottom of the socio-economic hierarchy, and that 'the problems of unemployment, underemployment and downward mobility are affecting the managerial and professional middle-class, whose members are experiencing substantial anxiety and insecurity'. He argues that those with credentials and appropriate employment experiences may accumulate, through their succession of jobs, an appropriate mix of experiences that considerably enhances their employability. Thus

> the CV-rich can face redundancy with greater confidence because they have built up skills and competencies and have acquired a variety of economically relevant social contacts and access networks providing information and have established networks for effective performance. This accumulation of cultural and social capital can be added to accumulated financial capital held in domestic property, insurance and pension rights. Not everyone sees the loss of a job, as traditionally considered, as a great disadvantage.

However, Pahl considers that 'workers at the other end of the spectrum with no secure job history, no established skills and reputation, with limited contacts and no stores of accumulated social, cultural or financial capital are extremely unlikely to be able to turn their redundancy to positive account' (p. 333). He cites Harrison and Bluestone (1988), who show that in the United States a succession of low-end jobs of varying duration interspersed with periods of unemployment generates considerable insecurity and anxiety, and Warr (1987), who indicates a causal link between job insecurity and various physical and psychosomatic complaints. Pahl considers that the differential ability among employees to acquire financial and human capital may produce a new kind of social differentiation based on the ability to cope with flexibilization. However, Pahl also believes that there are indications that flexibilization of working time may reduce over-strong commitment to employment with its attendant damaging effects, and that the potential exists for a reorganization of employment in order to make people's main experience of the market place more enjoyable.

Future scenarios

In Chapter 12 Stanley Parker outlines four possible scenarios for the future of work and leisure: conservatism, reactionism, reformism and revolutionism. Conservatism views the future as more or less the same as today with a continuation or perhaps slowing down of recent technological and consumer trends. Reactionism is based on the perception of a past 'golden age' to which it is thought desirable to return. Reactionist approaches seek to restore in the future a past attitude to, and experience of, work which is threatened by modern and impersonal mass production methods, and a return to full employment. This view of leisure looks back to ancient Greece, seeing leisure as a state of being in which activity is performed for its own sake or as its own end. The reactionist view of the work–leisure relationship considers that we have lost the earlier integration of the two spheres and should seek to restore the seemingly harmonious condition of the past. Reformism presumes the continuation of some form of capitalist free-market or mixed-economy system and aims to improve work and leisure life. This is the area in which most proposals for change fall, and Parker discusses several of these. Revolutionism is considered as any change in work, leisure or the relationship between the two that is post-capitalist. Parker notes that the meaning and experience of work have undergone revolutionary change in the past, and that they will no doubt do so again in the future. In the short to medium term, he considers that we need to insist that leisure is not the means to any work end, but that work and leisure interpenetrate one another; and that work, and the work–leisure relationship, should be at the centre of our concerns.

UNEMPLOYMENT, LEISURE AND LIFE TRANSITIONS

Unemployment and well-being

There are now comprehensive reviews of the effects of unemployment on well-being (e.g. Fryer and Payne, 1986; Warr, 1987; Dooley and Catalano, 1988; Warr et al., 1988; Fryer, 1992). Warr (1987, p. 207) concludes that 'Extensive research into the effects of unemployment indicates that it impairs mental health, even though the effect is not universal, and a small minority of people show gains in mental health after job loss'. This impairment can involve increased psychological distress, including anxiety and depression, lowered self-esteem, resigned apathy, helplessness and powerlessness, social isolation and disintegration. These disorders have been confirmed in many countries (Fryer, 1992).

A few people tolerate unemployment, preferring to have an in-and-out-of-work lifestyle rather than accept unsuitable jobs (Roberts et al., 1982); while a minority see it as a challenge and opportunity to develop their interests (Fryer and Payne, 1984). The wide variations among individuals in the mental health costs of unemployment are highlighted by Fryer (1995) while emphasizing that research has demonstrated beyond reasonable doubt that unemployment causes, rather than merely results from, poor psychological health. Fryer also perceptively indicates the wider ramifications of unemployment for increased mental health risks for the families of the unemployed, those on training schemes, those re-employed, those anticipating unemployment, or left in insecure employment, those trapped in psychologically stressful jobs and others who are subject to the ramifications of recession and labour-market disadvantage and economic insecurity.

Unemployment and leisure

In the 1970s in the UK the central government had come to regard leisure as a vital contributor to quality of life. With unemployment and urban dissent increasing in the early 1980s, improved leisure provision was advocated as part of a solution. The Sports Council of Great Britain launched a number of experimental schemes with the appointment of sports leaders who developed a varied activity programme at existing or new facilities, free of charge or at very low cost, and with equipment and transport provided. An important evaluation of these schemes, and a review of the role of leisure in unemployment, has been undertaken by Glyptis (1989, 1994). She notes that the schemes had their success among the unemployed both in stimulating new participation and recruiting back into sport a number of lapsed participants, but failed, for most, to *sustain* participation. She also reports that surveys of a large number of local authorities indicated that considerable attention was given to the needs of the unemployed, mainly through the provision of activities in leisure centres, but that most authorities reported little response by the unemployed. Most users appreciated the provision primarily for the social benefits and secondarily for their sports opportunities, although for a minority this provided a central life interest. Glyptis concludes that 'What people want, first and foremost are jobs. Even if financial inequalities are resolved, it seems unlikely that many people in our work oriented society would be eager to adopt leisure as a substitute for employment' (1989, p. 92); and that 'what leisure cannot provide, by its very nature, is a sense of compulsion and purpose beyond the pursuit of activity for its own sake. It cannot provide the central core of structure and purpose on which we have come to depend' (1989, p. 159).

Nevertheless, the provision of leisure opportunities for the unemployed, while not substituting for a job, is important. Glyptis (1994) notes that many unemployed people find sport a rewarding leisure activity to take part in occasionally and that the provision of opportunities is important, as is the removal of barriers to participation such as lack of income, transport and loss of self-esteem and purpose. Glyptis stresses the importance of providing a fuller choice of activities, far broader than sport, and the key role for good management and publicity, flexibility to adapt to varied and changing needs and a willingness to work with, rather than merely for, unemployed people.

Life transitions: young people

Many studies have shown that rates of unemployment are highest among young people and considerable concern has been expressed about the lifestyles of the unemployed. While leisure does not compensate for unemployment for adults in general, some young unemployed people have an active leisure lifestyle. The question has been raised as to whether this could constitute a leisure pattern for the future. But the answer appears to be no.

Kay (1989) studied a small number of unemployed young adults who were committed users of sports schemes. The study found that the high level of activity of respondents was not confined to participation in the sports scheme, but was evident in their lifestyle as a whole. Activities included studying at home or at college, voluntary work, and substantial involvement in clubs and societies. Most of these purposeful activities in which the respondents engaged had been taken up since they had become unemployed. They were not regarded as leisure by the respondents but were labelled as 'work' or 'work-like'. These work-like activities provided a contrast which was important to the enjoyment of those activities which were regarded as 'leisure', such as playing squash. Nearly all those interviewed, however, were protected from the main practical hardship of unemployment: a shortage of money. A number had deliberately chosen to become unemployed to escape an unsatisfying job. Others had initially become unemployed involuntary, but chose to remain so rather than return to forms of employment which they would dislike. None of the interviewees, though, envisaged themselves being permanently unemployed. Kay (1989, p. 425) notes that the 'committed user's high level of activity occurred within the context of a lifestyle which few unemployed people could emulate'.

Studies of young unemployed adults reported by Evans and Haworth (1991), Haworth and Evans (1987) and Haworth and Ducker (1991) are summarized and discussed in Chapter 10. These studies show that engagement in activity is associated with enhanced well-being, but that this is less than that for a matched sample of employed people. It is also noted that young people in this age group are still in a stage of transitional development and that while some unemployed people may engage in beneficial activity, the question of life goals is crucial, and that for most individuals these are provided by a job, marriage, children and life lived within conventional standards of morality.

In Chapter 10 Ken Roberts examines young people's changing experience of work and leisure and identifies typical problems that are likely to ensue. He notes that recent trends alert us to the hazards of trying to gaze even into the medium-term future, but that some features of modernity have retained their pivotal positions over the last hundred years, including the role of science and technology in economic change, paid occupations in governing individuals' social levels, and educational qualifications in distributing labour-market chances. Roberts points out that in Europe the vanishing youth labour market has been accompanied by an expansion of education and training for work, and that getting employment, and preparing for employment, remain extremely important for both males and females, but that there has been a devaluation of qualifications in terms of their labour-market returns. Many young people, he notes, remain in education simply because they feel they have no alternative. At the same time it is estimated in Britain that approximately one in seven 16- and 17-year-olds are 'status zero', meaning that they are not in education, training or employment. There has also been a sustained growth of part-time and other forms of precarious employment which generate only low levels of psychological commitment to a particular job, even though the individuals may have strong work values. The decline of youth employment has not left most young people with time on their hands. The opposite problem has become more common: coping with studies, paid employment, maintaining leisure interests and social relationships and still finding some time to be with families and to relax. It has also increased dependence on families for financial and social support.

These trends, Roberts considers, are leading to prolonged adolescence and an increase in individualization – an increase in individual experience and more variety within all social categories, while not necessarily diminishing the differences associated with social backgrounds and gender. Each individual nowadays tends to have an individualized network of relationships, and the youth population is linked through interlocking webs rather than clearly divided into groups, all with distinctive subcultures, between which there is little contact. Individuals may feel strong attachments to groups, but often only fleetingly. They may feel that their opportunities, achievements and problems are personal rather than shared by large numbers of peers. Individualization is also seen as coupled with increased uncertainty and risk, and that it is impossible for today's teenagers to know the types of adults they will become, and when transitions have ended. Young people's prospects have become less certain mainly because the links between their routes onwards from compulsory education to types of eventual adult employment, have weakened. Prolonged transitions, uncertain prospects and individualized predicaments are normal facts of life for young people in the 1990s, and can be simultaneously liberating and threatening.

Roberts sees the need for prolonged family support or an effective substitute. He recognizes that young people from less privileged backgrounds may be unable to accumulate the economic and cultural capital needed for jobs, and that this can result in polarization between those who feel that success is down to their own efforts and see little reason to share the benefits, and 'socially excluded groups' whose only strategy for maintaining self-respect set them apart, and keep them apart, from the remainder of the population. He considers that the chances are that, for the foreseeable future, individuals' occupations will continue to act as a major foundation for social identities. Leisure may help the transition to adulthood, but there will have to be enough decent jobs for everyone to complete their transitions to their own satisfaction.

Psychologists have also shown the importance of employment for developmental transitions and well-being in young people. Dooley and Prause (1995) review several longitudinal studies of the school-to-work transition, which show that young people with jobs are better off psychologically than those without jobs. In a large-scale longitudinal study of American young people they showed that the percentage of time unemployed since leaving school was negatively related to self-esteem. They conclude that their research agrees with several prior studies that unemployment blocks the normal progression to higher self-esteem in school leavers. They did not find a poor school-to-work transition to have affected young men more adversely than young women, and suggest this may indicate that work has become as important to women as to men in today's society.

Life transitions: retirement

The transition from employment to retirement is also a key area of study. In Chapter 11 John Kelly considers that unemployment and retirement now overlap in meaning. He points out that changing economic structures of production and markets are encouraging corporations to 'buy out' workers once considered in mid-careers or even forcing them out of the workforce, and that at the same time in the first three decades of the twenty-first century the number of those in traditional retirement age will nearly double. Glyptis (1989) documents a trend for the truncation of the working life in the UK through early retirement taking two forms: a decline in the proportion of people of pensionable age who carry on working, and a significant reduction in employment in men in the 60 to 64 age bracket. She also points to the longer time that people now spend in retirement due to increased life expectancy. She states that even after working until the statutory retirement age one can expect a decade or two of uncommitted time thereafter. Both Glyptis and Kelly consider that while many issues of retirement concern finance and health, others are social and psychological, concerning quality of life when traditional work roles have been left behind.

Kelly notes that for most people retirement is one more phase in the self-propelled journey of life in which they have had to cope with a series of transitions and traumas. Their values and routines reflect their histories despite some reorientations related to preparation for retirement. For those with enhanced financial and cultural capital, significant meaning may be found in a combination of family, work and leisure activities. For many with less resources their lives may be organized around the central commitment of family, where this is intact. Activity patterns can revolve around a core of relatively accessible and low-cost engagements. New routines are constructed around a core of companions and activities and take the place of the structuring of work schedules and work associates. Kelly also stresses the importance of differences between individuals: people are characterized by their diversity. Some individuals are so invested in their work that life loses meaning without it. Some have to reinvest in some activity that resembles work to cope with retirement; others focus on leisure and travel. There are also retirees who struggle to survive due to histories of irregular or low-income employment.

Kelly sees the basic requirements for satisfactory retirement as functional health and economic viability, coupled with social and leisure activity. While with increasing age there may be a constriction of activities, 'meaningful integration' of sharing and interaction remain central. Those most satisfied with their lives in later years are those who have maintained engagement with meaningful activities and associations with people. While participation in many kinds of recreational activities may diminish, this can obscure the relative stability in rates of participation in activities that are appropriate, possible and satisfying. For most older persons, Kelly notes, both the activity and relationships are an extension of histories that have been developed through the life course. Two critical elements in retirement are seen as challenge and social integration or community. The forms of activity that combine the two elements are almost infinite: the keys are that the engagement is regular, demanding and involves some kind of community. Kelly also notes that in the balance of a leisure style there needs to be relaxation and low-intensity engagements, but he argues that it is the highlights that produce extraordinary enjoyment in the routines of leisure.

The importance of personal history, or life trajectory, for adaptation to retirement has also been suggested in other studies. Grossin (1986), for example, indicates that an integrated employment/leisure lifestyle prior to retirement is important for successful adaptation to retirement. Long and Wimbush (1985) showed that respondents who participated in a large number of leisure activities in retirement tended to be those who had done so before retirement. The philosopher Merleau-Ponty (1962) considers that we live and create by personal style, a distinctive way of patterning the world, one which is not something developed consciously to depict the world, but instead has issued forth from perception, one's world being carried forth by lines of intentionality which trace out in advance at least the style of what is to come. He emphasizes the importance of lived experience and personal history in our understanding of the world. For people making the transition to retirement their experience of work and leisure will have a significant influence. And in part this will be influenced by the transition to adulthood and the opportunities available to experience satisfactory work and leisure.

WORK, LEISURE AND WELL-BEING

Leisure and health

The importance of leisure for well-being and health is reviewed by Seppo Iso-Ahola in Chapter 9. He points out that leisure, in distinction to free time, has to be discovered and that lack of information and attitudes are major constraints to experiencing leisure. He argues that seeking and escaping are the two fundamental dimensions of motivation for leisure, and that while participating in any leisure activity is motivated by these two forces, an important issue is which dimension dominates one's overall leisure involvement. A person's leisure can be mainly characterized by the seeking of interpersonal rewards or by escaping one's personal or interpersonal world. Iso-Ahola considers that evidence suggests that people who are predominantly 'seeking'-orientated in their leisure are healthier than those who are predominantly 'escapist' in their leisure.

Iso-Ahola cites evidence to indicate that participation in various forms of active leisure, including both physical and non-physical activities, is associated with increased psychological well-being, self-esteem and self-concept, social interaction, life satisfaction and happiness and with reduced depression; and that older adults may age more successfully from a cognitive standpoint if they have active leisure. An active leisure lifestyle is also viewed as beneficial to physical health, particularly if it includes physical exercise. Active leisure may enhance well-being and health directly by its influence on mood and the immune system. Active leisure may also act indirectly by buffering the deleterious effects of stress, whereas a passive leisure lifestyle may fail to do so. An active leisure lifestyle may buffer stress because it enables people to feel self-determined. Research has also indicated that leisure-related social support moderates the stress–illness relationship. Iso-Ahola concludes that the effect of leisure on health is mainly a psychological problem, and that leisure cannot protect or enhance health if people think leisure is not important or if they have little of it.

Serious leisure

Stebbins (1981, 1982, 1992) has studied participants committed to leisure activities such as astronomy, archaeology, music and singing. He introduced the term 'serious leisure' to denote the systematic pursuit of an amateur, hobbyist or volunteer activity which participants find so substantial and interesting that, in the typical case, they launch themselves on a 'career' centred on acquiring and expressing its special skills, knowledge and experience. He noted that people engaged in serious leisure are more obliged to engage in their pursuits than their unserious counterparts, while being less obligated than breadwinners to follow their occupation. In Chapter 8 Robert Stebbins presents an overview of several basic elements of serious leisure theory and research.

Serious leisure has six distinctive qualities: (1) the occasional need to persevere at it; (2) the development of the activity as in a career; (3) the requirement for effort based on specialized knowledge, training or skill; (4) the provision of durable benefits or rewards including personal enrichment, feelings of accomplishment, enhancement of self-image, social interaction and a sense of belonging; (5) the identification of the person with the activity; and (6) the production of an ethos and social world.

Social worlds may be local, regional, multi-regional, national and even international. Members may vary in degree of involvement. A rich subculture may be found there, and each social world can have a set of special norms, values, beliefs, styles, moral principals, performance standards and shared representations. These elements can help to explain social stratification in social worlds.

Serious leisure entails costs as well as rewards, including dislikes, tensions and disappointments. It can also require considerable effort in the development of skills and knowledge, and introduce conflicting demands between leisure, family and work. Stebbins emphasizes that, unlike family and work activities where institutional supports sustain involvement, such support for equivalent activities in leisure is absent, producing a marginal status for serious leisure. Notwithstanding this marginality, however, Stebbins indicates that serious leisure makes many significant contributions to the community in the generation of a great variety of social worlds: the pursuit of leisure as more than pure hedonism, communal and societal integration, and improvement of the general welfare of the community.

Stebbins concludes that serious leisure can foster enjoyment and hence well-being but that the relationship between serious leisure and well-being seems destined to be far more complicated than current levels of theory and research would suggest.

The importance of enjoyment

Enjoyment is considered to play a pivotal role in well-being. Chapter 6 examines the studies of enjoyment and the related concept of 'flow', where challenges met with equal skills are considered to give rise to optimal experience important for both well-being and psychological growth. Csikszentmihalyi (1975) and Csikszentmihalyi and Csikszentmihalyi (1988) report a series of pioneering studies conducted by themselves and colleagues into the experience of enjoyment and the structural contexts in which it occurs. Using self-reports by artists, athletes and creative professionals of when they were performing well, the main characteristics of enjoyable flow were identified as: intense involvement, clarity of goals and feedback, deep concentration, transcendence of self, lack of self-consciousness, loss of a sense of time, intrinsically rewarding experience, and a balance between skill and challenge. Other studies using diaries to record events in daily life show the importance of macro-flow, where challenge and skill are both high, for subjective well-being in the daily lives of college students and people at work. However, not all macro-flow has been found to be enjoyable, and low-challenge situations can provide positive subjective states, including enjoyment (Clarke and Haworth, 1994; Haworth and Evans, 1995).

Circumstances conducive to enjoyable flow experiences have been found to be diverse. Contrary to expectations, Csikszentmihalyi and Le Fevre (1989) found that the vast majority of flow experiences – measured as perceived balanced skill-challenge experiences above the person's average level – came when people were at work, rather than in 'free time'. However, they also found differences among individuals in their ability to obtain flow in similar situations. While this may be a result of personality factors, there is no evidence to suggest that these traits are innate and there is some evidence that the ability to enjoy flow experiences may be learned. Rathunde (1988) and Furnham and Steele (1993) suggest that positive life experiences can enhance internal locus of control dispositions, the expectation of control, which in turn can lead to more successful experiences and well-being.

Csikszentmihalyi (1988) argues that flow is not a luxury but is a staple of life, and that any activity can be adapted to improve life by making it more enjoyable and meaningful. The function of flow is to induce the organism to grow – in the sense of fulfilling the potentialities of the organism. To continue to experience the exhilaration of flow 'it is necessary to take on a slightly greater challenge and to develop slightly greater skills. So the complexity of adaptation increases, propelled forward by the enjoyment it provides' (p. 367). Csikszentmihalyi argues that both external and internal factors are necessary to improving quality of experience: 'without concrete challenges, a set of skills, a symbolic discipline, it is impossible to focus attention long enough on a limited stimulus field to begin experiencing flow. At the same time it is also true that no matter how many possibilities the environment offers, one cannot enter flow unless the challenges become personally meaningful, unless they are engaged by one's psychic energy' (p. 382).

The emphasis placed on the importance of flow for individual and social well-being has not gone unchallenged. Mullet (1988) claims that Csikszentmihalyi's notion of flow reduces the intrinsic value of things to the subject's experience of them, to intrinsic rewards. She proposes a notion of human flourishing which recognizes the importance of enjoyment but which goes beyond this to include the values of 'character' and 'excellence', the achievement of which, she claims, may sometimes involve sacrifice and may not be pleasurable. While she recognizes that an important aim of society would be to organize work, play and learning so as to facilitate the subjective experience of enjoyment or flow, she considers that 'there is, nevertheless, an even higher ideal that must be acknowledged and repeated in every possible context of discourse if we are to have an adequate understanding of ourselves. That is the idea of people engaged in practices, extending their powers to achieve human excellence by means of the cultivation of virtues' (p. 81).

The importance of the social dimension in life is acknowledged by Csikszentmihalyi (1991). While his thesis on flow emphasizes the importance of growth in individual complexity, he notes that complexity consists of integration as well as differentiation. In *The Evolving Self* (1993) he also notes that 'The development of unique individuality (is) no longer sufficient to give life a meaningful purpose . . . it is not just our personal advantage we must seek, or that of the causes we believe in now, it is the collective well-being of all life' (p. 252). Equally, he advocates that 'In order for the majority of people to take an active role in evolution, social institutions must also come to support flow and preserve order in mind' (p. 252).

Practice theory, work and quality of life

Practice theory

A paradigmatic change is now occurring in our conception of what it is to be a human being in the world, and how we come to act in innovatory and creative ways. This change, focusing on 'practice theory' has considerable implications for work and quality of life and is discussed in Chapter 7. The conceptions presented in practice theory indicate that perception is not consciousness of an existing factual situation, and learning is not simply a process in which the learner consciously internalizes a ready-formed body of objective knowledge; rather, knowledge and understanding are now viewed as tentative and generated through lived experience and histories of mutual involvement and social relationships, and can largely reside below the level of conscious awareness, but nevertheless significantly influence behaviour. In his *Phenomenology of Perception* (1962), Merleau-Ponty argues that perception can no longer be considered the constitution of the true object but as our *inherence* in things. Consciousness is in the first place not a matter of 'I think', but of 'I can'; and perception is a temporal synthesis which gradually clarifies itself and proceeds by dialogue with itself and others. Merleau-Ponty emphasizes the importance of lived experience and personal history in our understanding of the world. He stresses the importance of prereflexive thought in perception and consciousness. On this thesis we come to know things primarily by living; by engaging in activity however general, rather than primarily by reflection, though this is acknowledged as important. His thesis emphasizes the temporal dimensions of understanding, adaption and reaction to change. Research in social anthropology also suggests that learning should be understood as a process of apprenticeship, and as an integral part of generative social practice in a lived-in-world. Ingold (1996), for example, argues that common understanding comes about through the body acting in similar ways, through undertaking common activity in the 'practical business of life', which is then interpreted according to one's own cultural customs.

These new approaches to knowledge and understanding stress a dynamic intertwining between the individual and the environment. Interestingly, this can also be seen in the experiential characteristics of enjoyable flow identified by Csikszentmihalyi and colleagues, which resonate with the concepts of inherence identified by Merleau-Ponty as the fundamental process of perception. Conceivably, enjoyment may be an integral part of inherence in the world; buttressing the argument by Csikszentmihalyi that enjoyable flow is not a luxury but a staple of life.

Work and quality of life

Training for work is now a major concern of industrialized countries. In Britain, for example, the Learning Society is concerned with training for skills, competence, innovation and creativity. Yet in all Member States of the European Community a gap is perceived between the content of training programmes and the knowledge actually used in the work place. This 'work process knowledge' is the knowledge people need for successful performance at work. It is more than the procedural knowledge required to operate new technologies, for it implies an understanding of work organization in general. This vital human factor is often neglected, both in the design of work and in the planning of vocational education and training. However, some research based on practice theory is being undertaken. This shows that a concern for the dialectical character of human thinking is necessary for production, maintenance and design in industry. Arguably, the case can also be made that enjoyment may enhance inherence in situations with a concomitant increase in perception and understanding of the working process. If this is true, it would seem important that enjoyment is not designed out of work, either consciously or inadvertently, in the quest for greater short-term efficiency.

Social institutions and personal agency

The new conceptions of what it is to be a human being in the world espoused in practice theory have parallels in an analysis by Jahoda of social institutions and behaviour. In a penetrating analysis of employment and unemployment, Jahoda (1979, 1981, 1982, 1987) argues for the centrality of the social institution of employment in providing five categories of psychological experience which are conducive to well-being and that, to the extent that the unemployed are deprived of these experiences, this contributes to the decline in their well-being. These experiences are time structure, social contact, collective effort or purpose, social identity or status and regular activity. The wage relationship present in employment, its manifest function, is considered to impel people into situations which provide these categories of experience, or latent functions, as an unintended by-product of purposeful action. While the detrimental effects of poverty on the well-being of the unemployed are acknowledged, Jahoda is concerned to bring into visibility the important supportive effect social institutions can have on behaviour, habits and traditions.

Jahoda (1984, p. 64) believes that

> The relation between ideologies and the external life, or . . . the problems of habits and traditions in thought, is extremely difficult to grasp, because what is commonly called thinking represents a mixture of elements determined by tradition, emotion, social conditions, and speech habits of which only one thing is clear from the outset; it has almost nothing in common with the logical laws which often are supposed to determine our thinking.

She argues that if it were not for the comparative stability of traditional thinking, the capacity of the human mind would probably be insufficient to deal with reality; and that without traditions and habits of thought the infinite variety of life would overwhelm us. But, she states, that 'on the other hand its existence accounts for the discrepancy between ideas and behaviours and for the logical unreliability of a world in which the great majority of individuals is not capable of bringing behaviour and ideologies into harmony with one another' (p. 65). The process of adaption to change, she emphasizes, takes time.

While recognizing that the five categories of experience identified by Jahoda are of enduring significance, reflecting human needs, an extensive criticism of Jahoda's emphasis on the primary importance of the social institution of employment in supplying these experiences has been made by Fryer and Payne (1984, 1986), Fryer (1986a, 1986b, 1990, 1992, 1995) and Fryer and McKenna (1989). Some of the criticisms, and in particular those which impinge on the importance of social institutions for behaviour and well-being, have been challenged by Jahoda in an interview with Fryer (1986c) and by Jahoda (1984, 1986, 1992). In essence, the criticism made of Jahoda's theory is that it places too great an emphasis on the role of social factors in shaping behaviour, while presenting too passive a view of human beings, one which neglects the key role of personal agency and the factors which can restrict this, such as lack of money, and the bureaucratic features of social organizations with which the unemployed have to contend.

In reply to these criticisms, Jahoda (1986) agrees with proponents of agency theory that human beings are striving, coping, planning, interpreting creatures, but adds that the tendency to shape one's life from the inside out operates within the possibilities and constraints of social arrangements which are passively accepted and which shape life from the outside-in. A great deal of life, she argues, consists of passively following unexamined social rules not of our making but largely imposed by the collective plans of our ancestors; and that some of these rules meet basic human needs, even if we become aware of them only when they are broken by, for example, the enforced exclusion from an institution as in unemployment. Jahoda regards dependency on social institutions not as good or bad but as the *sine qua non* of human existence.

This debate is examined in detail in Chapter 2 where it is stressed that social institutions can both support and restrict personal agency. Current research into access to categories of experience in unemployed people is summarized and discussed in Chapter 3. This shows that the unemployed can gain access to the five categories of experience proposed by Jahoda, and that those with better access have better well-being. Access can come from work-like activities, leisure and general social interaction. Comparison with an employed sample, though, showed the unemployed to have less access to the categories of experience and worse well-being. However, it is still an open question as to whether or not the unemployed would have had access to all categories of experience and better well-being if their main activities had been embedded in a valued social structure. The research also shows that variations in access to the categories of experience in the leisure time of employed people appears to be important for well-being, contrary to Jahoda's predictions. It may well be that for some people there is not a strict division between important categories of experience obtained in work and those obtained in leisure.

A model of mental health

Warr (1987) has proposed a model of mental health which incorporates the five categories of experience advocated by Jahoda, along with features relating to personal agency highlighted by Fryer and Payne. This model emphasizes the importance of nine 'principal environmental influences' (PEIs) which interact with different 'enduring' characteristics of individuals to influence well-being, measured on a range of dimensions. Different social environments are considered to afford the PEIs to different degrees for different persons. The model thus stresses the importance of person–situation interactions for well-being, but studies these as discrete categories, in contrast to the 'flow' model proposed by Csikszentmihalyi which highlights the dynamic and reciprocal intertwining of the person and the situation. Warr points out, however, that the two approaches are complementary (p. 138).

The nine principal environmental influences are: opportunity for control, environmental clarity, opportunity for skill use, externally generated goals, variety, opportunity for interpersonal contact, valued social position, availability of money, physical security. Each PEI is thought to be harmful at low values but to have a constantly beneficial effect across a wide range of values, while some will have a negative effect on well-being at high values. An 'opportunity' can become an 'unavoidable requirement' at high levels.

A particular strength of the model highlighted by Warr is that it can be used in all kinds of environments, including work and leisure, and that it lends itself better to application and development than do many other models. Warr (1987, p. 21) considers that 'Through presenting a systematic categorical model, identifying social processes, and suggesting measurement approaches, the approach aims to yield recommendations for enhancing mental health by changing those environments identified as harmful'. He argues that there can be good and bad jobs and good and bad unemployment, though he concludes that in general unemployment is more adverse in terms of the principal environmental influences important for mental health than employment.

This model is examined in some detail in Chapter 4. Research using the model, conducted by the author and colleagues is examined in Chapter 5. This shows that different patterns of principal environmental influences seem to be significant for well-being for different groups of people in different life situations. 'Valued social position' was found to be a primary 'predictor' of well-being for a sample of managers, whereas 'environmental clarity', knowing what people expect of one, was of primary importance for a sample of female clerical workers. The study of working women also found that 'internal' locus of control, the expectation that the outcomes of behaviour are due more to one's actions than to chance, luck or fate, was associated with enhanced positive psychological states and access to principal environmental influences. 'Internals' were also shown to have more influence on enjoyment and feelings of control in daily life, particularly in leisure, measured by a diary method. The possibility exists that leisure may enhance internal locus of control, which in turn may lead to enhanced mental health, directly or indirectly through greater access to PEIs in work or leisure. This research shows the significance of studying both work and leisure in relation to well-being, and the necessity of undertaking this for different groups of people in different situations. As with the studies into the relationship between work and leisure discussed at the beginning of this Introduction, the research emphasizes the need to recognize the rich diversity of experience in the complex interplay between work, leisure and well-being.

TOUCHSTONES FOR POLICY

This Introduction to *Work, leisure and well-being* has highlighted a number of important parameters or 'touchstones' concerning our human condition – diversity; uncertainty; threats and opportunities; the social and temporal nature of human endeavour; and the importance of enjoyment. Together, they constitute a framework for policy, or at least a set of factors which cannot be ignored in the practice of shaping our future.

The *diversity* of human experience and individual requirements has been well illustrated in this Introduction. Theories of the relationship between work and leisure, pointers to trends influencing behaviour, the dynamics of well-being, and the temporal and emergent nature of social 'practices', all feature diversity, with the implication that there is no one correct policy for work and leisure. Some young people, for example, will prefer an in-and-out-of-work lifestyle for a period, while others will flourish better with secure employment. Similarly, for a section of working adults, a 'portfolio' of jobs may be preferred to a single career trajectory, which is still likely to be available for some individuals. The retirement phase of life will be welcomed early by certain individuals, while for others prolonged employment will be the desired option, and may best benefit both the individual and society.

The necessity for our social institutions to respond to this diversity is now acknowledged, even if it is not widely accepted (e.g. The Report of the Commission on Social Justice, 1994; Wilkinson and Mulgan, 1995; Hutton, 1996; Galbraith, 1996). In education, for example, a life-long learning society is advocated where individuals can develop their skills and interests at different phases of their life. A corollary of this is the necessity for the reshaping of our financial institutions concerned with tax, welfare and pensions to accommodate the diverse requirements of individuals; and the reshaping of our social institutions to ensure fair and proper rights for all. Mulgan and Wilkinson (1995) argue that micro-solutions offering individuals a range of choices to customize work time have had better results than macro-solutions which have tried to legislate for a set number of working hours to the working week. They point out that some people may prefer to work longer hours at certain periods of their life, whether for financial or other reasons. However, solutions will vary for different societies and groups of people. Perhaps what is more important is a general recognition, as Galbraith (1996) advocates, of a need for a compassionate base to sustain well-being, even if there is some abuse of arrangements.

The *uncertainty* of the future for individuals and societies reinforces the necessity for accommodating diversity. Predictions of the future remain as problematic as ever. What is becoming more common, though, is the experience of uncertainty. Many young people experience the uncertainty of not knowing whether they will get a job, and if they do for how long it will last. Adults in employment are increasingly experiencing the introduction of 'flexible' work contracts, or the uncertainty as to whether this will happen to them. The nature of the social practices to which people have become accustomed is changing radically, with uncertainty becoming an ingrained feature for many.

Yet with this uncertainty and diversity there are both *threats* and *opportunities*. The difficulties associated with individualization of experience and uncertainty of labour-market opportunities can diminish a sense of self as a participant in the valued community of practice of employment. Where there are considerable differentials in access to financial and cultural capital, this can produce a polarization of opportunities and experiences, and ensuing social differentiation, with some individuals becoming more deprived and having less and less stake in conventional society. Yet the opportunities of individualization of experience and uncertainty can lead to enhanced well-being and psychological growth when a range of challenges are met with skills afforded by appropriate human and economic resources.

The experience of differences in opportunities and difficulties in society raises the fundamental issue of social justice: the opportunity for all for access to resources necessary to meet the challenges of life. Crucial to this issue of social justice is the recognition of *the social and temporal nature of human endeavour*. The social nature of human endeavour necessitates the opportunity to participate in a community of practice, the form of which will be influenced by its participants and those in wider communities of practice. As such, it is imperative that we question and appraise ourselves and society, the practices we support and institute and the values these embody. Equally, the ownership and distribution of knowledge engendering practices become crucial considerations for quality of life; issues of participation, citizenship, sociality and justice become central concerns; and the politics of participation becomes fundamental to work, leisure and well-being. As our human condition is not only social but also temporal, with human beings perhaps best seen as temporal creatures embedded in changing social relationships, then organizing the appropriate social institutions to accommodate change, and providing the necessary time for change to be assimilated, is essential. This is even more the case when we recognize that the diversity of individual experience and requirements is not something which is merely a function of rational knowledge, but is built into the fibre of experience, the social networks of practice and horizons of transitions. Time is needed for individuals to become assimilated into institutions and practices, and time is needed for adaptation when individuals leave, voluntarily or otherwise, one form of social practice and enter another, as in the move from employment to unemployment, or retirement. Equally, it takes time for social practices to change to meet new requirements, necessitating the monitoring and evaluation of the relationship of social institutions to individual well-being.

Finally, the *importance of enjoyment* for both individual well-being and the structure and function of valued social practices should be acknowledged as a most providential touchstone of our human condition, one which needs to be cultivated and understood in its multi-faceted complexity.

REFERENCES

Clarke, S.G. and Haworth, J.T. (1994) '"Flow" experience in the daily lives of sixth form college students', *British Journal of Psychology* 85, 511–23.
Commission on Social Justice (1994) *Strategies for National Renewal*, London: Vintage.
Cross, G. (1995) 'The all-consuming work ethic', *Demos* 21–2.
Csikszentmihalyi, M. (1975) *Beyond Boredom and Anxiety*, San Francisco: Josey-Bass.
Csikszentmihalyi, M. (1988) 'A theoretical model of optimal experience', Introduction, in M. Csikszentmihalyi and I.S. Csiksentmihalyi (eds), *Optimal Experience*, Cambridge: Cambridge University Press, 3–14.
Csikszentmihalyi, M. (1991) *Flow: The Psychology of Optimal Experience*, New York: Harper & Row.
Csikszentmihalyi, M. (1993) *The Evolving Self*, New York: Harper & Row.
Csikszentmihalyi, M. and Csikszentmihalyi, I.S. (eds) (1988) *Optimal Experience*, Cambridge: Cambridge University Press.
Csikszentmihalyi, M. and Le Fevre (1989) 'Optimal experience in work and leisure', *Journal of Personality and Social Psychology* 56, 815–22.
Dooley, D. and Catalano, R. (1988) 'Do economic variables generate psychological problems? Different methods, different answers', in A.J. MacFadyen and H.W. MacFayden (eds), *Economic Psychology: Intersections in Theory and Practice*, 503–46, Amsterdam: Elsevier Science.
Dooley, D. and Prause, J. (1995) 'Effect of unemployment on school leavers' self-esteem', *Journal of Occupational and Organisational Psychology* 68, 177–92.
Dubin, R. (1956) 'Industrial workers' worlds: a study of the central life interest of industrial workers', *Social Problems* 3, 358–90.
Evans, S.T. and Haworth, J.T. (1991) 'Variations in personal activity, access to categories of experience and psychological well-being in unemployed young adults', *Leisure Studies* 10, 249–64.
Fryer, D. (1986a) 'Employment deprivation and personal agency during unemployment', *Social Behaviour* 1, 3–23.
Fryer, D. (1986b) 'On defending the unattacked: a comment upon Jahoda's "Defence"', *Social Behaviour* 1, 31–2.
Fryer, D. (1986c) 'The social psychology of the invisible: an interview with Maria Jahoda', *New Ideas in Psychology* 4, 107–18.
Fryer, D. (1990) 'The mental health costs of unemployment: towards a social psychological concept of poverty', *British Journal of Clinical and Social Psychiatry* 7: 4, 164–75.
Fryer, D. (1992) 'Psychological or material deprivation: why does unemployment have mental health consequencies?', in E. McLaughlin (ed.), *Understanding Unemployment*, London: Routledge.
Fryer, D. (1995) 'Benefit agency? Labour market disadvantage, deprivation and mental health', *The Psychologist*, 265–72.
Fryer, D. and McKenna, S. (1989) 'Redundant skills: temporary unemployment and mental health', in M. Patrickson (ed.), *Readings in Organisational Behaviour*, New South Wales: Harper & Row.

Fryer, D. and Payne, R. (1984) 'Proactive behaviour in unemployment: findings and implications', *Leisure Studies* 3, 273–95.

Fryer, D. and Payne, R. (1986) 'Being unemployed: a review of the literature on the psychological experience of unemployment', in C.L. Cooper and I. Robertson (eds), *International Review of Industrial and Organisational Psychology*, London: John Wiley.

Furnham, A. and Steele, H. (1993) 'Measuring locus of control: a critique of general, children's, health and work related locus of control questionnaires', *British Journal of Psychology* 84, 413–79.

Galbraith, J.K. (1996) *The Good Society: The Humane Agenda*, Boston: Houghton Mifflin.

Glyptis, S. (1989) *Leisure and Unemployment*, Milton Keynes: Open University Press.

Glyptis, S. (1994) 'Leisure provision for the unemployed: imperative or irrelevant?', *World Leisure and Recreation* 36: 34–9.

Godbey, G. (1975) 'Anti-leisure and public recreation policy', in S.R. Parker *et al.* (eds), *Sports and Leisure in Contemporary Society*, Brighton: Leisure Studies Association.

Grossin, W. (1986) 'The relationship between work time and free time and the meaning of retirement', *Leisure Studies* 5, 91–101.

Harrison, B. and Bluestone, B. (1988) *The great U-turn. Corporate Restructuring and the Polarising of America*, New York: Basic Books.

Haworth, J.T. and Ducker, J. (1991) 'Psychological well-being and access to categories of experience in unemployed young adults', *Leisure Studies* 10, 265–74.

Haworth, J.T. and Evans, S.T. (1987) 'Meaningful activity and unemployment', in D. Fryer and P. Ullah (eds), *Unemployed People*, Milton Keynes: Open University Press.

Haworth, J.T. and Evans, S. (1995) 'Challenge, skill and positive subjective states in the daily life of a sample of YTS students', *Journal of Occupational and Organisational Psychology* 68, 109–21.

Haworth, J.T. and Smith, M.A. (eds) (1975) *Work and Leisure: An Interdisciplinary Study in Theory, Education and Planning*, London: Lepus Books.

Hutton, W. (1996) *The State We're In*, London: Vintage.

Ingold, T. (1996) 'Culture, perception and cognition', in J.T. Haworth (ed.), *Psychological Research: Innovative Methods and Strategies*, London: Routledge.

Jahoda, M. (1979) 'The impact of unemployment in the 1930s and the 1970s', *Bulletin of the British Psychological Society* 32, 309–14.

Jahoda, M. (1981) 'Work, employment and unemployment: values, theories and approaches in social research', *American Psychology* 36, 1983–91.

Jahoda, M. (1982) *Employment and Unemployment: A Social Psychological Analysis*, Cambridge University Press: Cambridge.

Jahoda, M. (1984) 'Social institutions and human needs: a comment on Fryer and Payne', *Leisure Studies* 3, 297–9.

Jahoda, M. (1986) 'In defence of a non-reductionist social psychology', *Social Behaviour* 1, 25–9.

Jahoda, M. (1987) 'Unemployed men at work', in D. Fryer and P. Ullah (eds), *Unemployed People*, Milton Keynes: Open University Press.

Jahoda, M. (1992) 'Reflections on Marienthal and after', *Journal of Occupational and Organisational Psychology* 65, 355–8.

Kabonof, B. (1980) 'Work and non-work: a review of models, methods and findings', *Psychological Bulletin* 88, 60–77.

Kabonof, B. (1982) 'Occupational and sex differences in leisure needs and leisure satisfaction', *Journal of Occupational Behaviour* 3, 233–45.

Kabonof, B. and O'Brien, E. (1986) 'Stress and the leisure needs and activities of different occupations', *Human Relations* 39: 10, 903–16.

Kay, T. (1989) 'Active unemployment – a leisure pattern for the future?', *Society and Leisure* 12: 2, 413–30.

Kohn, M. and Schooler, M. (1983) *Work and Personality: An Inquiry into the Impact of Social Stratification*, Norwood, NJ: Ablex.

Lane, R.E. (1995) 'Time preferences: the economics of work and leisure', *Demos* 5, 12–14.

Long, J.A. and Wimbush, E. (1985) 'Continuity and change: leisure around retirement', Sports Council/ESRC Report, London.

Merleau-Ponty, M. (1962) *Phenomenology of Perception*, London: Routledge & Kegan Paul.

Mulgan, G. and Wilkinson, H. (1995) 'Well-being and time', *Demos* 5, 2–11.

Mullet, S. (1988) 'Leisure and consumption: incompatible concepts?', *Leisure Studies* 7, 241–53.

Pahl, R. (1996) 'Reflections and perspectives', in C.H.A. Verhaar *et al.* (eds) *On Challenges of Unemployment in Regional Europe*, Aldershot: Avebury Press.

Parker, S. (1972) *The Future of Work and Leisure*, London: Paladin.

Parker, S. (1976) *The Sociology of Leisure*, London: Allen & Unwin.

Parker, S. (1983) *Leisure and Work*, London, Allen & Unwin.

Rathunde, K. (1988) 'Optimal experience and the family context', in M. Csikszentmihalyi and I. Selega Csikszentmihalyi (eds) *Optimal Experiences*, Cambridge: Cambridge University Press.

Reisman, D. and Blomberg, W. (1957) 'Work and leisure: fusion or polarity?', in C.M. Arensberg *et al.* (eds), *Research in Industrial Human Relations*, New York, Harper & Row.

Rifkin, J. (1995) 'The end of work as we know it', *Demos* 5, 17–20.

Roberts, K., Noble, M. and Duggan, J. (1982) 'Out-of-school youth in high unemployment areas: an empirical investigation', *British Journal of Guidance and Counselling* 10, 1–11.

Schor, J. (1995) 'The new American dream', *Demos* 5, 30.

Stebbins, R.A. (1981) 'Science amateurs? Rewards and costs in amateur astronomy and archeology', *Journal of Leisure Research* 13, 289–304.

Stebbins, R.A. (1982) 'Serious leisure: a conceptual statement', *Pacific Sociological Review* 25, 251–72.

Stebbins, R.A. (1992) *Amateurs, Professionals and Serious Leisure*, Montreal/Kingston: McGill-Queen's University Press.

Tyrrell, B. (1995) 'Time in our lives: facts and analysis on the 90s', *Demos* 5, 23–5.

Warr, P. (1987) *Work, Unemployment and Mental Health*, Oxford: Clarendon Press.

Warr, P., Jackson, P. and Banks, M. (1988) 'Unemployment and mental health: some British studies', *Journal of Social Issues* 44, 37–68.

Wilensky, H.L. (1960) 'Work, careers and social integration', *International Science Journal* 4, 32–56.

Wilkinson, H. and Mulgan, G. (1995) 'Freedom's children: work relationships and politics for 18–34 year olds in Britain today', *Demos* 5.

Chapter 2

Categories of psychological experience and well-being

This chapter examines two theories of the psychological effects of unemployment: the 'deprivation theory' proposed by Jahoda, and the 'agency theory' proposed by Fryer. Both theories, or meta-theories as they have been termed by Fryer (1995), have significant implications for how we view ourselves and society. While the theories emphasize different facets of human behaviour, they have in common a recognition of the importance of various categories of psychological experience for well-being. They also give a complementary picture of the way in which social structures can influence behaviour.

In a penetrating analysis of employment and unemployment, Jahoda (1979, 1981, 1982) argues that employment provides five categories of psychological experience which are vital for well-being, and that to the extent that the unemployed are deprived of these experiences this contributes to the decline in their well-being. These experiences are time structure, social contact, collective effort or purpose, social identity or status and regular activity. The wage relationship present in employment, its manifest function, is considered to impel people into situations which provide these categories of experience, or latent functions, as an unintended by-product of purposeful action. While the quality of experience within these latent functions of employment can vary from the pleasant to the unpleasant, *some* experience in each of these must occur. It is this which Jahoda considers distinguishes sharply between employment and unemployment. Jahoda recognizes that the consequences of unemployment are intricately interwoven with the consequences of poverty, but considers that there are other consequences, including the lack of enforcement of these categories of experience, where the connection with poverty is less strong or, at least, less obvious. Although the detrimental effects of poverty are acknowledged, Jahoda is concerned to bring into visibility the supportive effect social institutions can have on behaviour.

The importance of employment for these categories of experience is clearly stated in Jahoda and Rush (1980, p. 12):

Employment of whatever kind and at whatever level makes the following categories of psychological experiences inevitable: it imposes a time structure on the waking day; it compels contacts and shared experiences with others outside the nuclear family; it demonstrates that there are goals and purposes which are beyond the scope of an individual, but require a collectivity; it imposes status and social identity through the division of labour in modern employment and, last but not least, it enforces activity – there is no other institution in modern societies which combines a necessary manifest function with enforcing all of these latent consequences in an obligatory fashion. Of course one can engage in leisure activities, but the absence of the social compulsion in such activities requires a degree of initiative from individuals which only few psychologically privileged human beings can muster on a regular basis.

SOCIAL INSTITUTIONS AND CATEGORIES OF EXPERIENCE

The important role that social institutions play in relation to these categories of experience has been outlined further by Jahoda (1982).The experience of *time* is seen as being shaped by public institutions, with the school system structuring the day of a child, and most employment involving a fixed time schedule, which people complain about. But when this time structure is removed, as it is in unemployment, its absence is seen as presenting a major psychological burden: 'Days stretch long when there is nothing that has to be done; boredom and waste of time become the rule, particularly once the first shock has been overcome and the search for employment has been given up as futile' (p. 22). *Social contacts* are enforced by employment, and whether these are liked or not they are seen as an inescapable source for enlarging a person's social horizon: 'In employment, even a shy and withdrawn person cannot help but enlarge his knowledge of the social world as he observes the similarities or differences, compared with his own, of the habits, opinions and life experience of others around him' (p. 25). During unemployment, impoverishment of social experience follows necessarily from the change in the structures of daily life.

Jahoda stresses that while industrialized societies have been described as emphasizing individualism as a dominant value, an ever increasing division of labour does not diminish but rather intensifies the social needs and *purposes* of the human species, and that individualism has to be embedded in a social context to be valued at all. She argues that 'Outside the nuclear family it is employment that provides for most people this social context and demonstrates in daily experience that "no man is an island, entire of itself", that the purpose of a collectivity transcended the purposes of an individual. Deprived of this daily demonstration, the unemployed suffer from lack of purpose, exclusion from the larger society and relative social isolation' (p. 24). Jahoda stresses the importance of employment for personal *identity*: 'Because of widespread consensus in public life about the social status assigned to varying jobs, people tend to adopt this assignation as one clear element in defining themselves to themselves and are reluctant to dispense with this support for their personal identity' (p. 26). She recognizes that the nature of the activity undertaken in employment has a bearing on the way in which its cessation is experienced in unemployment; but notes that the available evidence for manual workers points to a sharp break in *activities* before and after unemployment.

Jahoda (1982, p. 23) states that: 'To blame the unemployed for their inability to use their time in a more satisfactory way is pointless; it would amount to asking that they single-handedly overthrow the compelling social norms under which we all live and which provide a supportive frame within which individuals shape their individual lives. There are at all times only a few who can manage without it'. While Jahoda and Rush (1980, p. 15) note that the latent consequences of employment were originally identified by looking at the experiences of those without employment in a variety of situations including unemployment, retirement, mental and physical handicap and the 'housewife syndrome'. They point out that in all these situations people experience similar psychological deprivation: difficulty in organizing time, isolation, a sense of purposelessness, uncertainty about status and identity and nothing to do. They conclude that the desirable latent consequences of employment in industrial societies lie in these categories of experience, and that the *quality* of experience in each of these can vary considerably in degree of desirability. 'Many derive pleasure from employment; many others find the reality to which they are thus tied near intolerable in one or more of the five components. It is not employment as such, but the variety of conditions under which it is offered which produces qualitative differences in the latent consequences and hence differing experiences in the employed'.

Jahoda (1982) stresses that these categories of experience are not at the whim of a good or bad employer, but are a result of the structural forms of modern employment. While recognizing that other institutions may enforce one or more of these categories on participants, Jahoda stresses that none of them combines them all with as compelling a reason as earning one's living. Employment as a social institution does not exist for the purpose of providing these categories of experience, but it is seen as an unintended, albeit inevitable, consequence of its own purposes and organization to enforce these categories of experience on all participants. While the unemployed are left to their own devices to find experiences within these categories if they can and suffer if they cannot, the employed take them for granted: 'What preoccupies them is not the category but the quality of the experience within it' (p. 39). Jahoda recognizes that the quality of experience of some jobs can be very poor and stresses the importance of improving and 'humanizing' employment.

ENDURING NEEDS

In attempting to explain the psychological implications of these latent consequences of employment Jahoda (1981, p. 189) draws on Freud's 'elliptic aphorism' which states that work is a person's strongest tie to reality. She considers that 'we all need some tie to reality so as not to be overwhelmed by fantasy and emotion . . . . But the reality to which we are thus bound may have little, if any, pleasurable content. Time structures can be too rigid, contact with supervisors unpleasant, the purposes unclear or unacceptable, thé status too low, and the activity boring and exhausting'.

In her 1982 work, Jahoda argues that the five categories of experience correspond to more or less deep-seated needs. In an interview with Fryer (1986c, p. 111), she considers that

> As human beings, we all have some very basic needs which we do not formulate to ourselves . . . they are not repressed needs that one does not want to recognise. [Rather] They are so taken for granted that they do not engage the explicit conscious thought of a person as long as the world is reasonably normal. Only when this taken for granted satisfaction of a need – to have a time structure for example – disappears through no action of your own does the question of how to structure your time become a conscious, deliberate problem.

Jahoda (1992, p. 356) again indicates that her theory 'emphasises the habitual use people make of social institutions in meeting some psychological need'.

Jahoda (1982) considers that these needs are not necessarily biologically determined nor are they necessarily a product of social determinism – imposed on pliable human organisms by the power of prevailing social structures. Instead, she believes that it is necessary to avoid the extremes of biological or social determinism by studying the actual interplay between individual needs and available social structures, keeping in mind the possibility that either one may change gradually or suddenly. This interactionist position is amplified in her statement (Jahoda, 1986, p. 112) on personal factors involved in attempts to find alternatives to employment:

> Whether a person does or does not find an alternative for the environment of employment depends very much on personal qualities and personal history. But these personal qualities and personal history have in the past been shaped by the type of environment to which the person was exposed. Before unemployment hits, you have the impact of the industrial climate on people, their social background, the opportunities they have or have not had to develop themselves fully, and you have all these in interplay with the gifts and abilities and qualities of individuals. A few can escape from the pressure that the previous environment has exercised on them, but not many. The difficult question is to decide whether the explanation for the inability to take a creative initiative should be blamed on the previous social experience or has something to do with the make-up of the individual that is relatively independent of the previous social experience.

A study

In the 1930s Jahoda conducted a study of a subsistence production society (SPS) for unemployed minors, in Monmouthshire, South Wales. This study was published by Jahoda in 1987 and illustrates the complex interplay which can exist between social institutions and the individual. The unemployed men in the SPS produced goods to be used for their own subsistence, but not for sale on the open market. They got no wages and purchased goods from their social benefits, the prices calculated on the basis of the cost of the raw materials plus 20 per cent for overheads. The society was established to give men the psychological benefits of work, while also trying to ameliorate some of the economic disadvantages of unemployment. The society was also based on the idea that only voluntary work with a complete absence of compulsion would allow for the growth of the creative urge so as to give satisfaction and happiness in work.

About 17 per cent of the unemployed in the valley had first-hand experience of the SPS. Many of the men were dissatisfied with the SPS and felt that the goods produced should be sold on the open market, which was in line with their traditions deeply rooted in the industrial system. However, some of the men in the 60-plus age group gained new functions and social contacts, more so than they may have ordinarily expected, and were happy and satisfied members of the SPS. Again, individuals in the 45 to 59 age group found that the bitter hopelessness of the years of unemployment with the feeling of a premature, prolonged and useless old age was taken away. However, individuals in the 24 to 44 age group felt that their normal development and experience in the industrial system were being prevented. Many members of the SPS in this age group thought and said that they were losing their best years in the Society instead of getting along with normal employment in the normal course of life. Jahoda considers that these men did not want an experiment, they wanted industrial reality; and that the SPS was not quite real for them due to two factors. First, the economic benefit was not large enough to permit them to live a normal life; second, their habits of thought did not permit them to envisage any development that did not imply enjoying normal wages and working conditions in the prime of their lives. Jahoda notes that men up to 24 years old were also not satisfied with the Society. They objected to its lack of prospects for the future and to its 'humdrum' character.

Jahoda considers that the thought system then current was rooted in the tradition of mining and that these habits of thought, well established in the minds of working men, did not fit the new social reality, but were not abandoned at once. When many of the unemployed men were asked why they were not in the Society they answered either that the idea had never occurred to them or that they were strictly against it. The women had a far simpler and more single-minded attitude towards the SPS than the men. They seemed less burdened by traditions and habits of thought, as in the past they had no opportunity to acquire fixed habits of thought regarding unionism and industrialism. There was no ideology in their minds preventing them from seeing the immediate economic advantage in the SPS.

In reviewing this study, Jahoda considers that 'The relation between ideologies and the external life, or . . . the problems of habits and traditions in thought, is extremely difficult to grasp, because what is commonly called thinking represents a mixture of elements determined by tradition, emotion, social conditions, and speech habits of which only one thing is clear from the outset; it has almost nothing in common with the logical laws which often are supposed to determine our thinking' (Jahoda, 1987, p. 64). She argues that if it were not for the comparative stability of traditional thinking the capacity of the human mind would probably be insufficient to deal with reality; and that without tradition and habits of thought the infinite variety of life would overwhelm us. But she notes that traditions and habits can also greatly hinder the process of bringing behaviour and ideologies into harmony with one another. The process of adaptation, she emphasizes, takes time. The general description of normal industrial work in the mines was one of a complex work atmosphere which had a compelling force, which did not, however, exist in the SPS. Work in the pit formed the basis of existence, work in the SPS raised the level of living, but did not form its basis. Thus in the eyes of its members it lacked social and economic reality compared to the compelling effect of working in normal industry.

IN SUMMARY

Jahoda (1982, pp. 83–4) summarizes her position as follows:

> The structure of employment in the modern world has developed over at least two centuries. While the power of organised labour and changing technologies have significantly influenced this structure, it has remained virtually unaltered in at least two aspects; first it provides the means whereby the vast majority of people earn their livelihood; and second as an unintended by-product of its very organization it enforces on those who participate in it certain categories of experience . . . . These enforced categories can be experienced as pleasant or unpleasant; as categories, however, they are inescapable whatever their quality. These categories of experience correspond to more or less deep-seated needs in most people, who strive to make some sense out of their existence . . . . Modern employment is certainly not the only structure in industrial societies that meets these needs. But it is the dominant one at the moment and the only one that combines the automatic provision of these categories with the overwhelming economic necessity for most people to work for a living.

CRITICISMS

An extended criticism of Jahoda's thesis on the importance of social institutions for categories of experience, and the detrimental consequence for well-being of the deprivation of these in unemployment, has been made by Fryer and Payne (1984, 1986), Fryer (1986a and b, 1990, 1992, 1995), and Fryer and McKenna (1989). Some of the criticisms, and in particular those which impinge on the importance of social institutions for behaviour and well-being, have been challenged by Jahoda in an interview with Fryer (1986c) and by Jahoda (1984, 1986, 1988 1992). In essence, the criticism made of Jahoda's deprivation theory is that it places too great an emphasis on the role of social factors in shaping human behaviour, while presenting too passive a view of human beings, one which neglects the significance of personal agency and the factors which can restrict this, such as lack of money. Fryer and Payne (1984, p. 289) recognize the importance of the five categories of experience delineated by Jahoda, accepting them as 'enduring and widespread areas of human experience, though not necessarily the only ones relevant to an understanding of unemployment'. They reject, however, that these must be tied to employment for the majority of people and consider that some of the psychological problems associated with unemployment are not just the result of withdrawal of supports on which people depend but are a consequence of trying to understand and cope with the situation.

Fryer (1995, p. 270) states that 'Two factors in particular are emphasised as central in the mental health costs of unemployment for many people because they restrict personal agency. Firstly, unemployment cuts the unemployed person off from any future, making looking forward and planning very difficult. Secondly, unemployment generally results in psychologically corrosive experienced poverty'. He cites a large-scale study of the unemployed by Whelan (1992) who concluded that 'The findings presented here clearly demonstrate the role of poverty in mediating the impact of unemployment not only for the individuals involved but also for members of their families' (p. 270) Fryer (1995, p. 270) summarizes the assumptions underlying agency theory:

> Firstly that people are socially embedded agents actively striving for purposeful self-determination, attempting to make sense of, initiate, influence and cope with events in line with personal values, goals and expectations of the future in a context of cultural norms, traditions and past experience. Secondly that, whilst personal agency is sometimes empowered in interaction with labour market social settings and systems, agency is frequently undermined, restricted and frustrated by formal and informal social forces.

Fryer considers that personal agency can be restricted by persistently adverse labour-market experience, including both relative poverty and economic insecurity. He emphasizes what unemployment, scheme attendance, psychologically satisfactory and unsatisfactory employment share conceptually, rather than what distinguishes them: 'All are social relationships between parties involving psychological contracts in which work determined by one party is done in exchange for income by another party . . . unemployed people can be

. . . regarded as essentially poorly paid, low status, insecure, public sector workers with virtually no negotiating rights whose work (persistent near hopeless job search, humiliating benefit related rituals, management of households on inadequate resources etc.) carries a high risk of occupational strain' (p.271). Psychologists and others, he stresses, must engage with the mental health costs of psychological and material deprivation which is part and parcel for many of their labour-market careers.

This perceptive statement of agency theory by Fryer is a development of the ideas and concepts proposed by Fryer and Payne (1984). They undertook a study of a small group of unemployed people who were experiencing material but not psychological deprivation and who had adopted a proactive stance towards unemployment. The interviews showed that all the participants made a distinction between employment and doing meaningful work. The majority indicated the importance of having values which gave direction to one's life, including political, religious and personal development beliefs. Many of the interviewees also showed a desire to be active, had the capability to structure time, saw unemployment as an opportunity to develop oneself or achieve desired goals: features which indicate the nature of proactive behaviour. Other frequently mentioned aspects were those indicating achievement, high standards, consistency and commitment, emphasizing the high level of internal motivation which most of the respondents possessed. The financial and material difficulties of being unemployed were stressed, as was the receipt of psychological support which helped even these resilient individuals to cope. The study revealed that most of the sample had been proactive in coping with situations long before they were unemployed: 'proactivity in unemployment seems to a great extent to be an extension of proactivity in employment, full-time education or before' (p. 286).

The authors note that having goals encourages high activity and that energy is both encouraged and channelled by the support received from those with whom they are involved. The study also showed that the psychological categories of experience highlighted by Jahoda were important for this sample of proactive unemployed people. There was an active self-adoption of an internal approach to *time structure*: 'routines which I insist on sticking to'; of self-pacing, of setting oneself tasks and projects, 'it comes down to . . . disciplining yourself to do something'. All the samples were involved in regular *shared experience* outside the home. While a majority talked of the importance to them of receiving support to enable them to do what they are doing, all but one of these received crucially supportive regular experience inside the home. The majority of the sample had transcending *goals and purposes* which stemmed not from employment but from their personal values. *Status and identity*, while not topics which cropped up frequently, were obtained by things such as being leader of a community project, being 'a convenor, a person who's involved with people' (p. 289). The sample manifest *regular activity* which in part derived from personal commitment, but also through the expectations of others.

The authors believe that the 'congruence between the categories and our findings indicates the fact that Jahoda has pointed to enduring and widespread areas of human experience, though not necessarily the only ones relevant to an understanding of the problems of unemployment' (p. 289). While accepting that for most people unemployment is associated with many psychological problems, they 'suggest that these more typical cases to a great extent experience distress because efforts to assert agency are frustrated over time by inadequate resources, low social power and perhaps lack of exposure to solving varied problems due to having performed routine jobs whilst in employment' (p. 291). They add (p. 291):

> It follows that increases of resources and social power would cause distress to ameliorate or disappear. The deprivation approach, on the other hand, would predict that distress would not lessen or disappear unless the persons were employed or engaged in some other substitute social institution. The prediction from the agency approach is that given material and social freedom, individuals will create their own social institutions or seek existing ones which satisfy their social and psychological growth needs.

According to Fryer and Payne, Jahoda's latent consequence account of employment and unemployment misses much of what is important in understanding the experience and behaviours of their sample: 'in particular the extent to which they are active, coping, interpreting agents' (p. 290). In the conclusion to the study (p. 293) they also note that:

> It has become increasingly clear that access to categories of experience is not an all or nothing categorical matter, as seemed first implied. There is a range of access to the categories across the unemployed and, one supposes, across the employed too. We do not think the latent functions account is the whole story of the impact of unemployment but it is clearly a part of the story and well worth further refinement – the choice of a person to take up the opportunity of access or not to do so, and the reason lying behind that choice, is still to be explained. As has long been suggested with respect to poverty a central psychological issue of unemployment is why the unemployed make less and less use of the dwindling opportunities available.

In discussing other empirical evidence supporting the agency theory and critical of the deprivation theory, Fryer (1986a) cites studies by McKenna and Fryer (1984) and Fryer and McKenna (1987) which compared men laid off for a set period of seven weeks with a group of men from a similar but separate factory laid off indefinitely. The authors argue that according to deprivation theory both groups would be equally deprived of the latent functions of employment. The temporarily laid off men, however, were found to be active and appeared to be functioning well, whereas the redundant men showed a psychological profile very similar to that revealed by other studies of unemployment. The authors consider that it was a difference in orientation towards the future which characterized the two groups.

Winefield *et al.* (1993) have also been critical of Jahoda's theory, in particular her emphasis on the benefit of any form of employment over being unemployed. In an impressive longitudinal study of a large sample of young people in Australia making the transition from school to employment or unemployment, the researchers found that those who were dissatisfied with their jobs had worse affective well-being than the satisfied employed whose affective well-being had improved since school, and were also not different from the unemployed. They interpreted this as a criticism of Jahoda's theory. However, using a comprehensive measure of anomie, and making cross-sectional comparisons later in the study, they found that the unemployed had worse well-being than each of the other groups (p. 74). The authors state that while the results of their research seem to support agency theory rather than deprivation theory, they believe that any global view of human nature must be mistaken. They stress that 'the only realistic assumption to be made about human nature is its diversity' (p. 96).

REPLY

Commenting on Fryer and Payne's research, Jahoda (1984) makes two points. The first is that Fryer and Payne's sample demonstrates that access to the five categories of experience and hence satisfaction of the corresponding needs are met in work, even if this is not in employment. The second point is that this work is located in informal institutions, although no evidence is given for this.

Jahoda stresses that she shares the view of Fryer and Payne that human beings are 'active, coping, interpreting agents' adding that 'The maintenance of life itself depends on every living organism being active, interpreting the environment and coping with it'. However, she emphasizes (p. 298) that

> The degree to which these basic tendencies can be expressed depends on the nature of the environment which can be encouraging or repressing their manifestations. In complex human societies there are formal and informal institutions that affect the degree to which people have to exert themselves in meeting their basic needs. The supportive character of many institutions is so taken for granted that it becomes visible only when they break down, as in unemployment.

Jahoda argues that the real difference between the deprivation and the agency approach lies not in whether human beings are viewed as active or passive, but in the role assigned to the power of social institutions. She sees the institution of employment as so powerful that it has shaped the way of life in all industrialized countries. Not only has it led to the development of other institutions such as the trade unions, employers' organizations, educational and training facilities, leisure and holiday sites, but it has also given rise to the idea of solidarity and has influenced the way people think about themselves and others, their plans and aspirations and their family life. All this is in addition to being the locale in which the five basic needs can be met and from which financial independence derives.

These points, acknowledging the importance of personal agency and emphasizing the vital role of social institutions in encouraging or expressing basic tendencies, are stressed further by Jahoda (1986, pp. 28–9):

> Once again I agree in broad principle [with the specification of 'agency' as an attribute of being human] but the tendency to shape one's life from the inside-out operates within the possibilities and constraints of social arrangements which we passively accept and which shape life from the outside-in. A great deal of daily life consists of passively following unexamined social rules, not of our own making but largely imposed by the collective plans of our ancestors. Some of these rules meet basic human needs, even if we become aware of them only when they are broken by, for example, the enforced exclusion from an institution as in unemployment. I regard dependency on social institutions not as good or bad, but as the *sine qua non* of human existence. What the current situation requires is the creation of institutions for the unemployed on which they can depend in unfolding their full humanity, preferably employment opportunities with radical change in the *quality* of their unavoidable structural properties.

Jahoda argues that she has striven for a theory 'where causation lies *both* in the person and in the situation, where institutions are both "enabling" by meeting needs and "empowering" by imposing rules, where people can exercise their degrees of freedom better when their basic needs are met' (p. 29).

CONCLUSION

Jahoda and Fryer both stress the importance for well-being of the psychological categories of experience of time structure, social contact, collective effort or purpose, social identity or status and regular activity. Although Jahoda emphasizes the role of social institutions in facilitating access to these categories of experience, Fryer points to the inhibitory influence which poverty, social arrangements and cultural practices can have on personal agency, thereby restricting access to positive categories of experience, particularly in the unemployed. In many ways, these two 'theories' are complementary. Both 'theories' also recognize to some extent the crucial influence on behaviour of individual life experience or 'personal history'.

Finally, it seems pertinent to return to the views of Jahoda and Rush (1980) on the importance of studying unemployment. Although they stress the role of the social institution of employment in providing the five psychological categories of experience they state (p. 53):

> To establish whether the latent consequences of employment meet indeed relatively enduring needs seems to us important for several reasons: it could

contribute to a better understanding of the various speeds of change in human affairs: it could identify whether arrangements other than employment meet social needs if they are demonstrated to exist; and it could inform policy about unemployment. The best way to establish whether these needs are relatively enduring seems to us to look once again, at the life pattern of the currently unemployed.

Current research into access to categories of experience in unemployed and employed people constitutes the subject of the next chapter.

REFERENCES

Fryer, D. (1986a) 'Employment deprivation and personal agency during unemployment', *Social Behaviour* 1, 3–23.

Fryer, D. (1986b) 'On defending the unattacked: a comment upon Jahoda's "Defence"', *Social Behaviour* 1, 31–2.

Fryer, D. (1986c) 'The social psychology of the invisible: an interview with Maria Jahoda', *New Ideas in Psychology* 4, 107–18.

Fryer, D. (1990) 'The mental health costs of unemployment: towards a social psychological concept of poverty', *British Journal of Clinical and Social Psychiatry* 7: 4, 164–75.

Fryer, D. (1992) 'Psychological or material deprivation: why does unemployment have mental health consequences?', in E. McLaughlin (ed.), *Understanding Unemployment*, London: Routledge.

Fryer, D. (1995) 'Benefit agency? Labour market disadvantage, deprivation and mental health', *The Psychologist*, 265–72.

Fryer, D. and McKenna, S.P. (1987) 'The laying off of hands: unemployment and the experience of times', in S. Fineman (ed.), *Unemployment and the Experience of Time: Personal and Social Consequences*, London: Tavistock.

Fryer, D. and McKenna, S. (1989) 'Redundant skills: temporary unemployment and mental health', in M. Patrickson (ed.), *Readings in Organisational Behaviour*, New South Wales: Harper & Row.

Fryer, D. and Payne, R. (1984) 'Proactive behaviour in unemployment: findings and implications', *Leisure Studies* 3, 273–95.

Fryer, D. and Payne, R. (1986) 'Being unemployed: a review of the literature on the psychological experience of unemployment', in C.L. Cooper and I. Robertson (eds), *International Review of Industrial and Organisational Psychology*, London: Wiley.

Jahoda, M. (1979) 'The impact of unemployment in the 1930s and the 1970s', *Bulletin of the British Psychological Society* 32, 309–14.

Jahoda, M. (1981) 'Work, employment and unemployment: values, theories and approaches in social research', *American Psychology* 36, 1984–91.

Jahoda, M. (1982) *Employment and Unemployment: A Social Psychological Analysis*, Cambridge: Cambridge University Press.

Jahoda, M. (1984) 'Social institutions and human needs: a comment on Fryer and Payne', *Leisure Studies* 3, 297–99.

Jahoda, M. (1986) 'In defence of a non-reductionist social psychology', *Social Behaviour* 1, 25–9.

Jahoda, M. (1987) 'Unemployed men at work', in D.M. Fryer and P. Ullah (eds), *Unemployed People: Social and Psychological Perspectives*, Milton Keynes: Open University Press.

Jahoda, M. (1988) 'Economic recession and mental health: some conceptual issues', *Journal of Social Issues* 44: 4, 13–23.

Jahoda, M. (1992) 'Reflections on Marienthal and after', *Journal of Occupational and Organisational Psychology* 65, 355–8.

Jahoda, M. and Rush, H. (1980) 'Work, employment and unemployment', SPRU, Occasional Paper No 12, University of Sussex, Brighton.

McKenna, S.P. and Fryer, D.M. (1984) 'Perceived health during lay off and early unemployment', *Occupational Health* 36: 5, 201–6.

Whelan, C.T. (1992) 'The role of income, life-style deprivation and financial strain in mediating the impact of unemployment on psychological distress: evidence from the Republic of Ireland', *Journal of Occupational and Organisational Psychology* 65: 4, 331–44.

Winefield, A.H., Tiggemann, M., Winefield, H.R. and Goldney, R.D. (1993) *Growing Up with Unemployment: A Longitudinal Study of its Psychological Impact*, London: Routledge.

Chapter 3

Research into categories of psychological experience and well-being

In the previous chapter we saw that Jahoda (1982) considers that employment provides a number of categories of psychological experience important for well-being as an unintended by-product of its organization. Jahoda (1979) also claims that the psychological impact required to gain these five 'latent consequences' of employment on a regular basis and entirely under one's own steam is colossal. She states (Jahoda, 1981) that 'leisure activities from television to sports to self improvement are fine in themselves as a complement to employment but are not functional alternatives to work, since they lack its compelling manifest function' (i.e. earning a living). In other words, the wage relation is considered to impel people into situations which provide important categories of experience. Where people cope well with unemployment, as in a sample studied by Fryer and Payne (1984), Jahoda (1984) makes two points. The first is that Fryer and Payne's sample demonstrates that access to the five categories of experience, and hence satisfaction of the corresponding needs, are met in work, even if this is not in employment. The second point is that this work is located in informal institutions, though no evidence is given for this claim.

This chapter summarizes and discusses the results of several studies which directly measure the categories of experience proposed by Jahoda, and which also directly measure different aspects of psychological well-being. The studies show that employment is a stronger determinant of access to the categories of experience than is unemployment. They also show that there is variation in access to categories of experience in the unemployed and in the work and leisure time of the employed, and that this is associated with variation in well-being, measured on a range of dimensions. Finally, the studies show the importance of investigating person–situation interactions, and the processes involved in these interactions.

EMPLOYMENT AND UNEMPLOYMENT

The categories of experience of time structure, social contact, collective effort or purpose, social identity or status and regular activity are viewed by Jahoda as reflecting enduring human needs and, similarly, by Fryer and Payne (1984,

p. 298) as 'enduring and widespread areas of human experience'. It is recognized that these categories of experience are not of an 'all or nothing' type, but can vary in the extent to which they are experienced. In an innovative study of 300 unemployed and 100 employed men aged 21 and over, Miles (1983) devised a series of scales by factor analysis of the data from a wide range of questions which he used to measure variation in access to the categories of experience: the extent to which the categories were experienced. These he termed the ACE scales. The study showed that there was variation in access to the categories of experience in the unemployed, and that this was associated with variation in participation in sports, visits, voluntary activities, car maintenance and home activities. Thus the activities which may give rise to ACE were not confined to those of a traditional work variety, nor were they restricted to participation in the informal economy, which has been viewed as a possible alternative to the institution of employment. The study also showed that among the unemployed those with greater access to the categories of experience had better scores on standard measures of psychological well-being. However, the unemployed were found to have less access to the five categories of experience and worse psychological well-being than the group of employed people. Miles noted, though, that the employed sample was of a higher socio-economic status than the unemployed sample, thus making further comparative work necessary. He also suggested that it would be useful to refine the measures that had been developed to measure access to the five categories of experience.

Miles and Howard (1984), Henwood and Miles (1987) and Evans and Banks (1992) have also shown that Jahoda's categories of experience can be obtained by the unemployed, though not all to the same extent as by employed people of the same age group. In addition, Miles and Howard (1984) have shown the unemployed to be worse on some but not other measures of psychological well-being in comparison with the employed; and Evans and Banks (1992) have shown variations in ACE to be correlated with life satisfaction. The authors of these studies recognize, however, that the research would have benefited from the use of a wider range of more standard measures of psychological well-being.

The study by Evans and Banks (1992) is also notable because it shows the reliability of a refined version of the ACE scales produced by Evans (1986) in consultation with Miles. The sample studied by Evans and Banks consisted of 287 young people 16 to 19 years old and of various employment status (unemployed, Youth Training Scheme, full-time education, employed). In this study responses to the ACE items were made on a five-point scale, and each category of experience was measured by three items. The reliability analysis produced the following generally acceptable alpha co-efficients: activity (0.58), time structure (0.52), social contact (0.68), status (0.58) and collective purpose (0.62). A factor analysis was also performed which confirmed the existence of five separate factors, with the subscale items clustering together generally as expected. The authors concluded: 'we can assert with confidence that the five sub-scales are both reliable and independent of each other' (p. 286). They also noted that in the study by Evans (1986), factor analysis of the same items pooled together with a range of mental health measures confirmed that contrary to some suggestions, these items are tapping environmental rather than affective dimensions. They concluded that 'the measure of ACE represents the quality of a person's daily life, whereas the mental health measures tap their response to that quality (or lack of it)' (p. 286).

An important study using the refined measures of ACE and a range of standard measures of psychological well-being was undertaken by Evans (1986). This study, also reported and discussed in Evans and Haworth (1991), compared thirty-six unemployed adults aged 18 to 29 with thirty-six employed adults, matched in terms of age, marital status, education and socio-economic background. Three items were used to measure each of the five categories of experience. For example, 'activity' was measured by the responses 'My time is filled with things to do' (+ve (i.e. positively phrased) item), 'Things I have to do to keep me busy most of the day' (+ve item), 'Time often lies heavy on my hands' (-ve (i.e. negatively phrased) item). Each item was scored on a seven-point scale ranging from 'Completely disagree' (1) to 'Completely agree' (7). A mean score for each category was obtained from each set of three questions (having reversed the values of negative items), and used in analysis. If this mean score was 4 or above, then the respondent was also classed as having access to this category, and given a score of 1 in order to calculate the number of categories accessed, which could thus range from 0 to 5. The complete ACE questionnaire is given in Appendix 1.

Several standard psychological scales were used to measure different aspects of well-being:

1 The General Health Questionnaire (Goldberg, 1972) was administered in its twelve-item version (GHQ-12). Items cover strain and depression, loss of concentration, sleep, etc.
2 The self-esteem scale (Warr and Jackson, 1983) was used to assess respondents' feeling of personal worth. Four items measure positive self-esteem, and four items measure negative (unfavourable) personal self-esteem evaluations. Scores on the negative self-esteem items are reversed, so that a high score on both scales indicates favourable assessments of personal worth.
3 A life satisfaction scale based on Warr, Cook and Wall (1979) was administered. The scale included eleven items which refer to different aspects of the respondents' everyday lives and their environment. The sum of the scores to the eleven items constitutes a measure of an individual's total life satisfaction. The twelfth and final item on the scales asked respondents to rate their life as a whole at the present moment. Scores on this item provide the measure of an individual's overall life satisfaction. All items in the life satisfaction scale are answered using seven-point scales, ranging from 'Extremely dissatisfied' (1) to 'Extremely satisfied' (7).
4 An item measuring happiness, developed by Bradburn (1969), was also

administered. This asks 'Taking all things together, how would you say things are these days – would you say that you are very happy, pretty happy, or not too happy?', and is scored on a three-point scale.

The results showed that the unemployed sample exhibited consistently poorer mental health than the employed sample according to all the measures taken of psychological well-being. The unemployed were at greater risk of minor psychiatric disorder as indicated by scores on the GHQ-12 ($p < 0.001$). Levels of self-esteem were significantly lower among the unemployed, where negative self-esteem was substantially worse ($p < 0.001$), though positive self-esteem was also significantly lower ($p < 0.05$). The unemployed reported significantly lower levels of happiness in comparison to the employed sample ($p < 0.005$). The single-item measure of overall life satisfaction was significantly lower for the unemployed ($p < 0.001$) as was the eleven-item measure of total life satisfaction ($p < 0.001$).

The employed sample had access to a much greater number of Jahoda's five categories of experience. The mean number of categories to which the employed had access was 4.44 (SD = 0.7), (Max. 5.00), while the unemployed had on average access to only 2.86 categories (SD = 1.6) ($t = 5.333$, d.f. = 70, $p > 0.001$). Fifty-six per cent of employed respondents gained access to all five categories of experience, though 89 per cent reported gaining access to four or more. For the unemployed sample, only 19 per cent of respondents gained access to all five categories, though 42 per cent reported having access to four or more. Only 11 per cent of the unemployed reported having no access to any of the five categories.

In the unemployed group, correlation analysis showed that each of Jahoda's five categories of experience correlated significantly with at least one of the measures of psychological well-being, and that the category of activity correlated with the largest number, namely all the main measures of psychological well-being with the exception of positive self-esteem. To explore the effect of activity on psychological well-being in the unemployed, the sample was divided into two groups on the basis of a median split for scores on the category of activity. The more active group had much better psychological well-being than the less active group as indicated by their scores on the GHQ-12 ($p < 0.05$), the single item measure of overall life satisfaction ($p < 0.05$), and the composite measure of life satisfaction ($p < 0.05$). This more active group also reported more happiness in their daily lives ($p < 0.05$). However, there was no difference between the two groups on either of the measures of self-esteem. With regard to the other categories of experience (i.e. other than activity), the more active group had significantly greater access to all four categories, namely collective purpose, time structure, status, and social contact.

It is to be noted that the more active group were of higher educational level ($p < 0.005$) and came from higher socio-economic backgrounds ($p < 0.5$). They also had more previous experience of being without a job for a year or more

($p < 0.05$) and more experience of long-term (i.e. over one year) further education ($p < 0.005$).

The more active unemployed group was also compared with the employed group. There was no significant difference between these two groups in psychological well-being as measured by the GHQ-12, and in terms of their reported happiness. However, the active unemployed group exhibited significantly poorer mental health as indicated by the measures of self-esteem, including both positive self-esteem ($p < 0.05$) and negative self-esteem ($p < 0.05$). Overall life satisfaction was also lower in the active unemployed group ($p < 0.001$) as was the composite measure of total life satisfaction ($p < 0.001$). With respect to the various categories of experience, the active unemployed group reported significantly less access to the categories of status, social contact and time structure.

These results, using better measures of ACE and psychological well-being than those used by Henwood and Miles (1987), support their conclusions that many people lacking formal employment are failing to gain access to important categories of experience which contribute towards a sense of well-being. The results also concur with the suggestion of Henwood and Miles (1987) that different ways of using one's time when unemployed may be important determinants of well-being. The unemployed in the present study who were able to keep busy and fill their time had similar levels of happiness and freedom from negative mental health (GHQ-12) as the employed.

Although high levels of activity (keeping busy) can operate in a psychologically supportive manner during unemployment, the present study also shows that the benefits are limited in their extent in comparison to the levels of well-being of the individuals in employment. The more active unemployed respondents had significantly lower scores on both measures of life satisfaction and positive and negative self-esteem. If the motivation for keeping busy is to avoid apathy it may be limited in its effect on life satisfaction and self-esteem.

The study also measured the extent to which each unemployed person's activity was judged to be centred round a particular main activity of any type. Raters had to judge – from case notes of the activity of the unemployed – the extent to which the subject had a 'particular activity or interest which plays a significant or important part in their life at the moment'. Possible responses ranged from 'Definitely no' (scale value = 0) through to 'Definitely yes' (scale value = 6). Just over half the unemployed sample had a main activity, either work based, leisure based or general social interaction, which gave them a chance to use their abilities and be creative. These individuals had levels of self-esteem similar to the employed sample. However, they had worse affective well-being as measured by the GHQ-12 ($p < 0.01$), life satisfaction ($p < 0.001$) and happiness, ($p < 0.05$), and less access to the categories of experience of status ($p < 0.001$), social contact ($p < 0.001$), and time structure ($p < 0.001$) than the employed group.

The majority of the unemployed with a main activity reported that it gave them a sense of accomplishment, the chance to use their abilities, to be creative and to use their own judgement, and that it kept them busy. These characteristics were, in fact, more prevalent for this subset of the unemployed than they were for the employed sample. However, a majority of the employed sample, unlike the unemployed sample, reported that their job gave them a chance to do things for other people. This, perhaps, may contribute to the differences in self-perceived status (or social identity) between the employed and the active unemployed group, and which could be supported by the better 'social contact' among the employed.

The finding that the unemployed with a main activity did not differ from the employed in terms of self-esteem, and the category of experience of collective purpose, could be explained in terms of efficacious action. Gecas and Schwalbe (1983, pp. 79–85) argue that efficacious action is an important determinant of self-esteem: 'human beings derive a sense of self not only from reflected appraisal of others, but also from the consequences and products of behaviour that are attributed to the self as an agent in the environment'.

They also argue that it is important to consider the nature of the social context within which an individual functions; particularly with regard to the constraints imposed on individual autonomy, the degree of individual control and the availability of resources, which are necessary for producing intended outcomes. They note that the interaction between contextual resources and an individual's ability at mobilizing them, is important. Thus, they state, 'efficacy-based self-esteem depends upon an individual's opportunities to engage in efficacious action . . . (and) various social structural conditions both enable and constrain an individual's opportunities for engaging in efficacious action'. They also highlight the importance of the meaning which is ascribed to activity by an individual: 'even in the face of highly constraining objective conditions, actors may use whatever lattitude they possess to reconstruct the meaning of action such that efficacy-based esteem can be derived from it'.

This concept of self-esteem gives an indication of the way in which engagement in personally meaningful activity during unemployment can support self-esteem, whereby such activities provide an opportunity for engaging in efficacious action. It also stresses the necessity of studying purposeful forms of human behaviour which, as Feather and Bond (1983) have argued, are important both within and beyond the context of unemployment; and studying the factors which restrict personal agency, as emphasized by Fryer (1995). However, in arguing for a link between action, self-evaluation and social structure, Gecas and Schwalbe (1993) consider that the contribution of competent performance to self-esteem will depend, in part, on the meaning that is given to that performance both within the immediate context of actions and within the larger cultural community, and that in this regard social comparisons are likely to be especially crucial for self-esteem. In other words, personal agency in its influence on self-esteem is affected by social comparisons and cultural values. As such, the various social structural conditions which enable or promote action and its interpretation are also important, and require detailed study. This is in line with the views of Jahoda (1986) which stress the necessity of bringing into visibility the hidden social structures which support behaviour and well-being. While the present study was not designed to investigate this aspect, it is worth noting that many of the main activities of the unemployed did not seem to be embedded in informal institutional support systems. Although this perhaps shows the importance of personal agency in sustaining meaningful activity and aspects of well-being, it is still an open question as to whether or not this group of people would have had access to all categories of experience and better psychological well-being if their main activity had been located in a valued social structure.

Haworth and Evans (1987) briefly outline a number of case histories from the young unemployed studied by Evans (1986), which demonstrate the range of lifestyles adopted by these people and the variety of their experience of unemployment. Descriptions of main activities are given which demonstrate how they can range from more 'work-like' activities to more 'leisure'-based activities. There was considerable variety in what could constitute a main activity – busking, involvement with a local political party, involvement with a discussion group at a college of further education, casual repair work, listening to and playing music, flying radio-controlled aircraft, visiting friends, training for and competing in marathons, compiling a low-budget cookery book and being involved with a fringe theatre company. This variety emphasizes the fact that potentially any activity could be developed into a main activity by an individual during unemployment.

Young people in this age group (18 to 29), though, are still in a stage of transitional development. Csikszentmihalyi and Larson (1984) in their study of American adolescents claim that the development of a personal life theme – a meaningful arrangement of goals and means – is crucial to 'The meaningful interpretation of existence'. They report, however, that only a few individuals develop personal life goals themselves and that most are satisfied to pursue the goals society provides: a college education, a job, marriage, children and life within conventional standards of morality. They also recognize the notable part played by unconscious factors in the adoption of life goals, a point acknowledged by Csikszentmihalyi and Beattie (1979) in their study of life themes in adults. While young unemployed people may develop a main activity, the question of life goals is important, especially in situations where the prescribed goals of society are withheld from some sections of that society.

SUSTAINING ACTIVITY AND WELL-BEING IN THE UNEMPLOYED

Although, perhaps, the best encapsulating statement regarding the role and nature of personally meaningful activity for the unemployed is that by Warr (1984) when he notes that 'the large majority of people out of work today are clearly employable and clearly want a job', one can agree with the statement of Warr and Payne (1983) that 'sustaining activity levels . . . for unemployed people has a great deal to recommend it'.

A theory pertaining to psychological well-being, but one which has not received much attention in the study of unemployment, is that proposed by Csikszentmihalyi and colleagues (e.g. Csikszentmihalyi and Csikzsentmihalyi, 1988). They stress the importance of intrinsic motivation and enjoyment for quality of life. Their research uses experience sampling methodology (ESM) where people carry questionnaire diaries and electronic pagers which are bleeped to indicate response times. Results from the study of employed people show that as intrinsic motivation in daily life increases, individuals are more happy and less tense (Graef *et al.*, 1983). From their research on the employed, Csikszentmihalyi and colleagues argue that enjoyment plays a pivotal role in maintaining and enhancing quality of life and psychological well-being. In view of the potential of these factors for sustaining activity and well-being, a study was undertaken by Haworth and Ducker (1991) on a sample of twenty-two long-term unemployed young adults using the ESM and questionnaires to measure intrinsic motivation, enjoyment ACE and well-being. Questions were also asked on hope for the future, goals and career plans and financial strain.

Each respondent carried a time diary in which a series of questions had to be answered eight times a day for eight consecutive days, the first day being a practice day. Each respondent also carried an electronic paging device (watch or radio pager) which was 'bleeped' to indicate the response time for filling in the diary, between the hours of 11.30am and 11.30pm. Respondents were asked, 'What was the main thing you were doing?' and also, 'Why were you doing this activity?' Possible answers to the latter question were, 'I had to', 'I wanted to', and 'I had nothing else to do', one of which the respondents had to tick. They were also asked, 'Do you wish you had been doing something else'? The answer was given on a seven-point scale ranging from 'Not at all' (1) to 'Very much' (7). If respondents ticked either 1 or 2 on this question and had also ticked that they had wanted to do this activity then this was coded as *intrinsic motivation*. A question asking, 'How much were you enjoying this activity?', to be answered on a seven-point scale ranging from 'Not at all' (1) to 'Very much' (7) was used to calculate a mean enjoyment score over the duration of the study. Respondents also had to fill in seven-point scales on questions pertaining to the challenge of the activity and the skill level involved.

The study showed that this particular sample of unemployed young people had a generally low interest in conventional work roles. Only 41 per cent of the sample had any 'definite plans for a future career'. However, 77 per cent had definite hopes, plans or goals for the future which included 'setting up a co-op', 'learning practical skills so that I can be self-sufficient and independent of the state' and 'learning skills without having to pay or be paid'. Seventy-two per cent of the sample reported that they 'enjoyed being unemployed' and 94 per cent reported that unemployment provided a 'means to develop oneself'. Of the sample, 21 per cent were 'very happy', while 46 per cent were 'fairly happy' and 33 per cent were 'not happy' with their situation. The mean number per respondent of 'significant or important' activities in their lives was 3. Of the total number of such activities reported, 23 per cent were political; 20 per cent recreational (reading, writing, etc.); 16 per cent musical; 13 per cent social; 11 per cent sporting; 11 per cent artistic/creative and 6 per cent categorized as 'other'. The sample contains a significant proportion of 'proactive' unemployed people who apparently at this moment are willing to develop what Roberts *et al.* (1982) have called alternative lifestyles.

However, even within this sample that, in general, looks favourably on unemployment, 71 per cent of the responses recorded by the experience sampling method over the seven-day period showed that skill level exceeded the challenge level of the particular activity undertaken. The psychological health of the sample was also worse on a range of measures than that of the sample of thirty-six employed young adults reported in Evans and Haworth (1991) – i.e. general mental health (GHQ-12) (t = 2.73, p < 0.01), negative self-esteem evaluation (t = 1.84, p < 0.05), total life satisfaction (t = 2.06, p < 0.05), and overall life satisfaction (t = 2.63, p < 0.01).

Analysis of the correlates of well-being showed that intrinsic motivation did not correlate with any of the dimensions of psychological well-being. This is contrary to results obtained in employed people by Graef *et al.* (1983) indicating that intrinsic motivation correlated significantly with happiness and with reduced tension. It may be that the surfeit of free time in the unemployed reduces the importance of intrinsic motivation. Of the different 'categories of experience', activity, collective purpose, status and social contact correlated significantly with measures of psychological well-being. However, time structure did not correlate with any of the dimensions of psychological well-being. This is similar to the findings of Miles and Howard (1984), perhaps indicating the reduced importance of this category of experience for young people. Contrary to expectations, 'social contact' also correlated negatively with self-esteem, perhaps reflecting difficulties in maintaining reciprocity on social occasions (Kelvin and Jarrett, 1985). These results indicate the necessity of studying different life situations when investigating the correlates of psychological well-being and the importance of different categories of experience.

Hope for the future, enjoyment and decreased financial strain (money) all correlated highly and significantly in this sample with a number of measures of psychological well-being. An analysis of intercorrelations was also interesting. This showed that hope for the future and enjoyment, but not money, were significantly correlated with the ACE scales.

In view of the importance of the categories of experience, and particular activity for psychological well-being, a comparison was made of the type and patterns of activity engaged in by a subgroup of individuals with greater access to the five categories of experience and a subgroup of individuals with lower access. Individuals with the top seven scores for access to the five categories of experience were taken as a 'high-access' group, and individuals with the bottom seven scores as a 'low-access' group. The activities which individuals in these two groups were engaged in when 'bleeped' were divided into categories devised by Graef *et al.* (1983) and converted to percentage of things done over the week. The results showed that the high ACE group engaged in much more work and active leisure activities, and to a lesser extent more household chores. Whereas the low ACE group engaged in more passive leisure, idling and driving/travelling.

The results are interesting in that they suggest that respondents with better access to the five categories of experience participate in more positive and engaging activities or, in the terminology of White (1959), more 'competence'-serving activities than the low ACE group. It could thus be expected that the high ACE group would have better self-esteem and general levels of psychological well-being. This was borne out by t-test results. The high ACE group was statistically significantly better than the low ACE group on favourable negative self-esteem evaluations (t = 3.05, p < 0.01), total life satisfaction (t = 2.95, p < 0.01), GHQ–12 (t = 3.68, p < 0.01) and mean enjoyment (t = 3.03, p < 0.05).

The results from this study show that this sample of mainly long-term unemployed young adults contains a significant proportion of 'proactive' individuals in that they have activities which are important to them, viewing unemployment as a means to develop oneself, with the majority having definite hopes, plans or goals for the future. However, the vast majority of responses (71 per cent) recorded by the ESM over the seven-day period showed that skill level exceeded challenge level of the particular activity undertaken. Graef *et al.* (1983) have called these 'boring' experiences, though this categorization is open to doubt (Clarke and Haworth, 1994). Nevertheless, this sample of largely proactive unemployed people were worse off in comparison to employed young adults on several dimensions of psychological well-being, i.e. mental health (GHQ-12), negative self-esteem evaluations, total and overall life satisfaction.

The results showing that both hope for the future and enjoyment are significantly correlated with access to Jahoda's categories of experience perhaps indicate a notable interplay between these factors. It may well be, as Fryer and McKenna (1989) have argued, that proactivity is an important route into gaining access to categories of experience, and that the results in this study reflect variations in proactivity in the unemployed. At the same time, however, it may be that the work-like activities and active leisure engaged in by those with greater access to Jahoda's categories of experience provide some social structure and even obligation and commitment in the lives of these individuals (Haworth, 1984, 1986; Haworth and Evans, 1987). This warrants further research.

Another possibility is that enjoyment plays a significant role in these person–situation interactions. Csikszentmihalyi (1982) has argued that enjoyment is a crucial facet of quality of life and that it leads to psychological development. It may be that the correlation between enjoyment and access to categories of experience is a two-way relationship representing a dynamic intertwining between the person and the situation. Thus engagement in activity and other categories of experience could provide enjoyment, while at the same time enjoyment could provide the stimulus to continue with engagement in pursuits.

It is interesting that the results in the present study show that hope for the future correlated with more favourable GHQ-12 scores indicative of freedom from disturbance in normal mental functioning. While hope for the future may, to some degree, reflect personal characteristics, it could also be that this is both initiated and maintained through enjoyable interactions. Successful interactions can, of course, depend to some degree on adequate financial resources, or at least perceived freedom from financial strain. In the present study, lack of financial strain was a primary correlate of total life satisfaction, although, perhaps unexpectedly, it did not correlate with access to categories of experience.

In conclusion, this study of long-term unemployed young adults has shown that in this sample 'hope for the future', reduced financial strain, access to Jahoda's categories of experience (in particular, activity) and enjoyment are associated with critical and different dimensions of psychological well-being. It was also shown that there are important correlations between hope for the future, enjoyment and access to categories of experience, and it is suggested that these interrelations could be usefully explored further to study the processes involved in person–situation interactions pertinent to psychological well-being. Finally, the study has also shown that those unemployed individuals with better access to Jahoda's categories of experience have better psychological well-being and engage in more work-like and active leisure activities.

WORK AND LEISURE

We must be prepared to undertake research into categories of experience and well-being in the employed as well as in the unemployed. A study by Haworth and Hill (1992) examined the relationship between motivation, enjoyment, access to categories of experience and well-being in the work and leisure time of a sample of twenty 'white-collar' young employed adults. The study used a short questionnaire, psychological scales and the ESM for one week, respondents answering questions in a diary on the receipt of a signal eight times a day between the hours of 11.30am and 11.30pm.

Respondents were asked in the diary, 'What was the main thing you were doing'? and also 'Why were you doing this activity'?, possible answers to the latter question being 'I had to', 'I wanted to' and 'I had nothing else to do', one of which the respondents had to tick. They were also asked, 'Do you wish you had been doing something else?', the answer being given on a seven-point scale ranging from 'Not at all' (1) to 'Very much' (7). If respondents ticked either 1 or 2 on this question, and had also ticked that they wanted to do the activity, the response was coded as intrinsic motivation. Extrinsic motivation was indicated with a response 'I had to', coupled with 6 or 7 on the question 'Do you wish you had been doing something else'? Although Graef et al. (1983) in their study of employed people did not include activities in their analysis which could not be classified under the heading of either intrinsic or extrinsic motivation, it was deemed that such responses could be pertinent to the psychological well-being of the employed, as much as their time is spent in obligatory activities which they may wish to continue. Therefore, measures of 'positive motivational change' (PMC) and 'negative motivational change' (NMC) were included in the present study. PMC was measured as 'I had to' (do the activity) in conjunction with a tick of 1 or 2 on the seven-point scale for the question, 'Do you wish you had been doing something else?', where 1 indicates 'Not at all'. NMC was measured as 'I wanted to' (do the activity) in conjunction with a tick of 6 or 7 on the above question, where 7 indicates 'Very much'.

The motivational measure consisted of the frequency for each person of each motivational category (intrinsic, extrinsic, positive motivational change, negative motivational change) over the seven days of the study. Questions were also asked in the diary on affective states, competence and challenge in activities, and enjoyment and interest.

The results showed that when motivational variables are considered for daily life as a whole, intrinsic motivation correlated significantly with happiness, a finding shown in other studies (e.g. Graef *et al.*, 1983); but that extrinsic motivation, positive motivational change and negative motivational change, did not correlate with any of the measures of psychological well-being. When, however, the motivational variables were analysed separately for work and leisure a different pattern emerged. Intrinsic motivation for leisure, but not for work, correlated with happiness, and extrinsic motivation for work correlated with competence: the more one had to do things the more competent one felt. Somewhat similarly, 'positive motivational change' (i.e. having to do an activity but then wishing to continue) correlated with self-determination, while 'negative motivational change' (i.e. first wanting to do an activity but not wishing to continue) correlated negatively with self-determination and overall life satisfaction, and positively with scores on the GHQ indicating worse mental health. Thus extrinsic motivation at work, and the perception of this in a positive light (i.e. 'positive motivational change'), is associated in this sample with important beneficial aspects of mental health, while 'negative motivational change' is associated with a range of negative psychological aspects.

The results showed that enjoyment in daily life as a whole correlated with relaxation, total life satisfaction and happiness, which was similar to the findings for enjoyment in leisure. However, enjoyment in work correlated with total life satisfaction, and interestingly, hope for the future.

The results for access to categories of experience for work and leisure are also interesting. While there were some correlations between ACE at work and psychological well-being, there was a range of correlations with ACE in leisure. Social contact, collective purpose, status and a composite measure of the five categories of experience termed 'total access', all correlated with a measure of life satisfaction. Social contact and collective purpose also correlated significantly with happiness in daily life measured by the ESM. Status, time structure and total access all correlated significantly with a measure of self-esteem. Variations in access to categories of experience in the leisure time of employed people thus appear to be important in relation to well-being, contrary to Jahoda's predictions. It may well be that for some people there is not a strict division between the important categories of experience obtained in work and those obtained in leisure.

However, it may be that the mechanisms vary for obtaining ACE in work and leisure. When the seven individuals with the highest and lowest total ACE scores in both work and leisure were compared, the individuals with high ACE in leisure had significantly higher mean enjoyment scores than the individuals with low ACE in leisure (t = 2.30, p < 0.005), though this was not the case in work. Perhaps ACE at work can be provided to some extent irrespective of enjoyment, as Jahoda (1986) appears to indicate. Whereas, it seems that ACE in leisure requires more individual effort, reflected in higher enjoyment scores in leisure.

Work, however, is also important for enjoyment, as the correlation analysis reported earlier indicated. An analysis of skill (competence) and challenge in activities also showed the importance of work for enjoyment and interest. Csikszentmihalyi (1982) has shown that when skills and challenge are in balance this can result in enjoyable 'flow' experience, particularly when the challenge is high. In the present study activities in daily life were banded into balanced levels of skills and challenges for each point on the seven-point measurement scale, and the mean level of enjoyment and interest calculated for each point. Enjoyment and interest levels were found to increase in an approximately linear relationship as the level of balanced skill and challenge increased. To assess the relative importance of 'work' and leisure for balanced high skill/challenge activities, which Csikszentmihalyi (1982) has termed 'macro-flow', activities were coded into either work or leisure for each level of balanced skill and challenges. The results showed that 83 per cent of balanced skill/challenge activities at the 6 : 6 level were at work and 17 per cent at leisure and at the 7 : 7 level, 86 per cent were at work and 14 per cent at leisure. These states of macro-flow were highly enjoyable and interesting.

Overall, the results of this study show that for this sample of young adults in 'white-collar' employment, both work and leisure are important for positive subjective states and psychological well-being. While the results indicate, in line with other studies of employed people (e.g. Graef et al., 1983), that intrinsic motivation is a statistically significant correlate of happiness, they also show (not previously reported in other studies of employed people) that extrinsic motivation at work is correlated with competence, and that 'positive motivational change' (i.e. perceiving extrinsic motivation positively) is correlated with self-determination, the reverse being the case for 'negative motivational change'. The 'structured' situation of employment may be providing some psychological benefits for individuals, possibly by instigating purposive activity and 'traction' (Warr, 1987) and providing various categories of experience.

In addition, employment was found to be the main source of macro-flow, where high challenges and high skills are perceived as equal. In a study of employed people by Csikszentmihalyi and Le Fevre (1989) the great majority of flow experiences (transformed into Z scores) were experienced when working, not when at leisure. One of the experiential descriptions of flow is that it contains ordered rules which make action and the evaluation of action automatic and unproblematic, and in this connection (Warr, 1987, p.138) notes that: 'This description is very similar to Baldamus's account of traction', which is seen as similar to the 'rhythm', 'swing' or 'pull' of work (p.135).

The results on motivation and flow indicated the importance of studying person–situation interactions and the processes involved in these interactions. In some respects, this is also indicated in the present study in the relationships between ACE in leisure and psychological well-being. The results show that there are variations in ACE in leisure in the employed sample, and that these correlated positively with a range of measures of mental health. In addition, comparison of a low and high ACE group in leisure showed that individuals with high ACE had significantly higher mean enjoyment scores than individuals with low ACE. Fryer and McKenna (1989) have argued from studies of redundant people that the successful exercise of personal agency, or proactivity, is a major means for gaining access to important categories of experience. It may well be that enjoyment can be a key factor or process underpinning this interaction between the person and situationally afforded categories of experience.

Although enjoyment can be crucial in the context of structured person–situation interactions (flow and access to categories of experience) the results in the present study also show that it correlates with relaxation and happiness, which are the more 'traditional' aspects of leisure. Jahoda (1986) has postulated a set of categories of experience complementary to those she considers come primarily from work: namely unstructured time, privacy, individual effort, personal identity and periods of passivity. While Jahoda's theories suggest that leisure is mainly concerned with one set of categories of experience, and work (employment) with another, the present study and others indicate that this is too simplistic as a general premise. Although this hypothesis may be true for some groups of people, it seems more appropriate to study the contributions that both work and leisure can make to psychological well-being for different samples of people in different situations. Information obtained at this level of analysis may have a more direct bearing on the practical issues of well-being for particular groups of people in particular situations. The construction of a more general theory may arise from examining the processes and dynamics underpinning different person–situation interactions in work, leisure and psychological well-being.

CONCLUSION

The empirical studies of categories of psychological experience and well-being reported and discussed in this chapter support the case for the importance for well-being of time structure, social contact, collective effort or purpose, social identity or status and regular activity. While correlational studies cannot prove a causal connection between the categories of experience and well-being, they give grounds for their continued use in both theory and policy. Research using these categories of experience would benefit from the inclusion of additional variables which may be associated with well-being, as this reduces the risk of specification error: that the relationship between two variables is caused by a third unspecified variable. More inclusive models of well-being form part of the subject matter of the next chapter.

The studies in the present chapter have shown that it is possible for samples of unemployed people to gain access to Jahoda's categories of experience. Many of these studies, however, have been conducted on young people, and it may be that changing attitudes, values and expectations in this group make the reliance on the formal institution of employment for access to the categories of experience less than that for older people. Nevertheless, the studies have also shown that many young people lacking formal employment are failing to gain access to important categories of experience which appear to contribute towards a sense of well-being. It also remains the case that in these groups of young people employment is a stronger determinant of access to the categories of experience than is unemployment.

A number of studies reported in this chapter have showed that there is variability in access to the categories of experience in the employed, as well as in the unemployed. While it may be the case, as Jahoda and Rush (1980) assert, that some experience in each of the five categories must occur in employment, this may only be minimal in some cases, and do little to help satisfy enduring human needs. It is thus important that variability in access to categories of experience is studied in the employed as well as in the unemployed. This is also the subject matter of the next chapter.

REFERENCES

Bradburn, N.M. (1969) *The Structure of Psychological Well-being*, Chicago: Aldine Publishing Co.

Clarke, S.G. and Haworth, J.T. (1994) '"Flow" experience in the daily lives of sixth form college students', *British Journal of Psychology* 85, 511–23.

Csikszentmihalyi, M. (1982) 'Towards a psychology of optimal experience', in L. Wheeler (ed.), *Review of Personality and Social Psychology* (Vol. 2), Beverly Hills, CA: Sage.

Csikszentmihalyi, M. and Beattie, O. (1979) 'Life themes: a theoretical and empirical exploration of their origins and effects', *Journal of Humanistic Psychology* 19, 45–63.

Csikszentmihalyi, M. and Csikszentmihalyi, I.S. (1988) *Optimal Experience; Psychological Studies of Flow in Consciousness*, Cambridge: Cambridge University Press.

Csikszentmihalyi, M. and Larson, R. (1984) *Being Adolescent*, New York: Basic Books.

Csikszentmihalyi, M. and Le Fevre, J. (1989) 'Optimal experience in work and leisure', *Journal of Personality and Social Psychology* 56, 815–22.

Evans, S.T. (1986) 'Variations in activity and psychological well-being in employed young adults', unpublished PhD thesis, University of Manchester.

Evans, S.T. and Banks, M.H. (1992) 'Latent functions of employment: variations according to employment status and labour market', in C.H.A. Verhaar and L. Jansma *et al.* (eds), *On the Mysteries of Unemployment*, Netherlands: Kluwer, 281–95.

Evans, S.T. and Haworth, J.T. (1991) 'Variations in personal activity, access to categories of experience and psychological well-being in unemployed young adults', *Leisure Studies* 10, 249–64.

Feather, N.T. and Bond, M.J. (1983) 'Time structure and purposeful activity among employed and unemployed university graduates', *Journal of Occupational Psychology* 56, 241–54.

Fryer, D. (1995) 'Benefit agency? Labour market disadvantage, deprivation and mental health', *The Psychologist*, 265–72.

Fryer, D. and McKenna, S.P. (1989) 'Redundant skills, temporary unemployment and mental health', in M. Patrickson (ed.), *Readings in Organisational Behaviour*, New South Wales: Harper & Row.

Fryer, D. and Payne, R. (1984) 'Proactive behaviour in unemployment findings and implications', *Leisure Studies* 3, 273–95.

Gecas, V. and Schwalbe, M.L. (1983) 'Beyond the looking-glass self: social structure and efficacy-based self-esteem', *Social Psychology Quarterly* 46, 77–88.

Goldberg, D. (1972) *The Detection of Psychiatric Illness by Questionnaire*, London: Oxford University Press.

Graef, R., Csikszentmihalyi, M. and Gianinno, S.M. (1983) 'Measuring intrinsic motivation in people's everyday lives', *Leisure Studies* 2, 155–68.

Haworth, J.T. (1984) 'The perceived nature of meaningful pursuits and the social psychology of commitment', *Society and Leisure* 7, 197–216.

Haworth, J.T. (1986) 'Meaningful activity and psychological models of non-employment', *Leisure Studies* 5, 281–97.

Haworth, J.T. and Ducker, J. (1991) 'Psychological well-being and access to categories of experience in unemployed young adults', *Leisure Studies* 10, 265–74.

Haworth, J.T. and Evans, S.T. (1987) 'Meaningful activity and unemployment', in D. Fryer and P. Ullah (eds), *Unemployed People*, Milton Keynes: Open University Press.

Haworth, J.T. and Hill, S. (1992) 'Work, leisure and psychological well-being in a sample of young adults', *Journal of Community and Applied Social Psychology* 2, 147–60.

Henwood, F. and Miles, I. (1987) 'The experience of unemployment and the sexual divisions of labour', in D. Fryer and P. Ullah (eds), *Unemployed People*, Milton Keynes: Open University Press.

Jahoda, M. (1979) 'The impact of unemployment in the 1930s and the 1970s', *Bulletin of the British Psychological Society* 32, 309–14.

Jahoda, M. (1981) 'Work, employment and unemployment: values, theories and approaches in social research', *American Psychology* 36, 1984–91.

Jahoda, M. (1982) *Employment and Unemployment: A Social Psychological Analysis*, Cambridge: Cambridge University Press.

Jahoda, M. (1984) 'Social institutions and human needs: a comment on Fryer and Payne', *Leisure Studies* 3, 297–9.

Jahoda, M. (1986) 'In defence of a non-reductionist social psychology', *Social Behaviour* 1, 25–9.

Jahoda, M. and Rush, H. (1980) 'Work, employment and unemployment: an overview of ideas and research results in the social science literature', Occasional Paper series no. 12, Brighton: Science Policy Research Unit, University of Sussex.

Kelvin, P. and Jarrett, J.E. (1985) *Unemployment: Its Social-psychological Effects*, Cambridge: Cambridge University Press.

Miles, I. (1983) *Adaptation to Unemployment*, Science Policy Research Unit, Brighton: University of Sussex.

Miles, I. and Howard, J. (1984) 'A study of youth employment and unemployment', Occasional Paper, Science Policy Research Unit, Brighton: University of Sussex.

Roberts, K., Noble, M. and Duggan, J. (1982) 'Out-of-school youth in high unemployment areas: an empirical investigation', *British Journal of Guidance and Counselling* 10, 1–11.

Warr, P. (1984) 'Economic recession and mental health: a review of research', *Tidschrift voor Sociale Gezondheidzorg* 62, 298–308.

Warr, P. (1987) *Work, Unemployment and Mental Health*, Oxford: Clarendon Press.

Warr, P., Cook, J. and Wall, T. (1979) 'Scales for the measurement of some work attitudes and aspects of psychological well-being', *Journal of Occupational Psychology* 52, 129–48.

Warr, P.B. and Jackson, P. (1983) 'Self-esteem and unemployment among young workers', *Le Travail Humain* 46, 47–68.

Warr, P.B. and Payne, R. (1983) 'Social class and reported changes in behaviour after job loss', *Journal of Applied Social Psychology* 13, 206–22.

White, R. (1959) 'Motivation reconsidered: the concept of competence', *Psychological Review* 66: 5, 297–333.

Chapter 4

Principal environmental influences and mental health

This chapter focuses on a model of environmental influences important for mental health proposed by Warr (1986, 1987 and 1993). The model draws on that proposed by Jahoda (1982) emphasizing the importance for well-being of categories of experience provided by formal and informal institutions. It also encompasses features which Fryer and Payne (1984) highlight in their personal 'agency' account of people coping well with unemployment. The model is situation centred in that it emphasizes the importance for well-being of environmentally afforded categories of experience and is 'enabling' in that it recognizes that people can shape the character of their environment and influence its impact upon them. The model is thus concerned with person–situation interactions and processes, as well as with categorical features.

PRINCIPAL ENVIRONMENTAL INFLUENCES

Warr (1986) notes that his model seeks to explain variations in mental health within and between different environments in the same terms. These are nine broad features of the environment and are applicable in different situations. They are:

- opportunity for control;
- environmental clarity;
- opportunity for skill use;
- externally generated goals;
- variety;
- opportunity for interpersonal contact;
- valued social position;
- availability of money;
- physical security.

These nine principal environmental influences (PEIs), or environmental categories of experience, are considered to act together, in conjunction with person factors, to facilitate or constrain psychological well-being or mental health, which Warr divides into five main components: affective well-being, competence, aspiration, autonomy and integrated functioning.

Warr (1986, 1987, 1993) suggests that, like vitamins, the PEIs have non-linear effects, some improving mental health up to a certain point and then having no further effect, others producing benefits up to a certain level beyond which increases would be detrimental. The PEIs are proposed as determinants of mental health in all types of environments, including work and leisure. They are considered to be properties that an environment has relative to the capabilities and requirements of human beings (Warr 1987, p. 281). Warr also recognizes that individuals can have different enduring characteristics which may moderate the relationships between the principal environmental influences and the components of mental health, thus emphasizing the importance of studying person–situation interactions.

The principal environmental influences are described fully in Warr (1987), where he stresses that the division of the environment into nine principal categories which facilitate or constrain personally important processes and activities important for mental health, appears to be appropriately precise for most purposes, but that it is a matter of judgement, partly relating to applications, whether fewer or more categories would be preferable. In discussing the principal environmental influences he also notes that in many cases they can be divided into subcategories 'so that the fineness of categorization can be adjusted to meet a user's need' (p. 285). They can also be considered to fall into two broad categories covering *intrinsic* and *extrinsic* attributes.

The nine environmental categories have been devised in the light of considerable research into both jobs and unemployment, which Warr (1987) summarizes. Warr has deliberately set out to construct a categorical model wider in its coverage than perspectives restricted to intrinsic features of jobs. He considers that 'the evidence proposed for the nine factors is as convincing as that for other environmental models' (p. 283). The strength of this categorical model, he considers, is that it applies to any kind of environment and that it has considerable heuristic value, lending itself to application and development.

Central to the model is the proposition that the nine principal environmental influences are associated with mental health in a non-linear manner analogous to the influence of vitamins on physical health. Each PEI is thought to be harmful at low values but to have a constantly beneficial effect across a wide range of values, while some categories will have a negative effect in 'large doses'. This is illustrated in Figure 4.1.

While for diagrammatic purposes Warr presents one curve for all nine categories, he recognizes that there may be a family of curves for different PEIs and for the influence of a particular PEI on a particular component of mental health. Warr labels the 'additional decrement' part of the curve as AD, which is reflective of the fact that the vitamins AD can be toxic in large doses. The 'constant effect' part of the curve is labelled CE, which is reflective of vitamins CE appearing to have no ill effects, even in large doses.

The PEIs availability of money, physical security and valued social position

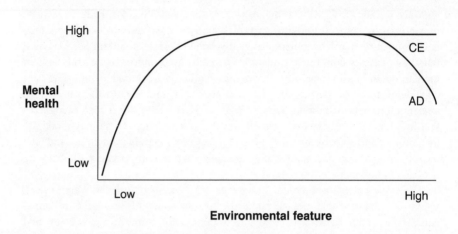

Figure 4.1 Principal environmental influences and mental health

are classified as being of the CE variety. The rest of the PEIs are considered to be of the AD variety. Thus PEIs such as opportunity for control, opportunity for skill use, externally generated goals and the like can turn from features which promote or facilitate into features which demand or coerce. 'It is this switch which causes the additional decrement at high levels' (Warr, 1986, p. 160). An 'opportunity' is thus liable to become an 'unavoidable requirement' at very high levels (Warr, 1987, p. 14). In addition, extremely high levels of one feature tend to have negative consequences for the level of certain other features.

Of all the environmental influences, 'opportunity for control' is assumed to be the principal 'foundation of mental health' (Warr, 1987, p. 4) as it not only contributes to psychological well-being in its own right, but also enables the individual to influence other levels of PEIs. It is defined as the opportunities provided by an environment for a person to control activities and events, and has two main elements: the opportunity to act in one's chosen way, and the potential to predict the consequences of one's actions. In employment, the former element may be subdivided into intrinsic control over the content of the job and extrinsic control over features of the job such as wages and company policy. Results from many studies have indicated that a relationship exists between perceived control and a wide range of subjective well-being measures, including life satisfaction and subjective competence. Environments which call for high levels of control through difficult decision-making and sustained responsibility are expected to give rise to overload strain, which in part may come about because of an associated shift to a high level of externally generated goals.

To enable an individual to make decisions and attain control, feedback from the environment is required, for without knowing the consequences of one's actions, suitable control of future events is almost impossible. This feature of the situation which is related to control has been termed 'environmental clarity' and three aspects appear to be particularly important: (1) feedback about the consequences of one's actions; (2) certainty about the future (this encompasses the degree of predictability of other people and systems in the environment so that one can foresee likely responses to one's own actions and, in the longer term, develop a conception of a likely life course); (3) clarity of role requirements and normative expectations.

Clarity has also been subdivided into 'intrinsic clarity' – that provided by the task itself; and 'extrinsic' clarity – that supplied by other people. Feedback implicit in the task appears to be an important feature of the environment, providing essential information regarding the attainment of goals and a basis for evaluating efficacy. Interpersonal contact may enable provision of environmental clarity as through discussion people gather information concerning their present environment and possible future changes, enhancing feedback, predictability and perceptions of the normative. Warr considers that environment clarity may be causally linked to aspects of affective well-being, though extreme clarity is expected to be harmful, as in perfectly predictable situations variety will be limited, with reduced requirements for exercising control or developing new skills.

The degree to which the environment inhibits or encourages the utilization and development of skills is notable and is often associated with 'control' and 'clarity'. Skilled performance can be satisfying in its smooth and familiar aspects and for permitting effective responses to novel or complex stimuli. It is psychologically important in assisting people to achieve targets, or to produce something useful or attractive.

The presence or absence of goals generated by the environment ('externally generated goals') is considered to be important for mental health. These can arise through obligations and targets deriving from roles within formal and informal institutions, as Jahoda (1982) has indicated. Warr (1987) notes that these roles introduce normative requirements to behave in certain ways, to follow certain routines and to be in specified locations at certain times; and that role-generated requirements give rise to organized sequences of actions, in which specific targets and their overall structure provide 'traction' which draws people along. Goals and plans are thus viewed as being generated by the nature of the environment, as well as through motivational characteristics of people themselves. This provides a direct synthesis of the 'agency theory' (Fryer and Payne, 1984) and the 'deprivation theory' (Jahoda, 1982) with their respective emphasis on the importance for well-being of personal agency and situational support (see Chapter 2). Warr's model also recognizes the importance of individual differences, noting that people differ in their tendency to establish goals themselves in the absence of environmental pressure. Externally generated goals can also be divided into intrinsic demands arising from tasks, and extrinsic demands arising from the context in which tasks, such as a job, are set.

While a certain level of externally generated goals may be beneficial for mental health, several investigators have reported significant associations between high job demand and low job satisfaction, life satisfaction, affective well-being and increased symptoms of physical ill health, including gastric complaints, headaches and nervous trouble. High job demands have been found to be associated with signs and symptoms of coronary heart disease, though research also indicates that this may be moderated by levels of personal control. Individuals with high work demands and low levels of control, typical of many blue-collar workers such as bus drivers, have been found to be at greater risk of heart disease than executives who are more in control of their working lives.

Variety is considered to be crucial for mental health since it can introduce novelty and break up excessive uniformity of activity and location, which externally generated goals can sometimes introduce, particularly within certain roles and jobs. Variety can be subdivided into intrinsic variety, concerning task features and the number of different operations performed, and extrinsic variety, which in the context of employment refers to aspects of the environment outside the content of the job, such as changes in location and working conditions. Extremely high levels of variety are considered to require constant switching of attention, with resulting low concentration and achievement in any single task. Conflict between contradictory goals may also be present, and extreme diversity may prevent development and use of substantial skills. Variety can also be considered in terms of the variability over time in the other PEIs.

Opportunity for interpersonal contact is considered to be important for at least four reasons. First, contact meets needs for friendship and reduces feelings of loneliness. Second, interpersonal contact can provide help of many kinds including emotional support, help with solving problems and encouragement to persist in efforts. Third, contact enables comparisons to be made with other people. Fourth, interpersonal contact arises from and makes possible the establishment and attainment of goals, which could not be realized by an individual alone. Opportunity for interpersonal contact provided by an environment can thus be seen to be linked with factors concerned with goals, variety, control, skill use and clarity. Extremely high levels of interpersonal contact may also be thought to be potentially harmful, through, for example, lack of personal control and excessive demands from other people. Studies of interpersonal contact have examined the significance of both quantity of contact and quality of contact for mental health.

Valued social position is defined as a position within a social structure which carries some esteem from others. Warr notes that in practice a person may be a member of several social structures – for example, a family, a company, a local community, society as a whole – and that the possibility of esteem arises from several sources. Perceptions of valued social position may thus be dependent upon three different types of evaluation: cultural (the general population), subcultural (the occupational population) and personal evaluations.

Warr considers that self-esteem within a social structure is generated primarily through the value attached to activities inherent in a role and the contribution these make to the social structure. Besides giving personal esteem, a valued social position may also give social esteem, or social status. Valued social position is associated with several other PEIs: a position and its role activities provide opportunities for social comparison, may enhance predictability and environmental clarity and impose goals and behavioural traction. More valued social positions in wider society may also carry with them larger incomes than those accorded lower status. Valued social position is considered to be a constant effect PEI, which we cannot have in excess.

Warr points out that money is often ignored in discussions of mental health, but that its absence can give rise to extensive psychological problems. Shortage of money means that payment of some bills is only possible if others are left unpaid. Entertainment requiring expenditure is not possible or is severely restricted, and life is impoverished in many senses beyond the merely financial. Poverty is also likely to influence other PEIs. Opportunity for personal control is reduced and skill use in hobby activities which require money is curtailed. Fryer (1995), discussed in Chapter 2, refers to many studies which show the enormous restrictive influence which poverty can have on the exercise of personal agency.

Physical security completes the list of principal environmental influence cited by Warr. Environments need to protect a person against physical threat and provide an adequate level of physical security. Work and home environments need to have reasonable physical conditions, in terms of temperature, noise and lighting, for example, so that the performance of tasks and hobbies are not unduly curtailed. Warr notes that 'physical security' often interacts with 'money'. He also makes a plea for research which examines physical working conditions to be undertaken in conjunction with other environmental categories, which is in line with the general theme of his model.

PERSON–SITUATION INTERACTIONS

'Persons affect situations, and situations affect persons; the process is a reciprocal one' (Warr, 1987, p. 291). Warr notes that his situation-centred model points to nine features of the environment which are assumed to be psychologically necessary, and asks why. Presumably, he says, because of certain characteristics of people. He uses the concept of 'affordances' developed by Gibson (1979) and used by Emery (1985) in relation to social planning. An affordance is a property that an environment has relative to the capabilities and requirements of a particular species: 'an affordance is neither an objective property nor a subjective property; or it is both if you like. An affordance cuts across the dichotomy of subjective–objective and helps us to understand its inadequacy. It is equally a fact of the environment and a fact of behaviour. It is both physical and psychical, yet neither. An affordance points both ways to the environment and to the observer' (Gibson, 1979, p. 129: quoted in Warr, 1987, p. 17). Affordances thus link together vital environmental features or categories and persons. The nine principal environmental influences are considered to facilitate personally important processes and activities. In more simplistic terms they are reflective of enduring human needs or requirements (Warr, 1987, p. 288).

Although Warr's model is situation centred, emphasizing the importance of various broad environmental features, 'it necessarily presupposes some characteristics of persons (and) . . . just as environments are recognised to differ so are variations expected between people' (Warr, 1987, p. 238). People vary in age, gender, nationality, ethnic group membership, socio-economic status and life-cycle stage, etc. There can also be differences between people in their styles of perceiving, thinking, valuing and behaviour, which can be fairly stable but which can change to some degree in response to situational pressures. Warr produces a classification of 'enduring' personal characteristics which identifies four key groups of attributes: (1) baseline mental health, (2) demographic features, (3) values; and (4) abilities. Baseline mental health includes several features often considered as elements of personality, such as neuroticism, self-confidence, hardiness, subjective autonomy or internal control beliefs. Demographic features include gender and age. Warr (1987, p. 253) considers that 'Persons with a particular value orientation are likely to seek out opportunities which match that orientation, to appreciate features which reward it, and to feel badly when those features are not available to them'. He also notes that individuals with high abilities in any given area will be particularly frustrated by very low opportunities to use their skills.

Warr believes that 'growth-need strength' or 'higher order need strength' has served as a possible modifying characteristic in many studies of work. Growth-need strength reflects the strength of the respondent's desire to obtain 'growth' satisfaction from work which presents challenges and permits independence, creativity and personal development. Warr sees this attribute as a set of preferences for certain sorts of intrinsic work characteristics, though, of course, such 'attributes' may in turn be a product of life opportunities and expectations.

Warr proposes that different patterns of relationships between environmental features and mental health are expected for people with different enduring characteristics. Phrased another way, different personal characteristics are expected to moderate the impact of different environmental features on different components of mental health. Warr stresses that we need to examine simultaneously a range of personal attributes, to learn about the impact of each upon controlling the other. Such research requires large samples and sophisticated statistical analysis. Warr recognizes, however, that this large-scale quantitative approach needs to be complemented by smaller scale in-depth qualitative approaches to understand the processes involved in the mutual, reciprocal influence between persons and situations.

Mental health

Warr (1987) points out that mental health is a value-laden concept and that definitions and assumptions can vary between times and between cultures.

Drawing on the theories and descriptions of many Western writers he identifies five components of mental health: (1) affective well-being; (2) competence; (3) aspiration; (4) autonomy; and (5) integrated functioning. He emphasizes variations in degrees of health and not whether individuals would be identified as ill or not in a medical sense. He views mental health as on a continuum ranging from very good mental health, through conditions considered moderately healthy, to those widely taken to be indicative of moderate and severe illness. Warr also rejects a 'passive, contentment' view of mental health, recognizing that healthy people often experience strain or anxiety (Warr, 1993, p. 15).

A related way of conceptualizing mental health is to distinguish between the degree of freedom from negative mental health, such as anxiety and depression and negative self-esteem evaluations, and the degree of presence of aspects of positive mental health, such as positive self-esteem, competence, etc. This view, arising from the work of Herzberg (1966), proposes that negative and positive mental health are not on the same continuum, and that different factors may influence each aspect. These two views on mental health have in common the proposition that freedom from negative mental health does not necessarily result in positive mental health, with the implication that mental health should be measured on a range of dimensions. This position is also advocated by Brief *et al.* (1993) from their studies of subjective well-being. They state that it can no longer be assumed that if a factor influences one aspect of subjective well-being it will also influence other aspects. The specification of a range of components of mental health, as well as a range of influencing factors, is therefore required.

The most comprehensively investigated measure of the five components of mental health proposed by Warr is affective well-being. Scales have been devised to measure affective well-being on three principal axes: the 'pleasure axis' (measuring displeasure to pleasure in context-free situations – i.e. life in general), the 'anxiety–contentment' axis and the 'depression–enthusiasm' axis, which have been used in the context-specific situations of work and leisure (Warr, 1987, 1989, 1990a, 1990b, 1993). The context-specific measures have been more widely used, and have been subject to development (Sevastos, Smith and Cordery, 1992; Warr, 1992). Examples of the questionnaires for the measurement of these three axes of affective well-being are given in Appendix 2. The pleasure axis contains questions on enjoyment, satisfaction and happiness in life as a whole. The other two axes note the frequency of a range of positive and negative mood states including tense, uneasy, worried, calm, contented and relaxed (measuring the anxiety–contentment axis), and depressed, gloomy, miserable, cheerful, enthusiastic and optimistic (measuring the depression–enthusiasm axis). There are also several established inventories of distress, life satisfaction, anxiety, depression, etc., which have been used to measure context-free affective well-being.

The importance of competence has been emphasized by many writers in terms such as 'environmental mastery' (Jahoda, 1958), 'self-efficacy' (Bandura,

1977) and 'effectance motivation' (White, 1959). Warr (1993) considers that competence refers to a person's ability to handle life's problems and act on the environment with at least a moderate amount of success, but that low competence is not always a sign of low mental health, since everyone is incompetent in some respects. Low competence which is not associated with negative affect is thus not normally a sign of low mental health.

Warr (1993, p. 15) notes that there are also difficulties in the measurement of aspiration, as a component of mental health. The healthy person, he states, 'is often viewed as someone who establishes realistic goals and makes active efforts to attain them (e.g. Herzberg, 1966; Maslow, 1970)' and that 'low aspiration is seen in apathy and acceptance of the status quo'. However, he adds that to characterize people in these terms in a context-free, general manner is problematic, since a person's aspirations can have many different targets. The measurement of aspiration in context-free situations through standard questionnaires is thus viewed as unlikely to be successful. In occupational settings, though, it may be appropriate to use questionnaires which cover aspects of intrinsic motivation or growth-need strength. Warr (1987, p. 31) cites the research of Csikszentmihayi (1975) who, in a review of positive experiences in a wide range of settings, has emphasized the importance of endeavours which involve 'a going beyond the known, a stretching of one's self towards new dimensions of skill and competence'. It is also recognized that overly high aspirations can give rise to chronic distress as actions lead to persistent failure.

In discussing autonomy Warr (1987) indicates that many Western writers have stressed the importance of a person's ability to resist environmental influences and to determine his or her own opinions and action. Autonomy has also been viewed in terms of internal locus of control, a general tendency to feel and act on the assumptions that one is influential rather than helpless in the face of life's difficulties. However, too much autonomy as well as too little is often seen as undesirable, and many writers have pointed out that it is successful interdependence rather than extreme independence which is a sign of good mental health. Both independence and interdependence are thus considered important for mental health. Warr (1993) notes that autonomy is a construct not easily measured by questionnaire and that more qualitative methods, including individual interviews, may be required.

The need for more qualitative methods also applies to the fifth component of mental health: 'integrated functioning'. This is seen as the smooth inter-dependence between autonomy, competence and aspiration to yield predominantly high levels of affective well-being. Warr notes that a healthy person has been viewed as someone who balances the three broad areas of social functioning (love, work and play), which cover family relations, employment and leisure. Integrated functioning may also be considered across time, either in terms of a balance between accepting strain during different phases of goal attainment, and relaxation during the intervening periods, or in terms of a development of the self through stages of life. The converse of integrated functioning is seen as a loss of coherence and mutual support between competence, autonomy and aspiration leading to low affective well-being extended over time in situations where this does not seem warranted. The rejection of a 'passive-contentment' view of mental health is re-emphasized by Warr (1993, pp. 15, 16), where he notes that 'Healthy people often experience strain or anxiety in coping with their environment, and indeed may create stressful situations as they identify and pursue different targets [and that] the components of mental health are not always positively inter-correlated'. He notes that research (Warr, 1990a, 1990b) has shown that people in higher level jobs report significantly less job-related depression than workers in lower level jobs, but also significantly more job-related anxiety.

APPRAISAL AND APPLICATION

Categorical features

In reviewing empirical evidence for his model of principal environmental influences important for mental health, Warr (1987, p. 283) concludes that 'The evidence for the proposed nine factors is as convincing as that for other environmental models'. He also points out that his model is more inclusive aiming to cover all the principal features, with no substantial omissions, as in the model proposed by Jahoda (1982), and other models of job characteristics and well-being. However, he notes that 'neither this model nor any other can be defined as "correct" in respect of the number of primary categories it proposes', and that 'it is a matter of judgement whether fewer or more categories would be preferable, and this assessment would partly depend upon the applications' (p. 285). Finally, he believes that the model has a better heuristic value, lending itself more easily to application and development. The fact that the model covers all kinds of environments is seen as a particular strength, and he advocates extensions to cover transitions and 'culture shock'. The framework could thus be used to map any changes in jobs across time and to characterize people's movements between jobs or from jobs to unemployment or into retirement.

Warr (1987) also points to three general difficulties or deficiencies in the model. First, there is a need to specify possible differences in the importance of a principal environmental influence according to which particular component of mental health is under consideration. Second, more attention must be paid to the likely mode of combination of different environmental features. Third, development in the measurement of each environmental feature is required in order to strengthen empirical tests. Warr notes that both objective measures of environmental features and subjective measures derived from reports made by individuals have their limitations. Ratings by other people are unlikely to provide completely accurate records of the environment as it actually impinges on a person. Subjective ratings of the environment can be influenced by a person's mood. A depressed person may be less likely than others to recognize the positive attributes of their environment. One strength of subjective indices noted by Warr (1987) is that they take immediate account of the fact that environmental features can have different meanings for different individuals. However, Warr (1993) notes that evaluative self-reports assessing whether work demands (externally generated goals) are excessive, are likely to be linked automatically with lower affective well-being, and thus produce an 'additional decrement' type of association.

Processes

Warr (1987) stresses that at the heart of his model is the non-linear association between the level of an environmental feature and the level of mental health. The model suggests that for some environmental features, low, moderate and high ranges will show different associations with mental health. Warr notes that despite the plausibility of this form of segmentation it has rarely been pursued conceptually or in empirical research. In a study of employed men and women, Warr (1990b) measured job demands and related this to job satisfaction, job anxiety–contentment and job depression–enthusiasm. Job demands were measured by a six-item self-report scale, including responses such as, 'My job makes almost no demands on me' and 'My workload is extremely heavy'. Using hierarchial multiple regression analysis it was found that job demands were significantly non-linearly related to each of the three axis of job-related well-being. Scores were low with least demand, increased with moderate demand, and then declined again at particularly high levels of demand. However, as Warr (1993, p. 23) notes, 'The curvilinear pattern, referred to as an "additional decrement" in the . . . model, is in practice likely to be tautologically present in many investigations that obtain perceptual measures [self reports] of job characteristics'. He recognizes that in seeking to avoid this problem it may be tempting to use rather bland statements of job demands such as 'a lot of work', but that this could produce an insensitive scale at the extremes of the range, which would be unlikely to reveal curvilinearity.

Warr emphasizes the importance of quantitative data in testing his model. He also notes that while correlational analysis may help in the exclusion of certain valuables, where no correlation is obtained, longitudinal investigations using multivariate analysis are required to make causal inferences that an environmental feature or combination of features causes a certain effect in given circumstances for people with particular enduring characteristics. He recognizes that in proposing a general model of environmental features the emphasis has been on quantitative evidence with somewhat reduced attention given to specific processes of interaction. The development of a processes model, he notes, requires in addition more qualitative enquiries into dynamic interactions and mutual interdependencies across time. He suggests that the processes which bring about impairment at high levels of an environmental feature are expected to differ from those which are important at low levels. He also calls for 'more descriptive and interpretive research . . . which can elucidate the processes whereby particular sets of environmental features work together to have their aggregate effects' (p. 290). Finally, he advocates qualitative research to deepen the understanding of the modes of person–situation interaction across time.

Warr (1987, p. 21) considers that 'through presenting a systematic categorical model, identifying causal processes, and suggesting measurement approaches, the approach aims to yield recommendations for enhancing mental health by changing those environments identified as harmful'. He argues that there can be good and bad jobs and good and bad unemployment, though he concludes that, in general, unemployment is more adverse in terms of the principal environmental influences important for mental health than employment. Unemployment, he believes, should be tackled by the creation of more jobs and expanding formal and informal institutions in areas of high local unemployment, since it is through roles within institutions that opportunities for personal control, skill use, variety and externally generated goals can be enhanced and interpersonal contact, environmental clarity and valued social position increased. With regard to people in employment, the model can be used to investigate the relationship between components of mental health and principal environmental influences in work and leisure. This can be undertaken for persons in different jobs, who have different personal characteristics, to produce knowledge of both practical and theoretical value. This is the topic of the next chapter.

REFERENCES

Bandura, A. (1977) 'Self-efficacy: toward a unifying theory of behavioural change', *Psychological Review* 84, 19–215.

Brief, A.P., Butcher, A.H., George, J.M. and Link, K.E. (1993) 'Integrating bottom-up and top-down theories of subjective well-being: the case of health', *Journal of Personality and Social Psychology* 64: 4, 646–53.

Csikszentmihalyi, M. (1975) *Beyond Boredom and Anxiety*, San Francisco: Josey-Bass.

Emery, F. (1985) 'Public policies for healthy workplaces', *Human Relations* 38, 1013–22.

Fryer, D. (1995) 'Benefit agency? Labour market disadvantage, deprivation and mental health, *The Psychologist*' 265–72.

Fryer, D. and Payne, R. (1984) 'Proactive behaviour in unemployment: findings and implications', *Leisure Studies* 3, 273–95.

Gibson, J.J. (1979) *The Ecological Approach to Visual Perception*, Boston: Houghton Mifflin.

Herzberg, F. (1966) *Work and the Nature of Man*, Chicago: World Publishing Co.

Jahoda, M. (1958) *Current Concepts of Positive Mental Health*, New York: Basic Books.

Jahoda, M. (1982) *Employment and Unemployment: A Social Psychological Analysis*, Cambridge: Cambridge University Press.

Maslow, A.H. (1970) *Motivation and Personality* (2nd edn), New York: Harper & Row.

Sevastos, P., Smith, L. and Cordery, J.L. (1992) 'Evidence on the reliability and construct validity of Warr's (1990) well-being and mental health measures', *Journal of Occupational and Organisational Psychology* 65, 33–49.

Warr, P. (1986) 'A vitamin model of jobs and mental health', in G. Debus and H.W. Schroiff (eds), *The Psychology of Work and Organisation*, North Holland: Elsevier Science.

Warr, P. (1987) *Work, Unemployment and Mental Health*, Oxford: Clarendon Press.

Warr, P. (1989) *The Measurement of Well-being and Other Aspects of Mental Health*, MRC/ESR Social and Applied Psychology Unit, Memo, Sheffield: University of Sheffield.

Warr, P. (1990a) 'The measurement of well-being and other aspects of mental health', *Journal of Occupational Psychology* 63, 193–210.

Warr, P. (1990b) 'Decision latitude, job demands, and employee well-being', *Work and Stress* 4: 4, 285–94.

Warr, P. (1992) *A Measure of Two Axes of Affective Well-being*, MRC/ERSC Social and Applied Psychology Unit, Memo 1392, Sheffield: University of Sheffield.

Warr, P. (1993) 'Work and mental health, a general model', in F. La Ferla and L. Levi (eds), *A Healthier Work Environment*, Copenhagen: World Health Organisation.

White, R.W. (1959) 'Motivation reconsidered: the concepts of competence', *Psychological Review* 66, 297–333.

Chapter 5

Research into principal environmental influences and mental health

The previous chapter outlined and commented on the model of principal environmental influences (PEIs) and mental health proposed by Warr (1986, 1987, 1993). This chapter looks in detail at research undertaken at Manchester using this model, and the associated model proposed by Jahoda (1982).

Warr (1987) indicates that the division of the environment into nine principal categories, which facilitate or constrain personally important processes and activities important for mental health, appears to be appropriately precise for most purposes, but that it is a matter of judgement, partly relating to applications, whether fewer or more categories would be preferable. His model subsumes the five categories of experience proposed by Jahoda (1982), namely: time structure, social experience (contact) collective effort or purpose, social identity or status, and activity. Jahoda (1986, p. 26) notes that 'people need some structure to the working day, (time structure), need an enlarged horizon beyond their primary group (social contacts), need to be involved in collective efforts, need to know where they stand in society (social identity or status) and need to be active'. Jahoda (1992, p. 356) emphasizes the 'habitual use people make of social institutions in meeting some psychological need'. While she considers that employment imposes the five categories of experience, research has shown that the level of experience within these categories can vary in both work and leisure, and that this variation is associated with variation in aspects of well-being (Haworth and Hill, 1992).

The validity of findings from correlational studies is dependent in part on there being no specification error (i.e. that relevant variables have not been excluded from the analyses, since the association between two variables can be the result of the variables co-varying with a third variable). The analyses of a broader range of variables, such as the nine principal environmental influences (detailed in Chapter 4), potentially reduces specification error and also permits a finer grain analysis. Besides subsuming the five 'categories of experience' identified by Jahoda, they also encompass features affording personal 'agency', considered vital for mental health. Warr considers that 'The evidence proposed for the nine factors is as convincing as that for other environmental models' (p. 283). The strength of his categorical model, he believes, is that it applies to any kind of environment and that it has considerable heuristic value, lending itself to application and development.

Two studies are considered in this chapter. The first is a sample of managers (Haworth and Paterson, 1995) and shows the importance for mental health of Jahoda's five categories of experience – in particular, collective purpose and status. Analysis of Warr's nine 'principal environmental influences' also supports the significance of collective purpose and status by showing that the PEI 'valued social position', which includes these two categories of experience, remained significantly associated with several measures of mental health. Analysis of the PEIs also showed that opportunity for use of existing skills in leisure, and variety in leisure, were significantly associated with several measures of mental health.

The second study, of a sample of working women (Haworth, *et al.*, in press) shows that while several principal environmental influences are associated with positive psychological states, the PEI 'environmental clarity' had the greatest range of associations, in contrast to 'valued social position' in managers. The study also found that 'internal' locus of control, the expectation that the outcomes of behaviour are due more to one's actions than to chance, luck or fate, was associated with enhanced positive psychological states and principal environmental influences. Possible processes of person–situation interactions are examined and discussed.

STUDY 1

The sample consisted of twenty-eight managers, fourteen females and fourteen males, aged between 21 and 56 years. Twenty-nine per cent of respondents were in the 21 to 30 age group, 32 per cent in the 31 to 45 age group, and 39 per cent in the 46 to 56 age group. Respondents worked in different economic sectors: 35 per cent in the financial sector, 21 per cent in publishing (editors), 21 per cent in advertising consultancy and 23 per cent in 'Other' e.g. technical director, solicitor. Of the sample, 64 per cent were married or living with a partner, 36 per cent were single or divorced, while 57 per cent had dependants. Recruitment was on a voluntary basis through personal contract. Respondents were sent the questionnaire package with an introductory letter and an explanatory note giving a brief outline of the study and the questionnaire package. Approximately two-thirds of respondents contacted returned the filled questionnaires. There was no particular bias in respondents not returning questionnaires.

Measures

Access to categories of experience (ACE)

The scales to measure the level of access to the five categories of experience of time structure, social contact, collective purpose, status and activity were those developed by Evans (1986), from those used by Miles (1983). Three items were used to measure each of the categories. For example, 'collective purpose' was measured by the responses, 'I'm doing things that need doing by someone' (+ve item); 'At this time in my life I feel I'm making a positive contribution to society at large' (+ve item); 'Nothing I'm involved in has much value for many other people' (-ve item). 'Status' was measured by the questions, 'I sometimes feel that people are looking down on me' (-ve item); 'Society in general respects people like me' (+ve item); 'Sometimes I feel like I'm on the scrap heap' (-ve item). Each item was scored on a seven-point scale ranging from 'Completely disagree' (1) to 'Completely agree' (7). A mean score for each category was obtained from each set of three questions (having reversed the values of negative items) and used in analysis. The scales are dispersed in the questionnaire to measure the principal environmental influences (see below). Respondents completed the scales for both their time at work and their time outside of work. Two separate questionnaires were used for this to reduce 'halo' and 'contrast' effects.

Principal environmental influences (PEI)

Each PEI was measured by a minimum of four questions in order to tap different sub-components. 'Physical security' and (problems with) 'Money' were measured once for life as a whole, questions being included with others in a short general questionnaire. The other seven PEIs were measured for the work and leisure contexts separately. Each of these PEIs – 'opportunity for control', 'opportunity for skill use', 'externally generated goals', 'variety', 'environmental clarity', 'opportunity for interpersonal contact' and 'valued social position' – was measured using seven-point scales with end points identical to those used to measure Jahoda's categories of experience, since these are subsumed within the PEIs. Scoring of these seven PEIs was similar to that for the categories of experience: a mean score for each PEI being obtained from each set of questions having reversed the value of the negative items. Full details of the questionnaire, which is being developed, are given in Appendix 3.

Mental health

Herzberg (1966) proposes that negative and positive mental health are not on the same continuum, and that different factors may influence each aspect. Warr (1989) also conceives of mental health as having positive as well as negative aspects, and advocates measurement on a range of dimensions. In this study several measures were used to assess freedom from negative mental health and positive mental health:

1 The General Health Questionnaire (Goldberg, 1972) was presented in its twelve-item version (GHQ-12). Items cover strain and depression, loss of concentration, sleep, etc. The scoring method used was that devised by Banks *et al.* (1980). A higher score is indicative of greater negative well-being.

2 Total life satisfaction (TLS) was measured by the sum of the scores on the first eleven scores of a life satisfaction scale based on Warr *et al.* (1979). These items refer to different aspects of a respondent's everyday life and his or her environment, and were answered on seven-point scales ranging from 'Extremely dissatisfied' (1), to 'Extremely satisfied' (7).

3 An affective well-being questionnaire, based on Warr (1989, 1990a, 1990b), was used to assess the presence of positive well-being along the three axes proposed by Warr (1987). (See Appendix 2.) The first part of the questionnaire, devised by Warr (1989), was used as a context-free measure of the 'pleasure axis' (AWB1). It consists of three questions concerned with the perceptions of enjoyment, happiness and satisfaction in life as a whole over the past few weeks. Each question was scored on a five-point scale (e.g. 1 = 'I do not enjoy it'; 5 = 'I really enjoy it') with the sum of the three scores averaged to find the mean score of the axis. The rest of the questionnaire, based on Warr (1990), was used to measure axis 2, anxiety–contentment (AWB2) and axis 3, depression–enthusiasm (AWB3) for the time respondents were at work, and then for when they were not at work. Subjects had to rate on a six-point scale, ranging from 'Never' (1) to 'All of the time' (6), how often during the past few weeks they had felt each of the twelve emotional states listed. The six adjectives measuring the anxiety–contentment (AWB2) axis were: tense, uneasy, worried, calm, contented and relaxed. Those measuring the depression–enthusiasm axis were: depressed, gloomy, miserable, cheerful, enthusiastic and optimistic. Scoring of the negative items on each axis was reversed. For this study, the mean scores for axis 2 at work and leisure was computed to give a context-free measure, in line with the other measures of mental health. This was also done for axis 3. Warr (1990) notes that the measures of in and out of work are likely to be intercorrelated in practice, rather than independent.

4 Aspiration was measured by two questions scored on seven-point scales, with the scores for work and non-work being combined. Scores from two questions from the General Health Questionnaire referring to life as a whole were added to give a composite context-free measure of aspiration.

5 Highly enjoyable challenging experiences, termed 'flow', were measured by a questionnaire based on Csikszentmihalyi and Csikszentmihalyi (1988), which described these experiences and asked respondents how often in the past week they had encountered such an experience, possible responses ranging from 'Not at all' (0), 'Once a week' (1), 'Several times a week' (2), 'Every day' (3) to 'More than once a day' (4). The incidence of 'flow' in daily life has been taken as an indicator of positive mental health.

The results

Each of Jahoda's categories of experience correlated significantly with at least one measure of mental health. To ascertain which of several variables associated with a particular measure of mental health were the more important ones, multiple regression analysis was undertaken separately for work and leisure. This showed that 'collective purpose' and 'status' in both work and leisure had moderate to large β coefficients,[1] indicative of their potential influence, for a considerable range of measures of mental health covering freedom from negative mental health and positive mental health. In addition, 'status', in both work and leisure has moderate to large β coefficients associated with 'flow' – the experience of highly enjoyable challenging activities. Other notable β coefficients were for aspiration with time structure at work and aspiration with activity in leisure.

Analysis of the principal environmental influences and mental health showed that, with one exception, all the PEIs in either work or leisure correlated with at least one measure of mental health. The exception was 'Money', which caused little or no problems in the sample. Analysis using stepwise multiple regression of PEIs which statistically significantly correlated with a particular measure of health, done separately for work PEIs and leisure PEIs, showed that valued social position at work was significantly associated with GHQ ($\beta = -0.40$), TLS ($\beta = 0.31$), AWB2 ($\beta = 0.71$), and AWB3 ($\beta = 0.71$). Valued social position at leisure was significantly associated with GHQ ($\beta = -0.63$), and AWB3 ($\beta = 0.59$). In this study the questions pertaining to the PEI 'valued social position' included the questions assessing the two categories of experience, 'collective purpose' and 'status'. The important association between collective purpose, status and mental health, identified in analysis of Jahoda's categories of experience, thus received support from the analysis of the PEIs which involved a wider range of variables, reducing the possibility of specification error. The analysis of the PEIs also showed other interesting statistical associations with mental health in this sample. 'Work variety' was associated with AWB1 ($\beta = 0.52$). Work 'clarity' was associated with 'flow' ($\beta = 0.48$). Leisure 'variety' was associated with AWB1, ($\beta = 0.69$), and also 'aspiration' ($\beta = 0.59$).

These results from the analysis of the PEIs, support those from the analysis using the categories of experience highlighted by Jahoda, and also present a finer grained account which shows the importance of additional variables. Thus, for example, the large β coefficients in the relationships between leisure skill and total life satisfaction, and 'flow', indicates the importance of active leisure for well-being in this sample of managers.

The study has indicated the apparently significant role of 'valued social position' at work for a range of measures of mental health. Valued social

1   The β coefficient (weight) indicates the average standard deviation change in y (mental health measure) with a standard deviation change in x (category of experience measure). The generality of the size of the βeta weight is restricted to samples with similar variance in the 'predictor' variables (x).

position, according to Warr (1987), refers to a position within a social structure which carries some esteem from others, generated primarily through the value attached to activities inherent in a role and the contribution that these make to the social structure. Besides giving personal esteem, a valued social position may also give social esteem, or social status. This PEI can thus be seen to encompass Jahoda's categories of experience of 'collective purpose' and 'status'. Warr (1987, p. 9) notes that the PEI 'valued social position' is associated with several other PEIs: 'a position and its role activities provide opportunities for social comparison, may enhance predictability and environmental clarity, and impose goals and behaviourial traction. More valued social positions in wider society may also carry with them larger incomes than those accorded lower status'. In the present study, the scores for 'valued social position' at work were: 5.2 (mean), 0.81 (standard deviation), 3.4 (minimum), 6.7 (maximum). The mean score in work is thus fairly high. Individuals in such situations may not always recognize or, when appropriate, articulate the importance of the contribution of the individual to the organization. Given this combination of circumstances, the 'valued social position' of the individual to the organization may inadvertently fall, with possible negative consequences for a range of dimensions of mental health. This argument presumes, of course, a direct relationship between 'valued social position' and mental health, which may well be the case. However, it could also be the case that 'valued social position', has an important indirect relationship with dimensions of mental health, operating through other PEIs, such as clarity, control, variety, skill use, money, etc. If this is so, maintenance of the appropriate levels of the PEIs operating in the indirect paths would also be necessary for maintaining or enhancing mental health.

The important association of levels of access to categories of experience and PEIs in the leisure sphere with mental health is also something which both organizations and individuals should recognize. Time for leisure pursuits in the everyday life of busy managers is not, it would seem, a peripheral consideration, one which can be forfeited without cost. 'Collective purpose' and 'status' or 'valued social position' in leisure were significantly associated with variations in mental health, as in work. Leisure 'variety' and 'skill use' were also positively associated with a range of dimensions of mental health. Leisure 'skill use' was associated with 'flow', the experience of highly enjoyable challenging activities, and total life satisfaction (TLS). Leisure may thus provide a vital arena for access to the categories of experience or PEIs for managers, or at least those of the type in this sample who may actively seek these out. Of course, the statistical association between two variables may be bidirectional in causal influence, in that, for example, those most satisfied engage in more leisure where they respond to tasks effectively and feel stretched, which in turn reinforces their feelings of satisfaction. Similarly, engaging effectively in challenging activities – one operational definition of 'flow' – may reflect the characteristics or current well-being of the individual. Nevertheless, such mutual interactions can enhance mental health and well-being.

STUDY 2

A sample of sixteen working women was chosen from occupations which involved a significant clerical component, including librarians, secretaries and administrative assistants. Ten of the sample were in the age group 41 to 50 years, five in the 30 to 40 group and one in the 26 to 30 age group. The majority (43 per cent) were married, 26 per cent had partners, 19 per cent were divorced or separated, 12 per cent were single and 56 per cent had dependants, all of which were children; 43 per cent had specific job qualifications while the other three categories, possession of school qualifications, university-level qualifications and no qualifications, were each represented by 19 per cent of the sample.

Two different methods were used to gather the data, a questionnaire package and the experience sampling method (ESM) (Csikszentmihalyi and Larson, 1987), where respondents fill in a diary several times a day for one week in response to signals from a pre-programmed watch. The questionnaire measured the principal environmental influences, life satisfaction and affective well-being on Warr's three axes, as outlined for Study 1. In addition, the social reaction inventory, (SRI) (Rotter, 1966) was included to measure the person-centred variable: locus of control. Rotter (1990) states that 'internal versus external control refers to the degree to which persons expect that a reinforcement or outcome is a function of chance, luck, or fate, is under the control of powerful others, or is simply unpredictable'. He emphasized that locus of control is a learned expectancy. People who hold expectancies that they can control reinforcements are considered to be *internals*, and people who hold expectancies that outside forces or luck controls reinforcements are considered to be *externals*. The SRI contains twenty-nine questions each comprising two statements, one congruent with an internal locus of control, the other congruent with an external locus of control. The twenty-nine questions included six filler items which were ignored in the scoring. Only answers indicative of an external locus of control were scored (1), with a possible overall score ranging from 1 to 23. Similar to Rotter (1966) the SRI was used as a unidimensional scale, with a higher response suggesting a more external orientation to perception of control, proposed to be associated with reduced psychological well-being. The SRI has also been used as a personality measure by various researchers (cf. Spector, 1982) classifying individuals scoring between 0 and 11 as 'internal' and individuals scoring between 12 and 23 as 'external'.

For the experience sampling method (ESM) first used by Csikszentmihalyi *et al.* (1977), subjects carried a watch (Seiko RC4000) for a one-week period, which was programmed to emit nine daily signals between the times of 9.30am and 11.00pm. The day was divided into blocks of 1½ hours and within each block into six 15-minute periods. A die was thrown to select one of these periods in each block for each separate day. Each subject received approximately sixty-three signals over the period of the week. An average of fifty-four responses per subject was completed (85 per cent of all signals sent) with all respondents completing more than 70 per cent.

When signalled, subjects were requested to answer a series of questions, taking about 2 minutes to complete, in the time diary which they kept with them at all times. As one of the advantages of the ESM is that it samples immediate experiences and is therefore less susceptible to recall problems and memory biases compared to other diary methods (Hormuth, 1986), signals were requested to be answered within a 20-minute period. A small number of signals were responded to after this period and these were classified along with those where no response was recorded (due to watch failure or subjects switching off the watches so as not to be disturbed) as missed signals.

The time diary included the following questions:

- *Current activity.* 'What was the main thing you were doing?' The responses, gathered at work to this question were later classified into six categories, with instances when the person was actually working (writing a report, typing) classed as work tasks, and responses when the person was discussing work issues (on the telephone, in a meeting) coded as productive interaction. The other four categories were general interaction, thinking, maintenance and miscellaneous. Responses given for time outside work were divided into nine categories including chores, social interaction, spectating, reading, hobbies, travelling, shopping, maintenance and miscellaneous.

- *Enjoyment, interest and control.* Questions asked, 'How much were you enjoying the activity?', 'How interesting did you find the activity?', and 'Were you in control of the situation?'. Each question was answered on a seven-point scale ranging from 1 = 'Not at all', to 7 = 'Very much' (cf. Larson, 1989).

- *Motivation.* Two questions referred to the subjects' perceived motivation at the time they were signalled. First, 'Why were you doing this activity?', responses being chosen from (a) 'I had to', (b) 'I wanted to', (c) 'I had nothing else to do'; and second 'Do you wish you had been doing something else?', the answers being given on a rating scale from 1 = 'Not at all' to 7 = 'Very much'. The two answers were combined to specify intrinsic and extrinsic motivation with strong intrinsic motivation indicated by wanting to do the activity and wishing to be doing something else not at all (score 1) and strong extrinsic motivation being indicated by having to do the activity and wished to be doing something else very much (score 7).

The results

The analysis of the questionnaire data, conducted at the person level, showed that several principal environmental influences in both work and leisure correlated with a range of positive psychological states, and that the context-free measure of 'Money' was highly correlated with total and overall life satisfaction and pleasure. Control at work was significantly associated with overall life satisfaction and measures of leisure well-being, though it was clarity at work which had the greatest number of significant associations. In leisure, both clarity and valued social position had the largest number of significant associations with positive states. Stepwise multiple regression, entering together significant correlations for work, leisure and context-free measures, highlighted the significance of money for total life satisfaction and pleasure, and the significance of clarity at work for total life satisfaction and work and leisure affective well-being. Valued social position in both work and leisure also had large β weights for a number of positive states.

Locus of control was found to be significantly associated with a range of measures of well-being, with internals having more favourable scores. Respondents were divided into two groups on the basis of their scores on the social reaction inventory (SRI). Subjects scoring between 0 and 11 formed an 'internal' group (N = 5) and subjects scoring between 12 and 23 an 'external' group (N = 10). One subject did not have a score on the SRI. Comparison showed the internal group to have statistically significantly better scores on the following principal environmental influences: 'clarity' at work, 'internal' mean 6.40, SD 0.137, 'external' mean 4.88, SD 1.244, F 82.59, P 0.001; 'Social contact' at work, 'internal' mean 6.88, SD 0.250, 'external' mean 5.45, SD 1.046, F 17.51, P 0.038 and, nearly significant, 'goals' in leisure, 'internal' mean 5.53 SD 0.558, 'external' mean 4.38, SD 1.622, F 8.45, P 0.055. Conceivably, while locus of control could have a direct influence on well-being, it could also be operating indirectly through better access to principal environmental influences. Path analysis was used to investigate this (Asher, 1976). The sample size permitted two principal environmental influences to be investigated. These were chosen on the basis of β weights and size of correlations for a particular positive state. Figure 4.1 shows the path analysis for the dependent variable total life satisfaction. The β weights for the paths were obtained by standard multiple regression (Davis, 1985). To make the presentation of results clear, internal locus of control is scored high.

The results show that while locus of control correlates highly with total life satisfaction (r = 0.72, p = 0.005), the association is occurring largely through the indirect effect (IE = β 0.72) with very little through the direct effect (DE = β 0.14). Similar results were obtained when valued social position at work was also entered into the analysis with clarity and money. The model suggests that individuals higher on internal locus of control have better total life satisfaction through greater 'clarity at work' and through less perceived money problems. However, path analyses with work affective well-being as the dependent variable, entering 'clarity at work' and 'VSP at work' along with locus of control, only showed a small indirect affect (IE = 0.28, DE = 0.23). Possibly the process of influence of locus of control is not the same in relation to all the positive subjective states with which it is associated. Future research using larger samples could usefully investigate this.

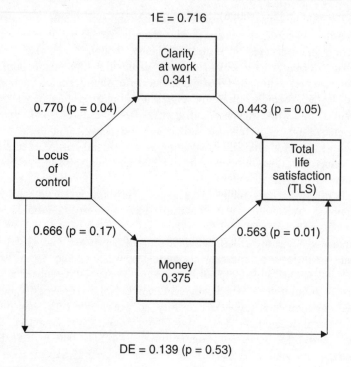

1E = 0.716

Clarity at work 0.341

0.770 (p = 0.04)

0.443 (p = 0.05)

Locus of control

Total life satisfaction (TLS)

0.666 (p = 0.17)

0.563 (p = 0.01)

Money 0.375

DE = 0.139 (p = 0.53)

Notes
Total effect, TE = 0.855
Indirect effect, IE = 0.716
Direct effect, DE = 0.139
Values are B Weights.
Pearson–product–moment correlation co-efficient r between
locus of control and total life satisfaction r = 0.72 p = 0.005.
Internal locus of control was scored high.

Figure 5.1 Path analysis of PEIs and locus of control against total life satisfaction

The time diary data were examined at the signal level (each case representing one signal), with analyses performed on the total sample of 827 responses for activity (181 missing or uncodable). Differences were examined, using univariate analyses of variance (ANOVA), in enjoyment, interest and control for 'internal' versus 'external' respondents, each signal being classified as belonging to an internal or external respondent. Differences were also examined in enjoyment, interest and control for work and leisure and for the separate activities categorized into these two domains. The results showed that for the week of the study the 'internal' locus of control group reported significantly greater levels of *enjoyment* (internal mean 5.38, SD 2.15, external mean 4.86,

SD 2.22, F = 11.7, P = 0.0006); *interest* (internal mean 4.93, SD 2.36, external mean 4.27, SD 2.41, F = 15.6, P = 0.0001) and *control* (internal mean 6.44, SD 1.52, external mean 5.91, SD 1.84, F = 18.9, P = 0.0000). The 'internal' group also reported more of their activities as 'intrinsically motivated' (44.3 per cent) than the 'external' locus of control group (29.7 per cent).

Comparison of the mean levels of enjoyment, interest and control during work and leisure showed that leisure was associated with significantly greater enjoyment (F = 30.4, p < 0.001) and control (F = 21.66, p < = 0.001) but with no difference showing in interest (F = 0.76, p = 0.06). In leisure, social interaction, spectating, reading, hobbies, shopping and self-maintenance had above-average levels of enjoyment, with many also showing above average levels of interest and control. Chores, and domestic activities including washing, cooking and general housework, were also very high on the positive experience of control, even though below average on enjoyment and interest. Work provided several areas where control was high including work tasks, general interaction and miscellaneous activities, with some of these not being very enjoyable. Work also provided highly enjoyable social interaction, and some individual tasks, such as word processing, were in the top ten most enjoyable activities along with leisure activities such as relaxing and reading. Thus both leisure and work are important for positive states in the daily life of these working women.

DISCUSSION

In this sample of working women path analysis suggests that the process of influence of locus of control on a particular positive state may be through better access to certain principal environmental influences, while also indicating that this may not be the case for each positive state with which it is associated. This differential effect is not unexpected. Parkes (1984) indicates that the more effective coping shown by internals is because they select particular strategies which are more adaptive in relation to their appraisal of specific situations, rather than solely using specific strategies in all situations. The need to differentiate between different aspects of subjective well-being has been made by Brief *et al.* (1993). In recognizing the multi-faceted nature of subjective well-being (SWB), they state that no longer should it be assumed that the relationship between any given life circumstance (e.g. health) and a particular aspect of SWB (e.g. positive affect) will generalize to another aspect of SWB (e.g. life satisfaction). In the present sample the analysis suggests that individuals higher on internal locus of control have better total life satisfaction through greater 'clarity' at work and through fewer perceived money problems. The four questions measuring 'clarity' were: 'In the things I do, I usually know the kind of results I will get' (intrinsic feedback); 'People often talk things over with me' (extrinsic feedback); 'Sometimes I just can't see where to go next in my life' (R) (future developments); 'Sometimes I feel I don't really know what people expect of me' (R) (role requirements). Furnham and Steele (1993, p. 144) note that 'Locus of control is seen to influence the particular goal expectancy in any given specific situation depending upon the novelty and ambiguity of the setting, as well as the degree of reinforcement that the individual has directly experienced in that setting'. In this sample of working women internals may thus perceive and experience more of the 'rewards' associated with 'clarity' in work environments which afford a range of these rewards.

In the General Model of Work and Mental Health proposed by Warr (1987, 1993), control is identified as the main principal environmental influence. In this study of working women control at work has a large β weight associated with overall life satisfaction, indicative of its potential importance for this aspect of well-being, and vice versa. However, it is clarity at work which shows the greatest range of significant β weights associated with positive states. In Warr's model, control is divided into intrinsic control, which is control over the content of what one does, and extrinsic control, which is control of features of the environment external to the task, such as wages and company policy. Clarity, as seen, involves knowing what people expect of one, and the likely result of actions, and low uncertainty about the future. For this sample of working women, who were mainly office workers, variations in what is perhaps general control (i.e. in what degree of choice one has in the tasks undertaken and what influence one has on company policy) may be associated with more responsible and better paid jobs, which in turn could be associated with variations in the appraisal of overall life satisfaction. Variations in clarity, on the other hand, are perhaps concerned in part with variations in more immediate aspects of the environment such as what is expected of one and what results one will get, and this could be reflected in the association of clarity with more transient positive states such as anxiety–contentment (AWB2) and depression–enthusiasm (AWB3) in both work and leisure. These results showing the importance of 'clarity' for well-being in women office workers have been replicated in other studies at Manchester.

The ESM data show that both work and leisure offer many opportunities for control measured as 'feeling in control of the situation', which was perhaps answered with reference to more immediate events, the question coming shortly after one asking what the respondent was doing. Work tasks, general interaction and miscellaneous activities at work were high on control. In leisure, feelings of being in control of the situation were high in chores, reading, hobbies, shopping and self-maintenance. Many activities which are high in feelings of control were also high in enjoyment and interest, though not in all cases, including chores. Iso-Ahola (1992) argues that leisure participation is an important contributor and developer of a sense of self-determination through providing opportunities to exercise personal control. Leisure experience, he contends, encourages the development, maintenance and enhancement of people's beliefs that they have capacities to initiate actions, persist and achieve successful outcomes and that by providing opportunities for exercising personal control leisure helps buffer against stressful life events. Iso-Ahola also notes that leisure participation facilitates coping with life stress by generating companionship, friendships and social support. In the present study social interaction in both work and leisure was a highly enjoyable aspect, and in work in particular it was also high in control. Larson (1989), conducting a within-person analysis of momentary experience using ESM data, found only a very low positive correlation between being in control and positive affect and concluded that normal people can experience ordinary occasions of discontrol without encountering substantial unhappiness, an essential requirement for psychological health given that there is much in life that we cannot control. An across-person analysis of average control over the week of the study showed that experiencing high control in life was related substantially but not strongly with maintaining an above-average affective state. Larson suggests that encountering many occasions of discontrol during the week might lead to generalized negative affect.

In discussing individual differences in locus of control beliefs, Furnham and Steele (1993) note that while these may influence experiences, the reverse can also be true. They suggest that positive successful life experiences probably increase internal locus of control beliefs through optimistic attributions. These may increase confidence, initiative and positive motivation and, in turn, lead to more successful experiences. The opposite may be seen to occur with negative, unsuccessful life experiences which leave the individual feeling at the whim of powerful and hostile forces beyond their control. They suggest that a pessimistic style may thus develop which will diminish one's sense of urgency and control, such that further unsuccessful experiences are likely. Judge and Watanabe (1993), studying a representative sample of the US workforce, found that job satisfaction and life satisfaction were reciprocally related, and that the effect of life satisfaction on job satisfaction was significantly stronger than the reverse. They recognize that a dispositional effect may in part account for the influence of life satisfaction on job satisfaction but also suggest that how individuals feel about their lives may influence how they process job information. The present study of working women has shown that 'internals' had greater levels of enjoyment, interest and control for the week of the study and reported more of their activities as intrinsically motivated than the external locus of control group. Locus of control also correlated with the work anxiety–contentment and depression–enthusiasm axes of positive affect, with internals having more favourable scores. The study also showed that for the sample as a whole leisure in comparison with work provided greater levels of enjoyment and feeling of control.

Rotter (1966, 1990) emphasizes that locus of control is a learned expectancy and (in Rotter, 1982) indicates the possible importance of what he terms 'enhancement behaviours'. Enhancement behaviours are 'specific cognitive activities that are used to enhance and maintain good feelings', which may explain why 'there are people who are happy, content and in a good mood much of the time, and that the objective circumstances of such people may not differ markedly from those of others who are mildly unhappy, discontent or worried about bad things that might happen' (p. 339). The possibility exists that enjoyment and feelings of control, which in this sample came more from leisure than from work, may enhance internal locus of control which in turn may lead to enhanced positive subjective states in work and leisure either directly or through greater access to principal environmental influences such as 'clarity' at work. Future research employing causal modelling, using larger samples than the present study, would be valuable in exploring these complex interactions between work, leisure and well-being.

Enjoyment and feelings of control in work and leisure may also have a general beneficial effect regardless of any effect on locus of control dispositions. Uleman and Bargh (1989) indicate the importance of subconscious processes including 'unintended thought' in the moderation of stress. Conceivably, enjoyment and feelings of control might help to buffer stressful life events and also enhance positive subjective states and mental health generally through non-reflexive interactions.

Future research could usually examine the intricacy of person–situation interactions with the instruments and methods used in the present studies. In addition, ethnographic methods including descriptive accounts and in-depth interviews would be useful in exploring what Warr (1987) has termed 'the complex inter-twining of simultaneous interactions between the person and the environment'. This would need to be undertaken on a range of specific focused groups, so that differential and common parameters and processes could be identified. The two studies considered in this chapter indicate that different patterns of principal environmental influences seem to be significant for different groups of people in different life situations, with the measures used to measure the PEIs having some discriminant validity. Thus 'valued social position' was the main predictor of a range of measures of well-being in managers, while in women office workers, it was 'clarity' of role requirements which was the most important PEI. The categorical models of Warr and Jahoda are useful in studying focused samples where the aim is to get information of practical value for a particular type of group in a particular situation. Such information could help both companies and policy-makers concerned with work and leisure in their understanding of factors associated with well-being and health. Although the specific findings from focused samples are only relevant in a 'predictive' sense to samples with similar characteristics, the utility of such research can be greater if 'findings' are used as 'insights' which policy-makers and companies use as a guide. The strategy of using focused samples can be further enhanced by studying the processes and dynamics underpinning person–situation interactions, which may help in the construction of general theory concerning mental health, work and leisure. Warr's model provides one overall perspective from which to develop this research.

The type of research considered in this chapter needs to be undertaken on people in different occupations, the unemployed and the retired, to gain a better understanding of factors influencing well-being and health for people with different enduring characteristics in different life situations. Using larger samples, causal modelling, using path analyses and other techniques, can be undertaken. More qualitative studies of the interaction of variables are also required. For example, research could usefully be undertaken comparing employed, unemployed, and retired samples using the ACE and PEI questionnaire as a starting point and undertaking in-depth interviews to obtain accounts from participants of their personal history, daily life and social networks. Csikszentmihalyi and Beattie (1979) and Csikszentmihalyi and Larson (1984) argue that the possession of a life theme is an important organizing force in the behaviour of an individual, and that both unconscious and conscious factors operate in the adoption of life goals. The seminal writings of Merleau-Ponty (1962) on the phenomenology of perception also stress the importance of lived experience and prereflexive thought in how we depict the world. These topics will be returned to in the next two chapters. At this point, it can be emphasized that a combination of quantitative and qualitative research could give a clearer picture of those who cope better and worse in different life circumstances.

REFERENCES

Asher, B.H. (1976) *Causal Modelling*, London: Sage.

Banks, M.H., Clegg, C.W., Jackson, P.R., Kemp, N.J., Stafford, E.M. and Wall, T.D. (1980) 'The use of the General Health Questionnaire as an indicator of mental health in occupational studies', *Journal of Occupational Psychology* 53, 187–95.

Brief, A.P., Butcher, A.H., George, J.M. and Link, K.E. (1993) 'Integrating bottom-up and top-down theories of subjective well-being: the case of health', *Journal of Personality and Social Psychology* 64: 646–53.

Csikszentmihalyi, M. and Beattie, O. (1979) 'Life themes: a theoretical and empirical exploration of their origins and effects', *Journal of Humanistic Psychology* 19, 45–63.

Csikszentmihalyi, M. and Larson, R. (1984) *Being Adolescent: Conflict and Growth in the Teenage Years*, New York: Basic Books.

Csikszentmihalyi, M. and Csikszentmihalyi, S.I. (1988) *Optimal Experience*, Cambridge: Cambridge University Press.

Csikszentmihalyi, M. and Larson, R. (1987) 'Validity and reliability of the experience-sampling method', *The Journal of Nervous and Mental Disease* 175: 9, 526–36.

Csikszentmihalyi, M., Larson, R. and Prescott, S. (1977) 'The ecology of adolescent activity and experience', *The Journal of Youth and Adolescence* 6, 281–94.

Davis, J.A. (1985) *The Logic of Causal Order*, Beverly Hills, CA: Sage.

Evans, S.T. (1986) 'Variations in activity and psychological well-being in employed young adults', unpublished PhD thesis, University of Manchester.

Furnham, A. and Steele, H. (1993) 'Measuring locus of control: a critique of general, children's health and work related locus of control questionnaires', *British Journal of Psychology* 84, 413–79.

Goldberg, D.P. (1972) *The Detection of Psychiatric Illness by Questionnaire*, Oxford: Oxford University Press.

Haworth, J.T. and Hill, S. (1992) 'Work, leisure and psychological well-being in a sample of young adults', *Journal of Community and Applied Social Psychology* 2, 147–60.

Haworth, J.T. and Paterson, F. (1995) 'Access to categories of experience and mental health in a sample of managers', *Journal of Applied Social Psychology* 25: 8, 712–24.

Haworth, J.T., Jarman, M. and Lee, S. (in press) 'Positive subjective states in the daily life of a sample of working women', *Journal of Applied Social Psychology*.

Herzberg, F. (1966) *Work and Nature of Man*, Chicago: World Publishing Co.

Hormuth, S.E. (1986) 'The sampling of experience *in situ*', *Journal of Personality* 54: 1, 262–93.

Iso-Ahola, S.E. (1992) 'On the theoretical and empirical relationship between leisure and health', paper presented at the International Conference on leisure and mental health, Salt Lake City, Utah.

Jahoda, M. (1982) *Employment and Unemployment: A Social Psychological Analysis*, Cambridge: Cambridge University Press.

Jahoda, M. (1984) 'Social institutions and human needs: a comment on Fryer and Payne', *Leisure Studies* 3, 297–9.

Jahoda, M. (1986) 'In defense of a non-reductionalist social psychology', *Social Behaviour* 1, 25–9.

Jahoda, M. (1992) 'Reflections on Marienthal and after', *Journal of Occupational and Organisational Psychology* 65, 355–8.

Judge, A.T. and Watanabe, S. (1993) 'Another look at the job satisfaction–life satisfaction relationship', *Journal of Applied Psychology* 78: 6, 939–48.

Larson, R. (1989) 'Is feeling in control related to happiness in everyday life', *Psychological Reports* 64, 775–84.

Merleau-Ponty, M. (1962) *Phenomenology of Perception*, London: Routledge & Kegan Paul.

Miles, I. (1983) *Adaptation to Unemployment*, Science Policy Research Unit, Brighton: University of Sussex.

Parkes, K.R. (1984) 'Locus of control, cognitive appraisal and coping in stressful episodes', *Journal of Personality and Social Psychology* 46: 3, 655–68.

Rotter, J.B. (1966) 'Generalised expectancies for internal versus external control of reinforcement', *Psychological Monographs* 80 (whole no.) 609.

Rotter, J.B. (1982) *The Development and Applications of Social Learning Theory*, New York: Praeger.

Rotter, J.B. (1990) 'Internal versus external locus of control of reinforcement: a case history of a variable', *American Psychologist* 45: 4, 489–93.

Spector, P. (1982) 'Behaviour in organizations as a function of employee's locus of control', *Psychological Bulletin* 91, 482–97.

Uleman, J.S. and Bargh, J.A. (eds) (1989) *Unintended Thought*, New York: The Guilford Press.

Warr, P.B. (1986) 'A vitamin model of jobs and mental health', in G. Debus and H.W. Schroiff (eds), *The Psychology of Work and Organisation*, North Holland: Elsevier Science Publishers.

Warr, P. (1987) *Work, Unemployment and Mental Health*, Oxford: Clarendon Press.

Warr, P. (1989) *The Measurement of Well-being and Other Aspects of Mental Health*, MRC/ESRC Social and Applied Psychology Unit, Memo, Sheffield: University of Sheffield.

Warr, P. (1990) 'The measurement of well-being and other aspects of mental health', *Journal of Occupational Psychology* 63, 193–210.

Warr, P. (1993) 'Work and mental health, a general model', in F. La Ferla and L. Levi (eds), *A Healthier Work Environment*, Copenhagen: World Health Organisation.

Warr, P., Cook, J. and Wall, T. (1979) 'Scales for the measurement of some work attitudes and aspects of psychological well-being', *Journal of Occupational Psychology* 52, 129–48.

Chapter 6

Enjoyment and well-being

INTRODUCTION

Enjoyment is considered to play a pivotal role in well-being (Csikszentmihalyi, 1975, 1982, 1991, 1993; Csikszentmihalyi and Csikszentmihalyi, 1988). In a pioneering study, Csikszentmihalyi (1975) set out to understand enjoyment in its own terms and to describe what characteristics make an activity enjoyable. Recognizing that enjoyment is an important but neglected aspect of human motivation, Csikszentmihalyi and colleagues conducted a series of studies of everyday life to 'describe as analytically and objectively as possible, the experience of enjoyment and the structural contexts in which it occurs' (p. xi). The goal of the study was 'to begin exploring activities that appear to contain rewards within themselves that do not rely on scarce material incentives – in other words, activities that are ecologically sound' (p. 5). For this reason the researchers started to look closely at such things as rock climbing, dance, chess and basketball. They also studied occupations which they considered one would expect to find enjoyable, including composers of music, surgeons and teachers. By understanding what makes particular leisure activities and satisfying jobs enjoyable it was hoped to be able to learn how to improve quality of life and decrease dependence on extrinsic rewards, such as money, power and prestige. The initial approach to the study was to contact people engaged in activities which required considerable commitment and energy but which provided few conventional rewards (autotelic activities), and ask them why they were performing these activities. Creative professionals, artists and athletes were also asked to describe the best times experienced in their favourite activities. The research concluded that the crucial component of enjoyment was the *flow* experience. A model of flow processes was developed to describe the common structure of activities that are experienced as enjoyable.

In his seminal article linking flow with optimal experience, Csikszentmihalyi (1982, p. 17) defines optimal experience as an ordered state of consciousness where a person's perception of what there is to do (challenges) and what one is capable of doing (skills) are equal. He notes that when artists, athletes, or creative professionals describe the best times experienced in their favourite activities, they all mention this dynamic balance between opportunity and ability as crucial (and that) optimal experience or flow as we came to call it using some of the respondents' own terminology, is differentiated from states of boredom, in which there is less to do than what one is capable of, and from anxiety, which occurs when things to do are more than one can cope with.

Several accounts of flow and its importance for subjective well-being are reported in Csikszentmihalyi and Csikszentmihalyi (1988). These include the experience of flow during work and leisure in men and women, and the experience of flow as a lifestyle and its relationship with life satisfaction. In Csikszentmihalyi (1991) it is emphasized that for flow experiences to be fully effective they should not just be piecemeal experiences but rather should be part of a general integrated experience, and that life themes can aid in this. Other studies reported in Csikszentmihalyi and Csikszentmihalyi (1988) use more empirical methods involving diaries where people record the level of challenge as well as its relationship with skills (equal, greater, or less) to enable the original three states of anxiety, boredom and flow to be more subtly defined. Using this approach, several studies show the necessity of macro-flow, where challenge and skill are both high for subjective well-being in the daily lives of college students, and people at work.

Empirical studies reported by Haworth (1993) replicate several of the findings showing the importance of flow for positive subjective states. However, they also show that not all macro-flow, where high challenge is met with equal skill, is enjoyable, and that it is enjoyable flow which is associated with better psychological well-being. In addition, the studies show the importance of low challenge situations, where skills are equal or greater, for positive subjective states. These qualifications on the relationship between flow, enjoyment and subjective well-being will be discussed later in the chapter. For the time being, it is important to focus on the pioneering findings of Csikszentmihalyi and colleagues on the characteristics of enjoyable flow and the common structure of activities that are experienced this way.

CHARACTERISTICS OF ENJOYABLE FLOW

Csikszentmihalyi and Csikszentmihalyi (1988) see the main dimensions of flow as:

- intense involvement;
- clarity of goals and feedback;
- deep concentration;
- transcendence of self;
- lack of self-consciousness;
- loss of a sense of time;

- intrinsically rewarding experience;
- a balance between skill and challenge.

The balance between skill and challenge is seen as a prerequisite for flow and is re-emphasized in Csikszentmihalyi (1991, p. 71) which summarizes the elements of enjoyable flow, or the common characteristics of optimal experience, as:

> a sense that one's skills are adequate to cope with the challenges at hand in a goal directed, rule bound action system that provides clear clues as to how one is performing. Concentration is so intense that there is no attention left over to think about anything irrelevant or to worry about problems. Self-consciousness disappears, and the sense of time becomes distorted. An activity that produces such experiences is so gratifying that people are willing to do it for its own sake, with little concern for what they will get out of it, even when it is difficult or dangerous.

Reviewing the results of the studies of rock climbing, dance, chess and other autotelic activities, Csikszentmihalyi (1975, p. 30) notes that 'The underlying similarity that cuts across these autotelic activities regardless of their formal differences, is that they all gave participants a sense of discovery, exploration, problem solution, in other words, a feeling of novelty and challenge'. He continues (p. 30):

> It would be difficult to overemphasise the importance of this finding. The fact that some people climb mountains whereas others make up tunes at a piano or push chess pieces across a board is in a sense incidental to the fact that they are all exploring the limit of their abilities and trying to expand them. Whatever the specific structure of an autotelic activity is like, it seems the most basic requirement is to provide a clear set of challenges. These can be of two types: the challenge of the unknown which leads to discovery exploration, problem solution, and which is essential to composing, dancing, climbing and chess; or the most concrete challenge of competition, which is important in activities like basket ball.

Csikszentmihalyi also notes that 'a warm feeing of closeness to others, or a loosening of ego boundaries, is important in at least some autotelic activities' (p. 30), and that this is similar to the state which has been called 'communitas' seen in certain religious rituals, feasts or initiation rites. In the flow state it is considered that 'action follows upon action according to an internal logic that seems to need no conscious intervention by the actor. He expresses it as a unified flowing from one moment to the next in which he is in control of his actions, and in which there is little distinction between self and environment, between stimulus and response, between past, present and future' (p. 36). Flow, it is considered, can be obtained in almost any activity, with the goals of activities serving as mere tokens that justify the activity by giving it direction and determining rules of action.

The phenomenological experience of flow is outlined further by Csikszent-mihalyi (1975, pp. 38–49). Six features are emphasized which constitute an integral part of the dimensions listed previously. First, flow is the merging of action and awareness. A person in flow is aware of his or her actions but not of the awareness itself. By paying individual attention to the task, one cannot reflect on the act of awareness itself. When awareness becomes split, so that one perceives the activity from 'outside', flow is interrupted. Therefore flow is difficult to maintain for any length of time without at least momentary interruptions. For action to merge with awareness the activity must be feasible. Flow seems to occur only when tasks are within one's ability to perform, which is why flow often occurs in activities with clearly established rules for action.

Csikszentmihalyi quotes an expert rock climber – 'You are so involved in what you are doing [that] you aren't thinking of yourself as separate from the immediate activity . . . you don't see yourself as separate from what you are doing' (1975, p. 59) – and a dancer describing how it feels when a performance is going well: 'Your concentration is very complete. Your mind isn't wandering, you are not thinking of something else; you are totally involved in what you are doing. Your body feels good. You are not aware of any stiffness. Your body is awake all over. No area where you feel blocked or stiff. Your energy is flowing very smoothly. You feel relaxed, comfortable and energetic' (p. 39).

This merging of action and awareness is made possible by a second feature of flow experiences: a centring of attention on a limited stimulus field. Rock climbing, for example, can force one to ignore all distracting stimuli by the knowledge that survival is dependent on complete concentration. In games, rules define the relevant stimuli and exclude everything else as irrelevant. The structure of games can also provide motivational elements which draw the player into play, the simplest of these inducements being competition.

A third feature of flow experiences has been variously described as 'loss of ego', 'self-forgetfulness', 'loss of self-consciousness' and even 'transcendence of individuality and fusion with the world'. Activities which allow flow to occur usually do not require any negotiation. As long as participants follow the same rules there is no need continually to negotiate the rules. The participants need no self to bargain with about what should or should not be done. 'As long as the rules are respected, a flow situation is a social system with no deviance' (p. 43).

Csikszentmihalyi (1991, pp. 64–6) stresses that self-forgetfulness does not mean that in flow a person loses touch with his or her own physical reality. He notes that 'A violinist must be extremely aware of every movement of her fingers, as well as of the sound entering her ears, and of the total form of the piece she is playing, both analytically, note by note, and holistically, in terms of its overall design' and concludes:

> So loss of self-consciousness does not involve a loss of self . . . but rather, only a loss of consciousness of the self. What slips below the threshold of awareness is the *concept* of self. The information we use to represent to

ourselves who we are. And being able to forget temporarily who we are seems to be very enjoyable. When we are not preoccupied with ourselves, we actually have a chance to expand the concept of who we are. Loss of self-consciousness can lead to self-transcendence, to a feeling that the boundaries of our being have been pushed forward . . . . Why this is so should be fairly clear. In flow a person is challenged to do her best, and must constantly improve her skills. At the time, she doesn't have the time to reflect on what this means in terms of the self – if she did allow herself to become self-conscious, the experience could not have been very deep. But afterwards, when the activity is over and self-consciousness has a chance to resume, the self that the person reflects upon is not the same self that existed before the flow experience: it is now enriched by new skills and fresh achievements.

Csikszentmihalyi is thus emphasizing the importance of flow for psychological growth. Elsewhere in his writings he also distinguishes between enjoyment and pleasure, which he views as being more concerned with homeostatic states, rather than psychological growth (e.g. Csikszentmihalyi, 1988, p. 25).

A fourth aspect of flow is that a person perceives him or herself as in control of his or her actions and of the environment. The individual has no active awareness of control but is simply not worried by the possible lack of control. Later, in thinking back on the experience, Csikszentmihalyi (1975) suggests that the person will usually conclude that for the duration of the flow episode his or her skills were adequate for meeting environmental demands, and that this reflection might become an important component of a positive self-concept. Thus a flow activity 'provides optimal challenge in relation to the actors skills' (p. 49).

A fifth quality of the flow experience is that it usually contains coherent, non-contradictory demands for action and provides clear, unambiguous feedback to a person's actions. This is made possible because one's awareness is limited to a restricted field of possibilities. Csikszentmihalyi (1975, p. 47) stresses that in flow one does not stop to evaluate the feedback; instead,

> action and reaction have become so well practised as to be automatic. The person is too involved with the experience to reflect on it . . . . The flow experience differs from awareness in everyday reality because it contains ordered rules which make action and the evaluation of action automatic and hence unproblematic. When contradictory actions are made possible, the self reappears to negotiate between the conflicting definitions of what needs to be done, and the flow is interrupted.

A sixth feature of flow is its 'autotelic' nature: it appears to need no goals or rewards external to itself. 'The purpose of flow is to keep on flowing' (Csikszenmihalyi, 1975, p. 47).

Csikszentmihalyi (1975, p. 48) concludes:

> The various elements of the flow experience are linked together and

dependent on each other. By limiting the stimulus field, a flow activity allows people to concentrate their actions and ignore distractions. As a result, they feel in potential control of the environment. Because the flow activity has clear and non-contradictory rules, people who perform in it can temporarily forget their identity and its problems. The result of these conditions is that one finds the process intrinsically rewarding.

In his 1991 study, Csikszentmihalyi emphasizes that autotelic activities need not be active in the physical sense, and that among the most frequently mentioned enjoyable activities are reading and being with other people. The 'passive' enjoyment that one gets from looking at a painting or sculpture is also considered to depend on the challenges that the work of art contain. Csikszentmihalyi (p. 52) stresses that productive work and the necessary routines of everyday life are also satisfying. Thus

> Everybody develops routines to fill in the boring gaps of the day, or to bring experience back on an even keel when anxiety threatens. Some people are compulsive doodlers, others chew on things or smoke, smooth their hair or hum a tune, or engage in more esoteric private rituals that have the same purpose: to impose order in consciousness through the performance of patterned action. These are the 'microflow' activities that help us negotiate the doldrums of the day. But how enjoyable an activity is depends ultimately on its complexity. The small automatic games woven into the fabric of everyday life help reduce boredom, but add little to the positive quality of experience. For that one needs to face more demanding challenges, and use higher-level skills.

Most things we do, he believes, are neither purely autotelic nor purely exotelic (activities done for external reasons only) but are a combination of the two; and that some things we are initially forced to do against our will turn out in the course of time to be intrinsically rewarding. He also recognizes that the flow experience is not good in an absolute sense and that whether the consequences of any particular instance of flow is good in a larger sense needs to be discussed in terms of more inclusive social criteria. Thus breaking into houses and lifting jewellery can be a flow experience. The importance of extrinsic motivation for flow and the topic of values will be returned to later in the chapter. At this point, it will be useful to examine some empirical studies of flow and enjoyment using the experience sampling method.

The experience sampling method

The experience sampling method (ESM) allows the random collection *in situ* of self-reports about a respondent's subjective states and daily experience. Respondents answer questions in a diary several times a day in response to signals from a preprogrammed device such as a watch or radio pager. First used by Csikszentmihalyi *et al.* (1977) and Brandstatter (1991), the ESM is regarded as complementary to more traditional methods. Brandstatter (1991) considers that traditional questionnaire measures have several shortcomings, and that time-sampling diaries can be designed to overcome some of the flaws and restrictions inherent in traditional rating methods used to measure subjective experience. The advantages of the ESM have been noted by Hormuth (1986) who states that it is less prone to problems of recall, distortions and anticipation of report completion than more conventional diary methods. Csikszentmihalyi and Larson (1987) review evidence for the reliability and validity of the ESM and present studies with both normal and clinical populations to demonstrate the range of issues to which the technique can be applied.

Several studies of flow and subjective states using the ESM are reported in Csikszentmihalyi and Csikszentmihalyi (1988). An important development of the three-channel model of flow (anxiety, flow, boredom) proposed by Csikszentmihalyi (1975) was made by Massimini and Carli (1988) by using the level of challenge (e.g. low, medium, high) as well as the skill–challenge ratio (e.g. greater, equal, less) to give more differentiated models. A four-channel model predicts that only high-challenge, high-skill situations produce flow, whereas apathy will be the result when challenges and skills are in balance but low, with these being below a person's mean level of skill and challenge experience over the period of study, which is typically one week. When the model was reformulated in this way the results of ESM studies on positive states were much more in line with the theoretical propositions concerning flow than they were for the three-channel model. People reported the most positive states when challenge and skills were in balance and when both were above the mean levels for the week of testing. In a sample of Milanese teenagers, eighteen of the twenty-seven dimensions of subjective experience measured on self-report scales were significantly more positive in this condition than any other. Teenagers concentrated much more, felt more in control, were more happy, strong, active, involved, creative, free, excited, open, clear, motivated and satisfied with their performance when both challenges and skills were in balance and above a person's mean level. Csikszentmihalyi and Csikszentmihalyi (1988, p. 260) note that 'when both challenges and skills are below what is customary for a person, it does not make sense to expect a person to be in flow, even if the two variables are perfectly balanced'.

Massimini and Carli (1988) have also used an eight-channel model in their research. In order to have a common reference point for comparison among subjects who they felt may have a bias to use different parts of the measurement scales, individual responses were standardized around individual mean scores, each response indicating the degree of deviation from the average response for the person (Z scores). The various combinations between the level of perceived challenges and skills were reported in terms of eight different ratios between the individual's standardized challenge and skill scores:

1   High challenge and average skills (arousal);
2   High challenge and high skills (flow);
3   Average challenges and high skills (control);
4   Low challenges and high skills (boredom);
5   Low challenges and average skills (relaxation);
6   Low challenges and low skills (apathy);
7   Average challenges and low skills (worry);
8   High challenges and low skills (anxiety).

In this model high challenges are those which are above the subject's average for the week, and low challenges are those which are below the subjects' average for the week. Challenge and skill were measured on nine-point self-report scales. The labels attached to the channels are based on what would be expected, rather than being empirically verified.

In a sample of teenage students in a classical lyceum in Milan, channel 2 (flow) was found to be the most positive of the eight channels, bringing together the positive extremes on almost every dimension of experience. When challenges and skills were both high respondents were concentrating significantly more than usual, they felt in control, happy, strong, active, involved, creative, free, excited, open, clear, satisfied and wishing to be doing the activity at hand. The opposite state of experience was reported in channel 6 (apathy), where both challenges and skills were below the person's average, and a similar although somewhat less negative state held in channel 7 (worry) and channel 8 (anxiety). Channel 4, which theoretically corresponds to the situation of boredom, reflected an essentially neutral experience: below-average concentration, a feeling that nothing important was at stake, an adequate sense of control, and otherwise average mood states. The study also showed that teenagers who reported a greater frequency of responses in channel 2 also reported being more happy, cheerful, friendly, sociable, excited, relaxed and satisfied over the course of the week.

Somewhat different results were obtained for a sample of American adolescent students in Chicago (Carli et al., 1988). For these students, the most positive responses tended to occur in channel 3 (control) where the ratio of skills is higher than the challenges. Ten positive experiences out of twenty peaked in the control channel and seven in the flow channel (2). For the Italian adolescents, fifteen out of twenty-three variables had their most positive mean in channel 2 (flow). The American teenagers thus reported a subjective preference for situations of higher personal control in which their skills are perceived to be more than adequate for coping with the situational opportunities for action. The American teenagers appear to split the optimal experience between channels 2 and 3 with the experience of 'activation' (interest) and potency, peaking in the flow channel, and the experience of positive affect and motivation, peaking in channel 3 where the ratio is more favourable to personal skills. For the Italian teenagers, all these dimensions of positive experience peak in channel 2. For the

American students, the most negative channel was channel 8 (anxiety) whereas for the Italian students, channel 6 (apathy) was the worst. This difference in preferred channels of experience in different samples of adolescents has also been obtained in research using the ESM at Manchester.

Research at Manchester

Several studies using the ESM have been undertaken from the Psychology Department at Manchester University. These have included studies of college students, adolescents on Youth Training Schemes undertaking training at work and at college, and working adults.

The questions used in our research at Manchester have included the following: 'What was the main thing you were doing?', 'Why were you doing this activity?', responses chosen from (a) 'I had to', (b) 'I wanted to' and (c) 'I had nothing else to do'; and 'Do you wish you had been doing something else?', the answer being given as a rating on a scale ranging from 1 ('Not at all'), to 7 ('Very much'). The answers from these two questions have been combined to specify which type of motivation is present. For example, if a respondent ticks either 1 or 2 on the question asking, 'Do you wish you had been doing something else?', and also ticked that they had wanted to do the activity, this can be coded as intrinsic motivation. Extrinsic motivation is indicated by a response, 'I had to' (do the activity) coupled with 6 or 7 on the question, 'Do you wish you had been doing something else?'. Affective states are measured by questions asking 'How much were you enjoying this activity?' to be answered on a seven-point scale ranging from 'Not at all' (1) to 'Very much' (7) and, 'How were you feeling at the time?', answers being rated on two seven-point scales, namely 'Very sad' (1) to 'Very happy' (7); and 'Very tense' (1) to 'Very relaxed' (7). Questions have also asked, 'Were you in control of the situation?', and 'How interesting did you find this activity?', answers being required on a seven-point scale ranging from 1 ('Not at all') to 7 ('Very much'); 'How challenging do you find the situation?', answered on a seven-point scale; and whether skills were 'equal to', 'greater than' or 'less than' the challenge, respondents selecting one answer. While the questions only take about 2 minutes in total to answer at each response signal, considerable commitment is required to complete the diary over seven days. A nominal fee may partially compensate respondents for their efforts, while not encouraging non-valid completion.

A study by Clarke and Haworth (1994) of thirty adolescent college students examined the importance of 'macro-flow' (high skills = high challenges) and other skill–challenge relationships for positive subjective states and psychological well-being measured by standard questionnaires. The study used the skill–challenge ratio and level of challenge to define channels of experience based on the eight-channel model developed by Massimini and Carli (1988). Channels were operationalized using absolute levels of challenge and not levels relative to the individual's average challenge level. High challenge was indicated by points

6 and 7 on a seven-point scale, with points 3, 4 and 5 taken as moderate challenge and points 1 and 2 as low challenge. This gives a more rigorous definition of flow as involving high challenge, than that used by Massimini and Carli (1988). Subjective feelings were measured along four dimensions: enjoyment, interest, happiness and relaxation. Surprisingly, previous studies of flow using the ESM had not measured enjoyment. Analysis of subjective states across the channels of experience produced results similar to the American college students. The 'control' channel – where skills are perceived to be higher than moderate challenges was found to be the 'preferred' channel of experience for the UK college students, in that this channel, and not the flow channel, where perceived skills equal high perceived challenges – was associated with high levels of enjoyment, interest, relaxation and happiness, although not differing significantly from other channels in all cases. Channel 2 (flow) had the highest level of interest, although this did not differ significantly from channel 3 (control). The theoretical states deemed by Massimini and Carli (1988) to be associated with the other channels of experience were found to be generally the case for the British college students, though channel 4, labelled 'boredom', was found to be high on positive subjective states.

The results, indicating that 'control' is the preferred channel of subjective experience for UK students, are similar to the results for the American college students showing that interest or 'activation' peaked in flow and that the positive extremes of affect peaked in control. For the British college students, like the American students, the worst experiences occurred when there was high challenge and low skill (anxiety). The results differ from those for the Italian students, reported by Carli *et al.* (1988), showing that the flow channel accounted for the positive extremes of activation and affect.

Results from another study, however, by Haworth and Evans (1995) of fifty-seven Youth Training Scheme (YTS) students show some similarity with the findings of the Italian students. When incidences of high challenge were matched by high skills, in the YTS students, enjoyment and interest both tended to be high in line with flow-model predictions. These results were obtained for both a raw score and a Z score analysis. They support the flow-model prediction that enjoyment and interest are associated with the flow channel, as this is experienced in the daily life of these YTS students. To this extent they are in line with the statement by Massimini and Carli (1988) that in these situations where experience in daily life closely approximates flow one would expect a positive convergence of dimensions of consciousness. In the YTS students analysis of the mean scores of individuals showed that as challenge increased this was perceived as more enjoyable and interesting. This is in contrast to the example of college students studied by Clarke and Haworth (1994) where higher challenges were perceived as less enjoyable even though they were more interesting. The YTS students were also similar to the Italian students in that the 'apathy' channel was the least enjoyable.

Interpretation of the findings from these different studies could benefit from a more detailed and descriptive account of the interaction of different groups of people in different situations, which in turn could have useful practical implications. For example, the British and American college students may be oriented to achieve successful 'approach behaviour' (i.e. the successful exercise of personal effort). Preference for moderate challenge might be interpreted in terms of the need for achievement (e.g. Atkinson and Feather, 1966). A challenge can be perceived as both an opportunity to be successful and as a threat of failure. A high need for achievement will result in high challenges being avoided and moderate challenges, with a high expectation of success, being sought. Control is described by Deci (1980) as being actively in charge of a situation, being in a position to achieve a particular outcome. Feeling in control can be an important positive experience, and may help to buffer stressful life events (Coleman and Iso-Ahola, 1993). However, the need to achieve this through moderate challenges could be a reflection of lower levels of self-determination (the inner feeling of being competent) in the British and American college students in comparison with the Italian students.

The British Job Training Scheme students, on the other hand, may to some degree be 'oriented' to avoid non-stimulation. As noted, apathy was the least enjoyable channel in this sample and, while the flow channel was high in enjoyment and interest (i.e. stimulation), these were also high in the arousal and anxiety channels. However, an alternative hypothesis could be that in the perception of skills in relation to challenges, the training scheme sample, which included hairdressers, car body builders, industrial trainees and hotel caterers, have a tendency to undervalue their skills in relation to the job, thereby moving what would be 'flow' experiences into the 'anxiety' channel.

High enjoyment

In line with other research, the previous analysis of the flow model was based on the levels of subjective states. Experiential descriptions of flow, however, feature high enjoyment. Further analysis was undertaken on enjoyment using the frequency of occurrence of scores 6 and 7 on the seven-point scale. In both the YTS and UK college students high enjoyment experiences occurred in each channel. However, the flow channel in both samples had a high proportion of high enjoyment experiences consonant with experiential descriptions of flow. But it should also be noted that in the YTS sample over 50 per cent of flow situations were not highly enjoyable, and in the UK college students, just over 60 per cent of flow situations in channel 2 were not experienced as highly enjoyable. The usage of 'flow' as synonymous with enjoyment is thus unjustified, as high enjoyment is associated with other channels and less than half of flow was found to be very enjoyable.

In the YTS students, analysing the distribution of high enjoyment experiences by activity showed that the greater percentage (21 per cent) came from undertaking the job at work, followed by 20 per cent from passive leisure including watching television, followed by 16 per cent from socializing.

In the UK college students, subjects who had flow experiences which were highly enjoyable were found to score significantly higher on several standard questionnaire measures of psychological well-being than subjects who did not experience flow as highly enjoyable. The enjoyable flow group also experienced significantly more happiness, relaxation and interest on average during the week than the group who did not experience flow as highly enjoyable. Thus enjoyable flow seems to be important for psychological well-being in the longer term, though this requires further validation.

Positive subjective states in low challenge channels

While the results from the British college and Youth Training Scheme students differed in relation to the significance of flow for enjoyment, the results agreed in relation to happiness and relaxation. When perceived challenges were low, and skills for coping with the situation were considered to be equal or more than adequate, both samples felt happy and more relaxed in comparison to the high challenge channels. This indicates that subjective experiences such as high levels of happiness and relaxation can be associated with channels other than flow and that these experiences may play important roles in people's lives in a context other than flow experiences. Shaw (1984), for example, considers mental and physical relaxation to be a major component of the 'leisure experience'.

The importance of low challenge experiences for positive subjective states in young people has also been obtained in a small study of American college students using a raw score analysis (Haworth 1993) and, as part of a larger study, using a Z score analysis. This showed the levels of relaxation, enjoyment and happiness to be related to seeing the situation as leisure, which was negatively related to seeing the situation as challenging (Kleiber et al., 1993). In both the UK college students and YTS students, passive leisure (watching television and listening to music) and socializing was important for positive subjective states.

Although these empirical studies of adolescents using the ESM show that high balanced skill–challenge experiences (flow) are necessary for positive subjective states and well-being, the research also indicates the potential importance of low challenge encounters for positive subjective states in daily life. Both low and high challenge encounters could be important for successful life transition in adolescents.

Situational and motivational correlates of flow

Circumstances conducive to enjoyable flow experiences are very diverse. In the YTS students highly enjoyable flow experiences in channel 2 came from a wide range of activities. The most frequent were associated with the job, followed by listening to music. Csikzentmihalyi and Le Fevre (1989) found, contrary to expectations, that the vast majority of flow experiences, measured as perceived balanced skill–challenge experiences above the person's average level, came when people were at work rather than in 'free time'. A study by Haworth and Hill (1992) of young adult white-collar workers shows similar results. When perceived skills and challenges were recorded as equal at point 6 on a seven-point scale, 83 per cent of these flow experiences were at work. When they were equal at point 7 on the scales, 86 per cent of these flow experiences were at work.

Both the studies by Haworth and Hill and Csikszentmihalyi and Le Fevre indicated that flow experiences were associated with a high degree of intrinsic rather than extrinsic motivation. In the Haworth and Hill study 71 per cent of flow activities, where the skill–challenge level was 7 : 7, were intrinsically motivated, in that respondents both wanted to do the activity and wished to continue doing it.

The finding that employment can be a major source of flow experiences may be indicative of the potential importance of work for well-being. However, this may also be a function of the type of person. The results from the white-collar sample studied by Haworth and Hill may not necessarily be replicated on samples in different occupations, which may attract different 'types' of people and also, of course, provide different opportunities. Csikszentmihalyi and Le Fevre (1989) identified in their research a group of individuals who were positively motivated in flow, while other individuals were more motivated in lower skill–challenge situations. The ability of some people to gain more positive (flow) experiences than others in 'uniform' situations may be indicative of an autotelic personality.

Autotelic personality

Csikszentmihalyi and Csikszentmihalyi (1988) consider that the ability to experience flow as enjoyable may be in part due to inborn characteristics but that it is an ability that can be learned. The term 'autotelic personality' has been used to describe individuals who gain more enjoyable flow experiences from situations than others. Although analysis of the aggregate data for the UK college students showed that channel 3 (control) seemed to be the channel which provided the adolescents in this sample with the best sense of immediate well-being, a certain section of this sample, those who experienced highly enjoyable flow, were identified as having better long-term psychological well-being. Arguably this group may be described as having an autotelic personality. To date, however, there is little empirical evidence for innate personality traits being responsible for individual differences in the experience of enjoyable flow. Graef, et al. (1983) were unable to find any significant differences in socio-economic variables to account for individual differences in the experience of intrinsic motivation and proposed inner quality as a causal factor. However, the importance of a conducive learning environment has emerged from a study of family context (Rathunde, 1988): adolescents who perceived their parents as offering a balance of choice, clarity, centring, commitment and challenge were found to be better able to enjoy flow experiences.

Locus of control and enjoyment

While there is no hard evidence of innate differences in the ability to experience enjoyment in situations, Feist *et al.* (1995) suggest there is a growing body of literature which provides evidence that some people, especially those high in extroversion and openness to experience and low in neuroticism, are dispositionally happier than others. They also indicate that general well-being dispositions such as optimism and negative affectivity can filter perceptions of daily experience, and that daily experience can in turn influence dispositions. One such area in which considerable research has been done is with the construct of locus of control: the degree to which an individual has the expectation that the outcomes of behaviour are due more to one's actions than to chance, luck or fate. Rotter (1966, 1990) emphasizes that locus of control is a learned expectancy, that it is based on social learning theory and that it does not imply fixed traits; rather that the basic unit of investigation in the study of personality is the interaction of the individual and his or her meaningful environment. This specificity in the influence of locus of control is stressed by Furnham and Steele (1993) who state that 'locus of control is seen to influence the particular goal expectancy in any given specific situation depending on the novelty and the ambiguity of the setting, as well as the degree of reinforcement that the individual has directly experienced in that setting'. They note that while 'internals' who hold expectancies that they can control reinforcements are more likely to take part in healthy and adaptive behaviours, it is questionable to assume that only positive attributes and activities are associated with internality. In discussing individual differences in locus of control beliefs they note that while these may influence experience, the reverse can also be true. They suggest that positive successful life experiences probably increase internal locus of control beliefs through optimistic attributions. These may increase confidence, initiative and positive motivation, and thus lead to more successful experiences. The opposite may be seen to occur with negative, unsuccessful life experiences which leave the individual feeling at the whim of powerful and hostile forces beyond their control. Furnham and Steele suggest a pessimistic style may thus develop which will diminish one's sense of urgency and control, such that further unsuccessful experiences are likely.

The study of working women reported in Chapter 5 (Haworth *et al.*, in press) showed that 'internals' had greater levels of enjoyment, interest and control for the week of the study and reported more of their activities as intrinsically motivated than the external locus of control group. Internals also had better scores on several principal environmental influences, and better scores on a number of standard measures of well-being. It was suggested that enjoyment and feelings of control may enhance internal locus of control which in turn may lead to enhanced positive subjective states in work and leisure either directly or through greater access to principal environmental influences.

Rotter (1982) indicates the possible importance of 'enhancement behaviours' which he viewed as 'specific cognitive activities that are used by internals to enhance and maintain good feelings'. Uleman and Bargh (1989) also indicate the importance of subconscious processes in well-being. Conceivable enjoyment, particularly when it is allied to control, as in macro-flow experiences, may enhance well-being through reflective and non-reflective interactions influencing locus of control dispositions, as well as by a direct influence. This model of well-being is shown in Figure 6.1.

Enjoyment and situational factors are conjoined. Enjoyment can give rise to well-being directly or through enhancing 'person factors'. Person factors may directly enhance well-being, or operate through situational factors or through enjoyment, and in turn be influenced by these. Well-being is measured on a range of dimensions, and relationships may be different for different dimensions. Person factors include dispositions, coping styles, life themes, etc.

Personal history, life themes and lifestyles

Some aspects of personality are obviously significantly influenced by personal history and use of time. Julkunen (1977) takes this further and points to the fact that the infrastructure of personality can only be regarded as a structure of activity and that this in turn is a temporal structure. The writings of Merleau-Ponty (1962) on the phenomenology of perception and the importance of lived experience (see Chapter 7) also emphasizes personal history. He stresses the key role of prereflexive thought in perception and consciousness. On his thesis we inhabit space and time, *inhering* in them. We come to know things primarily by living, by engaging in activity, however general, rather than primarily by reflection, though this is acknowledged as important. Perception, on this thesis, 'is subtended by *an intentional arc* which projects round us our past, our future, our human setting, our physical, ideological and moral situation, or rather which results in our being situated in all these aspects' (Merleau-Ponty, 1962, p. 136, his emphasis). Merleau-Ponty considers that while 'ahead of what I see and perceive there is nothing more actually visible, my world is carried forward by *lines of intentionality* which trace out in advance at least the *style* of what is to

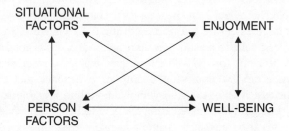

Figure 6.1 A model of well-being

come' (p. 416; emphasis added). He considers that we live and create by personal style, and that this is not something developed consciously to depict the world but is 'an exigency that has issued forth from perception. It is a style of being, a distinctive way of patterning the world' (p. 170).

One approach to incorporating the dimension of personal history is to study life themes and lifestyles. We have seen that Csikszentmihalyi and Larson (1984) argue that possession of a life theme by an individual is an important organizing force in behaviour. They consider that 'the ability to enjoy everyday experience is necessary, but not sufficient to avoid psychic entropy in the long run' (p. 261). They propose that long-term 'dissipative structures' are also required to produce order in consciousness, and that this includes the 'meaningful interpretation of existence'. The ultimate achievement in this, they consider, is perhaps 'the development of a personal life theme . . . a meaningful arrangement of goals and means' (p. 263). They also note that enjoyment and life themes are not the only hedges against psychic disorder but that political institutions, religious beliefs, feelings of solidarity and love are also vital. While Csikszentmihalyi and Larson (1984) and Csikszentmihalyi and Beattie (1979) emphasize the importance of conscious thought in the development of life themes, they also recognize the role of unconscious factors, stressing that most adolescents are satisfied to pursue the goals society prescribes.

THE FUTURE OF FLOW

Csikszentmihalyi (1988, p. 366) states that 'flow is not a luxury, it is a staple of life'. He considers that 'every activity including work, child care, and study can produce the focused well-being that is characteristic of flow. If one understands the requirements and structural feature of the experience, in theory any activity can be adapted to improve life by making it more enjoyable and meaningful' (p. 367). The function of flow is considered to 'induce the organism to grow . . . in the sense of fulfilling the potentialities of the organism, and then going beyond even those limits' (p. 367). To continue to experience the exhilaration of flow, 'it is necessary to take on a slightly greater challenge and to develop slightly greater skills. So the complexity of adaptation increases, propelled forward by the enjoyment it provides' (p. 367). Csikszentmihalyi considers that 'any skill that requires complex behaviour – and hence a great concentration of psychic energy – depends to a large extent on intrinsic motivation . . . cognitive abilities do not guarantee success; unless a person likes doing what he or she is good at doing, that skill will not develop' (pp. 373–4). He argues that both external and internal factors are necessary to improving quality of experience and that 'without concrete challenges, a set of skills, a symbolic discipline, it is impossible to focus attention long enough on a limited stimulus field to begin experiencing flow. At the same time it is also true that no matter how many possibilities the environment offers, one cannot enter flow unless the challenges become personally meaningful, unless they are engaged by one's psychic energy' (p. 382).

Obligation

Delle Fave and Massimini (1988) stress the importance of freely chosen obligations for setting the structure for flow to occur. In studying what *initiates* and *sustains* flow they found that getting involved and persevering with the activity was important. These findings were the result of studies of traditional cultures in Italy which illustrated the deep integration between flow and everyday activities. Obligation and commitment have also been found to be important for flow experiences in a study of retired people, using the ESM, by Mannell *et al.* (1988). They found, contrary to expectations, that freely chosen but extrinsically motivated activities produced the highest levels of flow. These activities appeared to demand more effort, commitment and obligation than the freely chosen and intrinsically motivated activities often associated with leisure. They consider that 'given the freedom to choose, some people may need the feeling of external compulsion, obligation to self or others or long term commitment to overcome resistance to engagement in activities that require an investment of effort but as a consequence produce higher levels of intrinsically satisfying flow' (p. 302).

In commenting on the characteristic of flow that it differs from awareness in everyday reality because it contains ordered rules which make action and the evaluation of action automatic and hence unproblematic, Warr (1987) considers that the description is very similar to part of Baldamus' account of traction in industrial jobs which can be widely present as sources of satisfaction. The intertwining of intrinsic and extrinsic motivation is obviously an important consideration for future research into flow.

Intrinsic values

The tension between intrinsic and extrinsic factors in flow is echoed in the wider consideration of the interaction of the individual and society in the question of values. Mullet (1988) claims that Csikszentmihalyi's notion of 'flow' reduces the intrinsic value of things to the subjective experience of them: to intrinsic rewards. She proposes a notion of human flourishing which recognizes the importance of enjoyment but which goes beyond this to include the values of 'character' and 'excellence', the achievement of which, she claims, may sometimes involve sacrifice and not be pleasurable. Mullet argues that the concept of 'flow' carries with it an exclusive individualism which lacks the tools to articulate the social character of our experience and values: the picture of human beings as separate centres of consciousness each seeking to maximize his or her utility or enjoyment mystifies the collaborative process of world-making.

In discussing the nature of intrinsic values, Mullett draws on the concept of 'practice' as articulated by MacIntyre (1981, p. 250): Practices provide 'the arena in which virtues are exhibited'; they include 'any . . . complex form of socially established co-operative human activity'. Associated with these activities are certain standards of excellence, peculiar to each activity, which have emerged historically as the result of accomplishments of previous practitioners of the activities. Mullet notes that there is a vast and open-ended list of human practices, including such things as the creation and sustaining of human communities, the making and sustaining of households, family life, cities and nations. She quotes MacIntyre (1981, p. 177) – 'A practice involves standards of excellence and obedience to rules as well as the achievement of goods' – and recognizes that practices vary from society to society as do the goods internal to these practices and the understanding of the virtues necessary for their realization. She adds (p. 251):

> while much of our activity associated with practices and the pursuit of the forms of excellence made possible by these practices affords us intrinsic pleasure, or 'flow', nevertheless we can distinguish the experience of enjoyment from the pursuit of the values intrinsic to these practices. In short, we often continue to pursue our most cherished values in the absence of enjoyment because we are drawn to the intrinsic value of the practice.

Mullet acknowledges the social science view that 'there are no facts about what is valuable', quoting MacIntyre (1981, p. 81). However, while it is acknowledged that a major aim of society would be to organize work, play and learning so as to facilitate the subjective experience of enjoyment or 'flow', Mullet considers that 'there is, nevertheless, an even higher ideal that must be acknowledged and repeated in every possible context of discourse if we are to have an adequate understanding of ourselves. That is the idea of people engaged in practices, extending their powers to achieve human excellence by means of the cultivation of virtues' (Mullet, 1981, p. 81).

The importance of the social dimension in life does not go unrecognized by Csikszentmihalyi (1991). While his thesis on flow has emphasized the importance of growth in individual complexity, in concluding he notes that complexity consists of *integration* as well as differentiation. He comments, 'the task of the next decades and centuries is to realise this underdeveloped component of the mind. Just as we have learned to separate ourselves from each other and the environment, we all need to learn how to reunite ourselves with other activities around us without losing our hard won individuality' (p. 240).

And in *The Evolving Self* (1993, pp. 236–7) he notes that 'the development of unique individuality [is] no longer sufficient to give life a meaningful purpose' so 'it is not just our personal advantage we must seek, or that of the causes we believe in now, it is the collective well-being of all life . . .' (p. 249). Equally, 'in order for the majority of people to take an active role in evolution, social institutions must also come to support flow and preserve order in mind' (p. 252).

CONCLUSION

This chapter has shown the study of enjoyment to be an important endeavour, one which should be pursued using both experiential and empirical methods if we are to enhance our understanding of motivation and factors necessary for well-being and quality of life. As we shall see in the next chapter, the study of enjoyment may also be central to enquiries into what it is to be a human being in the world and how we come to know and understand things to improve learning and performance.

REFERENCES

Atkinson, J.W. and Feather, N.T. (1966) *A Theory of Achievement Motivation*, New York: John Wiley.

Brandstatter, H. (1991) 'Emotions in everyday life situations. Time sampling of subjective experience', in F. Strack, M. Argyle and N. Schwartz (eds), *Subjective Well-being. An Interdisciplinary Perspective*, Oxford: Pergamon Press.

Carli, M., Delle Fave, A. and Massimini, F. (1988) 'The quality of experience in the flow channels: comparison of Italian and US students', in M. Csikszentmihalyi and I.S. Csikszentmihalyi (eds), *Optimal Experience. Psychological Studies of Flow in Consciousness*, Cambridge: Cambridge University Press.

Clarke, S.G. and Haworth, J.T. (1994) '"Flow" experience in the daily lives of sixth form college students', *British Journal of Psychology* 85, 511–23.

Coleman, D. and Iso-Ahola, S.E. (1993) 'Leisure and health: the role of social support and self-determination', *Journal of Leisure Research* 25: 2, 111–28.

Csikszentmihalyi, M. (1975) *Beyond Boredom and Anxiety*, San Francisco: Jossey-Bass.

Csikszentmihalyi, M. (1982) 'Towards a psychology of optimal experience', in L. Wheeler (ed.), *Review of Personality and Social Psychology* (Vol. 2), Beverly Hills, CA: Sage.

Csikszentmihalyi, M. (1988) 'The flow experience and its significance for human psychology', in M. Csikszentmihalyi and I.S. Csikszentmihalyi (eds), *Optimal Experience. Psychological Studies of Flow in Consciousness*, Cambridge: Cambridge University Press.

Csikszentmihalyi, M. (1991) *Flow: The Psychology of Optimal Experience*, New York: Harper Perennial.

Csikszentmihalyi, M. (1993) *The Evolving Self*, New York: Harper & Row.

Csikszentmihalyi, M. and Beattie, O. (1979) 'Life themes: a theoretical and empirical exploration of their origins and effects', *Journal of Humanistic Psychology* 19, 45–63.

Csikszentmihalyi, M. and Csikszentmihalyi, I.S. (1988) *Optimal Experience. Psychological Studies of Flow in Consciousness*, Cambridge: Cambridge University Press.

Csikszentmihalyi, M. and Larson, R. (1984) *Being Adolescent*, New York: Basic Books.

Csikszentmihalyi, M. and Larson, R. (1987) 'Validity and reliability of the experience-sampling method', *The Journal of Nervous and Mental Disease* 175: 9, 526–36.

Csikszentmihalyi, M. and Le Fevre, J. (1989) 'Optimal experience in work and leisure', *Journal of Personality and Social Psychology* 56, 815–22.

Csikszentmihalyi, M., Larson, R. and Prescott, S. (1977) 'The ecology of adolescent activity and experience', *The Journal of Youth and Adolescence* 6, 281–94.

Deci, E. (1980) *The Psychology of Self-determination*, Lexington, MA: Lexington Books.

Delle Fave, A. and Massimini, F. (1988) 'Modernization and the changing contexts of flow in work and leisure', in M. Csikszentmihalyi and I.S. Csikszentmihalyi (eds), *Optimal Experience. Psychological Studies of Flow in Consciousness*, Cambridge: Cambridge University Press.

Feist, G.J., Todd E., Bodner, T.E., Jacobs, J.F., Miles, M. and Tan, V. (1995) 'Integrating top-down and bottom-up structural models of subjective well-being: a longitudinal investigation', *Journal of Personality and Social Psychology* 68, 138–50.

Furnham, A. and Steele, H. (1993) 'Measuring locus of control: a critique of general, children's, health and work related locus of control questionnaires', *British Journal of Psychology* 84, 413–79.

Graef, R., Csikszentmihalyi, M. and McManama Gianinno, S. (1983) 'Measuring intrinsic motivation in people's everyday lives', *Leisure Studies* 2, 155–68.

Haworth, J.T. (1993) *Activity and Psychological Well-being in the Daily life of Young People: UK–USA Comparisons*. Research grant report to the ESRC. London: British Library.

Haworth, J.T. and Evans, S. (1995) 'Challenge, skill and positive subjective states in the daily life of a sample of YTS students', *Journal of Occupational and Organisational Psychology* 68, 109–21.

Haworth, J.T. and Hill, S. (1992) 'Work, leisure and psychological well-being in a sample of young adults', *Journal of Community and Applied Psychology* 2, 147–60.

Haworth, J.T., Jarman, M. and Lee, S. (in press) 'Positive subjective states in the daily life of a sample of working women', *Journal of Applied Social Psychology*.

Hormuth, S.E. (1986) 'The sampling of experience *in situ*', *Journal of Personality* 54, 262–93.

Julkunen, R. (1977) 'A contribution of social time and the economy of time', *Acta Sociologica* 20, 5–24.

Kleiber, D.A., Caldwell, L.L. and Shaw, S.M. (1993) 'Leisure meanings in adolescence', *Leisure and Society* 16: 1, 99–144.

MacIntyre, A. (1981) *After Virtue*, Notre Dame: University of Notre Dame Press.

Mannell, R.C., Zuzanek, J. and Larson, R. (1988) 'Leisure states and "flow" experiences: testing perceived freedom and intrinsic motivation hypotheses', *Journal of Leisure Research* 20, 289–304.

Massimini, F. and Carli, M. (1988) 'The systematic assessment of flow in daily experience', in M. Csikszentmihalyi and I.S. Csikszentmihalyi (eds), *Optimal Experience. Psychological Studies of Flow in Consciousness*, Cambridge: Cambridge University Press.

Merleau-Ponty, M. (1962) *Phenomenology of Perception*, London: Routledge & Kegan Paul.

Mullet, S. (1988) 'Leisure and consumption: incompatible concepts?', *Leisure Studies* 7, 241–53.

Rathunde, K. (1988) 'Optimal experience and the family context', in M. Csikszentmihalyi and I.S. Csikszentmihalyi (eds), *Optimal Experience. Psychological Studies of Flow in Consciousness*, Cambridge: Cambridge University Press.

Rotter, J.B. (1966) 'Generalised expectancies for internal versus external control of reinforcement', *Psychological Monographs* 80 (whole no.) 609.

Rotter, J.B. (1982) *The Development and Applications of Social Learning Theory*, New York: Praeger.

Rotter, J.B. (1990) 'Internal versus external locus of control of reinforcement: a case history of a variable', *American Psychologist* 45: 4, 489–93.

Shaw, S.M. (1984) 'The measurement of leisure in everyday life', *Leisure Studies* 7, 1–24.

Uleman, J.S. and Bargh, J.A. (1989) (eds) *Unintended Thought*, New York: The Guilford Press.

Warr, P. (1987) *Work, Unemployment and Mental Health*, Oxford: Clarendon Press.

Chapter 7

Embodiment and quality of life

INTRODUCTION

Previous chapters have examined the importance of situational and personal factors for well-being. Situational factors, such as social institutions and environmentally afforded categories of experience or 'principal environmental influences' have been largely examined separately from person factors, such as agency and personal dispositions including locus of control, although a model of interactions has been presented using the technique of path analysis.

Modern views on the nature of what it is to be a human being, however, see the relationship between the organism and the environment as a *dynamic-reciprocal intertwining*, where there is *not an objective world independent of the knower*, and where cognition is seen as *embodied action set in context*.

Warr (1987) used the concept of *affordance*, proposed by Gibson (1979), to explain why nine principal environmental influences are important for well-being. He noted that an affordance is neither an objective property of the environment nor solely a subjective property of the species, but is both. Thus affordances link together both important *environmental* features, or *categories*, and *processes* within *persons* (p. 17). He also recognized the '*complex intertwining of simultaneous interactions between person and environment*' citing the research by Csikszentmihalyi into the experiential characteristics of enjoyment as drawing attention to this, and providing an important balance to more deterministic research.

PARADIGMATIC CHANGE

A paradigmatic change is now occurring in several social science disciplines in our conception of what it is to be a human being in the world, and how we come to understand things and act in innovatory and creative ways. This change, focusing on the 'embodied mind', 'embodied practice' and 'situated cognition' is occurring with different but related emphasese in psychology, social anthropology and sociology. It is underpinned by philosophical views on the nature of perception and cognition. This chapter briefly reviews these concepts and discusses the implications of such a non-objectivist view of the world for research. This is not only important for fundamental questions concerning how we come to know things and act in innovatory and creative ways, but is also critical for improving economic competiveness and quality of life.

EMBODIED MIND

Traditional representationist views of the mind conceive the world as being independent of the observer, and perception being a representation of pre-given properties of the world, much like a camera records a picture of some object. This Cartesian dualism of mind and body is now being challenged. Perception and our knowledge of the world are considered to be generated by our interaction with the world which takes on a specific form due to the nature of our bodies and our individual and social experiences in the particular culture in which we live. This 'new' view emphasizes the roles in seeing and understanding of 'embodied mind', 'embodied practice' and 'situated cognition'. Perception is not simply consciousness of an existing factual situation, and learning is not simply a process in which the learner consciously internalizes a ready-formed body of objective knowledge. Rather, knowledge and understanding are tentative and generated through lived experience, histories of mutual involvement and social relationships, and can largely reside below the level of conscious awareness, but will nevertheless significantly influence behaviour.

Varela *et al.* (1991) in their book *The Embodied Mind*, note that one of the most entrenched assumptions of our scientific heritage is that the world is independent of the knower. In challenging this objectivist view of the world they say that the central insight of the non-objectivist orientation is the view that knowledge is the result of an ongoing interpretation that emerges from our capacities of understanding which are rooted in the structures of our biological embodiment, but which is lived and experienced within a domain of consensual action and cultural history. They present cognition as embodied action.

The central problem of perception is then seen as determining how action is guided, rather than the traditional concern with how the human mind processes information to represent the external world. Varela *et al.* quote Lewontin (1989) to emphasize that what an environment is cannot be separated from what organisms are and what they do: 'The organism and the environment are not actually separately determined. The environment is not a structure imposed on living beings from the outside but is in fact a creation of those beings. The environment is not an autonomous process but a reflection of the biology of the species. Just as there is no organism without an environment, so there is no environment without an organism'. In presenting cognition as embodied action, and emphasizing the temporal and reciprocal intertwining of the organism and the environment, they acknowledge the seminal influence of the philosopher and psychologist Merleau-Ponty.

The embodiment theory of Merleau-Ponty is in contradistinction to traditional philosophy which takes consciousness as its starting point and operates on sense data. It is in contrast to views arising from Plato and developed by Descartes, which locate knowing in consciousness, where the mind grasps the essence of things consistent through time and space and through which individuals can come to know the same thing. In the embodiment theory, consciousness is not seen primarily as a mental phenomenon but as a function of the integrated operation of all the senses. Our knowledge of the world is founded upon the body relating and habituating itself to things. It is not the knowing subject who brings about the synthesis of the senses but the body, and intersubjectivity occurs because of the communality of the body.

Merleau-Ponty (1962), in the *Phenomenology of Perception* (1962), argues that our fundamental knowledge of the world comes through our bodies' explorations of it. The body is not primarily a thing observing the world and being informed by its motivational and emotional state. Instead, primary meaning is reached through coexisting with the world as opposed to intellectual meaning which is reached through analysis. Primary meaning is brought about mainly by prereflexive thought in distinction to reflection. The body does not find meaning pre-existent in the world but calls such meaning into existence by its own activity and by virtue of it being combined with time and space, rather than it being in and conceiving time and space. The body has its world or understands its world without having to use its symbolic objectifying function: 'to perceive is to render oneself present to something through the body' and 'consciousness is in the first place not a matter of "I think", but of "I can"'.

In his *Phenomenology of Perception* (1962, p. 316) Merleau-Ponty emphasizes that contact with the world is not mediated just by thought:

> The person who touches and who recognises the rough and the smooth does not . . . think of them in any thorough going way. It is not consciousness which touches or feels, but the hand, and the hand is, as Kant says, 'an outer brain of man' . . . . I am able to touch effectively only if the phenomenon finds an echo within me, if it accords with a certain nature of my consciousness, and if the organ which goes out to meet it is synchronised with it. The unity and identity of the tactile phenomenon do not come about through any synthesis of recognition in the concept, they are founded upon the unity and identity of the body as a synergic totality.

Perception, it is argued, can no longer be considered a constitution of the true object but as our *inherence* in things. The world is not an object, it is not a sum of things even though it has an envelope of objective and determinate attributes. 'The thing and the world exist only in so far as they are experienced by me or by subjects like me since they are both the concantentation of our perspectives, yet they transcend all perspectives because this chain is temporal and incomplete' (1962, p. 333).

In *The Visible and the Invisible* (1968, p. 218) Merleau-Ponty stresses that 'Perception is not first a perception of things, but perception of elements . . . of rays of the world, of things which have dimensions, which are worlds, I slip on these "elements" and here I am in the world, I slip from the "subjective" to being' (p. 218).

This 'embodiment theory' of Merleau-Ponty proposes that the visible unfolds and is concentrated by the body over time. It has a style across time. We do not see the world but see with the world. Vision commences in things. It is not to apprehend first by constructing an intellectual immanence but by coexisting over time. Perception is seen as a temporal synthesis. This involves structures from the past sensory and affective life of a person sedimented in pre-reflexive thought and lines of intentionality which trace out at least the style of what is to come; that is, a certain manner of dealing with situations, which has issued from perception rather than being consciously imposed.

Merleau-Ponty in *The Primacy of Perception* (1964a) considers that because we are temporal beings 'the idea of going straight to the essence of things is inconsistent . . . what is given is a route, an experience, which gradually clarifies itself and proceeds by dialogue with itself and others' and that 'To experience a structure is not to receive it into oneself passively, it is to live it, to take it up, assume it and discover its immanent significance' (pp. 205, 258). While Merleau-Ponty does not accept that truth endures for all time, he recognizes that truth endures for a time. Euclidean geometry is still with us and useful, even if it is not the only geometry. But it is truth which results from an 'inherence in things'. It is truth which is relative to a system or medium, appearing when we allow ourselves 'to come to rest in it' (1962, p. 396). Truths and ideas are thus cultural objects rather than absolute certainties. Yet this does not detract from their organizing force: they may indeed give a firm focus to action and thought.

Merleau-Ponty does not deny the importance of reflection for knowing and understanding. In defending his embodiment thesis in *The Primacy of Perception* he states 'it is the unreflected which is understood and conquered by the reflective, left to itself perception forgets itself (and) is ignorant of its own accomplishments' (1964a, p. 203). He also recognizes in *Eye and Mind* (1964b) that there can be a different emphasis on the reflective mode of thought in some realms of life, such as scientific endeavour and philosophy.

The nature of awareness and the guiding of action are also of considerable interest to psychologists engaged in the study of 'unintended thought' (Uleman and Bargh, 1989). Bargh (1989) distinguishes between three major types of unintended thoughts: preconscious interpretive influences, where social and affective judgements may be made without intervention or conscious awareness; post-conscious automaticity, where how one feels can affect one's impressions of the world and behaviour, and goal-dependent automaticity, where the search for an answer to a particular problem can go on automatically. Posner and Rothbart (1989) note that, while considerable advances have been made in studying unintended thought, only rather slowly are cognitive psychologists coming to understand that much of our mental life is structured outside of consciousness and that our intentional control of mental events represents only one, perhaps small, part of the mind.

EMBODIED PRACTICE

In reviewing research on implicit learning, Berry and Dienes (1993) consider that evidence shows that subjects can learn to perform well in a task without being able to recall what they have learned or why they made the right decisions, and that knowledge can be below an objective threshold and influence performance. Although research on implicit learning has attracted considerable interest because of its association with the 'cognitive unconscious', it has tended to focus on 'traditional' processing issues, such as whether implicit and explicit learning are different modes of learning which produce a qualitatively different knowledge. There has been less emphasis on discussing the possible key influence of context on cognition. Yet in a literature review on factors influencing individual commitment to lifetime learning, Maguire et al. (1993) note that we need to broaden the research agenda to consider the importance of organizational structure for the process of skill acquisition and formation.

Social anthropologists (e.g. Lave, 1988; Bourdieu, 1990; Ingold, 1992, 1996) have also challenged the assumption that people construct the world, or what for them is 'reality', by reorganizing the data of sensory perception in terms of received and culturally specific conceptual schemata. Advocates of 'practice theory' argue that cultural knowledge, rather than being imported into the settings of practical activity, is constituted within these settings through the development of specific dispositions and sensibilities that lead people to orient themselves in relation to their environment and to attend to its features in the particular way that they do. Recent work in social anthropology also suggests that learning should be understood as a process of apprenticeship, as an integral part of generative social practice in a lived-in world.

Ingold (1996) argues that common understanding in a situation comes about through the body acting in similar ways, through undertaking common activity in the 'practical business of life' (Bourdieu, 1990), which is then interpreted according to one's own cultural customs, rather than by ordering sensory data as impressions of the world by acquired representations or concepts. The Cartesian dualism of mind and nature, which divorces the activity of the mind from that of the body as though the body were no more than a recipient of information to be processed by the mind, is rejected.

In discussing sociability, Ingold (1996, p. 112) states that 'the awareness of living in a common world . . . does not depend on the organisation of sensory data in terms of an objective system of representations . . . rather, sociality is given from the start, prior to the objectivation of experience in cultural categories . . . in the direct perceptual involvement of fellow participants in a shared environment'. Where knowledge is shared it is because people work together, through their joint immersion in settings of activity, in the process of its formation. These settings of activity are not confined to local situations, but encompass wide areas in the formation of a culture.

Ingold (1996) notes that conventional understanding sees culture as an ever-accumulating stock of knowledge which is available for transmission independently of the practical contexts of its application. He cites Lave (1988) as repudiating the view that cultural knowledge exists in such a context free from internalization – and with it the orthodox account of learning as a process of internalization – involving the literal transplantation of information from one mind to another. He adds, 'For although the novice of course listens to what other people say and watches what they do, words and deeds do not carry meaning into contexts of interaction but rather gather their meaning from the settings in which they are "in play"' (p. 106).

Ingold considers that how we conceive things comes about because we have been embedded in a certain tradition such as the objectivist scientific tradition, and that this influences what questions we ask, which can restrict one from conceiving alternative ways of viewing the world. Such alternatives may be productive in terms of insights, understandings and approaches to problems.

Yet Gergen (1982) notes that alternative approaches to knowledge and understanding such as ethnomethodology, where meaning is considered to be context dependent, and to arise through ongoing interpretation rather than being universal and objective, have received little attention in subjects such as psychology. He argues (Gergen, 1994 in the Introduction to the second edition of Gergen, 1982) that the 'new paradigm' approach to knowledge and understanding receives support from postmodernist theory, but that the critique has not displaced traditional representationalist views because to question these views challenges the forms of power relations in the culture. However, Gergen also acknowledges that there can be benefits in adopting classical approaches to research, even if the underlying paradigm needs revision (Haworth, 1996).

SITUATED COGNITION

Levine *et al.* (1993), in reviewing the social foundations of cognition, note that while cognitive psychologists have begun to recognize how situated cognition always is, realizing, for example, that domain-specific knowledge is important as well as general skills for problem-solving, little attention has been paid to intentions, motivations, social interpretations, or cognitive functioning in interaction with others (p. 586). One can add that even less attention has been paid to prereflexive cognition in individual and social situations, although notions of 'learning as apprenticeship' are now becoming important in the field, particularly in relation to situated cognition and education (p. 605). The 'pragmatic approach to perception' (Fiske, 1993) also acknowledges the possible utility for social interaction of both perceivers theories and the data given by the situation resulting in 'good-enough perception' that allows people to navigate their social environments, with 'automatic' processes playing a significant role.

Mowday and Sutton (1993) note that new approaches to micro-organizational behaviour, rather than concentrating on cognitive processes which rarely consider social contexts, are now focusing directly on the interplay between individuals and organizational contexts, with interdisciplinary perspectives coming to the fore. They state that the traditional approach to thinking about the context has been heavily influenced by rational design considerations and bureaucratic theory, such as the influence of technology and control systems on behaviour. They believe that if we are to move beyond simple assertions that the context is important we need to articulate more closely how contextual influences operate. They discuss the influence of organizational context on groups and individuals under the perspectives of context as opportunity and constraint, context as distal and/or proximate influence and context as similar and dissimilar groupings. They cite instances where the distinction between opportunity and constraint, when used as a research lens, benefits understanding. For example, in the case of musical ensembles, compared to less successful string quartets, more successful quartets were found to have implicit but well-established rules constraining talk about sensitive issues.

Anderson and Sharrock (1991), in discussing the sociology of cognition, draw on the affordance theory of perception proposed by Gibson (1979), and extend this to include social dimensions, noting that perception occurs in the context of patterns of social activities. They argue that we encounter the world of objects as our social world, which we have learned, and that information pick-up is not the passive processing of information, but the active construction of the world for the individual in particular contexts. It is situated cognition. Equally, they note that social institutions are constructed and reconstructed in and through courses of action in which we engage, and that knowledge and action are thus conjoined. This way individuals who have experienced a particular organization come to see at a glance, grasp unthinkingly, and recognize immediately what is going on around them. Anderson and Sharrock stress that an important task of the social sciences is to discover the processes involved in achieving this cultural competence, and that posing the questions as clearly as possible will be crucial to finding answers.

Macro-organizational contexts

The importance of macro-organizational contexts has been highlighted by Jahoda (1982) who argues that employment provides latent consequences or categories of experience additional to the manifest consequence of income. These categories of experience of time structure, regular activity, goals and purposes, status or social identity and social contact, which are examined in Chapter 2, are considered to support behaviour even if they are not appreciated at the time. Jahoda (1984) considers that since the Industrial Revolution the institution of employment has shaped the form of our daily lives, our experience of work and leisure and our attitudes, values and beliefs.

Jahoda (1986) agrees with proponents of agency theory that human beings are striving, coping, planning, interpreting creatures, but adds that the tendency to shape one's life from the inside-out operates within the possibilities and constraints of social arrangements which we passively accept and which shape life from the outside-in. A great deal of life consists of passively following unexamined social rules, not of our making but largely imposed by the collective plans of our ancestors. Some of these rules meet basic human needs, even if we become aware of them only when they are broken by, for example, the enforced exclusion from an institution as in unemployment (p. 28). Jahoda regards dependency on social institutions not as good or bad but as the *sine qua non* of human existence (p. 28).

Jahoda (1987, p. 64) points out that 'the problems of habits and traditions in thought, is extremely difficult to grasp, because what is commonly called thinking represents a mixture of elements determined by tradition, emotion, social conditions, and speech habits of which only one thing is clear from the outset; it has almost nothing in common with the logical laws which often are supposed to determine our thinking'. She argues that if it were not for the comparative stability of traditional thinking the capacity of the human mind would probably be insufficient to deal with reality; and that without tradition and habits of thought the infinite variety of life would overwhelm us. However, she also notes that the presence of established traditions and habits means that adaptation to change can be difficult and takes time.

The key influence of the institution of employment on individuals is also stressed in the literature review by Maguire *et al.* (1993) on 'Factors influencing individual commitment to lifetime learning'. They report research by Kohn and Slomczynski (1990), which found that work free from close supervision involving dealing with complex issues or making independent judgements and which is non-routine in nature, will have lasting positive effect on an individual, so that those in more complex jobs improve their intelligence and problem-solving ability while those in less complex jobs have this development impaired. As noted, Maguire *et al.* suggest that we need to broaden the research agenda to consider the importance of organizational structure for the process of skill acquisition and formation.

INHERENCE AND ENJOYMENT

In recognizing the 'complex interweaving of simultaneous interactions between person and environment', Warr (1987, p. 138) cites the noteworthy research by Csikszentmihalyi and colleagues into the characteristics of enjoyment as exemplifying this intertwining. It is interesting to see the resonance between in the account of the characteristics of enjoyment and Merleau-Ponty's concept of inherence.

As indicated earlier, Merleau-Ponty (1962) argues that perception can no longer be considered a constitution of the true object but as our inherence in things. The body does not find meaning pre-existent in the world but calls such meaning into existence by its own activity and by virtue of it being combined with time and space, as opposed to it being in and conceiving time and space.

The body has its world or understands its world without having to use its symbolic objectifying function: 'to perceive is to render oneself present to something through the body' and 'consciousness is in the first place not a matter of "I think" but of "I can"'. Merleau-Ponty (1962, p. 166) considers that 'Vision is not a certain mode of thought or presence to the self; it is the means given me for being absent from myself, for being present at the fission of Being from the inside'.

Analysis of the accounts of enjoyable flow experiences where people are performing at their best (Csikszentmihalyi, 1975; Csikszentmihalyi and Csikszentmihalyi, 1988) indicates that flow has several main elements. These are summarized in Csikszentmihalyi (1991, p. 49) as 'the elements of enjoyment':

> First, the experience usually occurs when we confront tasks we have a chance of completing. Second, we must be able to concentrate on what we are doing. Third and fourth, the concentration is usually possible because the task undertaken has clear goals and provides immediate feedback. Fifth, one acts with a deep but effortless involvement that removes from awareness the worries and frustrations of everyday life. Sixth, enjoyable experiences allow people to exercise a sense of control over their actions. Seventh, concern for the self disappears, yet paradoxically the sense of self emerges stronger after the flow experience is over. Finally, the sense of duration of time is altered; hours pass by in minutes, and minutes can stretch out to seem like hours. The combination of all of these elements causes a sense of deep enjoyment that is so rewarding people feel that expending a great deal of energy is worthwhile simply to feel it.

In commenting on the characteristic 'merging of action and awareness' in flow, Csikszentmihalyi (1991, p. 53) notes that 'When all a person's relevant skills are needed to cope with the challenges of a situation, that person's attention is completely absorbed by the activity . . . . As a result, one of the most universal and distinctive features of optimal experience takes place: people become so involved in what they are doing that the activity becomes spontaneous, almost automatic; they stop being aware of themselves as separate from the actions they are performing'.

Although high enjoyment can come from situations where challenges are not high, and where skills are greater than challenges (Haworth and Evans, 1995), this research has shown that balanced high challenge–skill experiences are most likely to produce high enjoyment. Research reported in Csikszentmihalyi and Csikszentmihalyi (1988) also shows that enjoyable flow experiences are associated with enhanced performance and learning. Enjoyment may thus be an integral part of inherence in the world.

WORK PROCESS KNOWLEDGE

There is now a considerable interest in Europe in achieving a 'learning society', one which systematically increases the skills and knowledge of all its members by learning undertaken inside and outside of formal education and training. In all Member States of the European Community a gap is perceived between the content of training programmes and the knowledge actually used in the work place. 'Work process knowledge' is the knowledge people need for successful performance at work. It is more than the academic content of textbooks; much of it is learned from direct experience of work itself. It is more than the procedural knowledge required to operate new technologies for it implies an understanding of work organization in general. This crucial human factor is often neglected, both in the design of work and in the planning of vocational education and training. Most research into training in high technology industries is using traditional models of cognitive science, which sees the operator as an information processor and attempts to model the cognitive structures involved. However, some research is based on activity theory, embodied practice and embodied mind, which emphasize the importance of situated learning and implicit knowledge.

Fischer (1994), reporting findings of studies of work process knowledge in skilled production and maintenance workers in Germany, indicates that work process knowledge about work organization could mostly be acquired within processes of informal cooperation: situations where unforseen events made collaboration necessary, beyond the boundaries of official work organizations. Informal personal relations were also found to be important: 'experience is a dominant factor in the structure and acquisition of work process knowledge . . . skilled workers' specific experiences of work organization are penetrated by thoughts and feelings, images and conclusions, which reveal profound competence as well as barriers to understanding – especially if people are confronted with new work tasks due to the change of work organization within modern production concepts' (p. 3).

The study of skilled maintenance work showed that this involved dealing with contradictions: technically appropriate solutions are sometimes not economical, while economic solutions can often endanger people's work safety. The planning and performance of maintenance work required communication processes and judgements on the persons who communicate who may lack expert knowledge. Work process knowledge also has a collective quality: knowledge about facts and functions is interpersonally transferred by hints concerning sensory experience (for instance, 'Look how . . .', 'Can you hear that . . .?', 'Don't you smell that . . .?'). Fischer notes that this is one reason apart from others why people have great difficulty in verbalizing their experience.

Fischer believes that 'to insist on the dialectical character of human thinking (concerning both analytical thinking as well as intuition and experience) is not just an academic attitude. This basic approach even leads to consequences concerning the design of computer-based tools' (p. 5). He advocates that 'understanding human work process knowledge does not mean trying to copy it by complex computer systems. It is that information which calls things back into the user's memory and inspires his imagination which needs to be represented' (p. 5).

Ingold (1995, p. 19) sees industrial tasks as socially embedded activities. Rather than simply operating a technology, the activity of industrial workers is interpreted as *coping with machines*: 'It is person-centred, it follows implicit "rules of thumb" rather than explicitly codified procedures, its objectives are set within the current of activity among all those involved in the work situation rather than following directives from above, it is continually responsive to other activities that are going on around it, and most importantly it is constitutive of personal and social identity'.

Ingold notes that whereas the operation of technology produces commodities for the owner of capital, 'coping with machines is part of the process of producing the worker as a skilled social agent' (p. 19), though one which operates 'within the straight jacket of a "Western" or commodity based institutional and ideological framework that seeks at every turn to deny the reality of situated social experience' (p. 27).

CONCLUSION

This chapter has examined 'new' conceptions of what it is to be a human being in the world, and how we come to understand things and act in innovatory and creative ways. This 'new' view, occurring with different but related emphasis in psychology, social anthropology and sociology, emphasizes the importance in seeing, understanding and being of 'embodied mind', 'embodied practice' and 'situated cognition'. Central to these conceptions is a complex intertwining of the person and the situation. Experiential descriptions of enjoyable flow experiences also emphasize this dynamic intertwining of the person and the situation and resonate with Merleau-Ponty's conception of perception as inherence in things, and with views on the importance of the cognitive unconscious.

These new conceptions have profound implications for economic competitiveness and quality of life. The report of the Commission on Social Justice (1994) indicates that 'flexible' working patterns will become the norm, with periods of unemployment being a feature of the working lives of perhaps the majority of people. Life-long training in a 'learning society' has been advocated as a potential solution to future uncertainty and flexible lifestyles. While conventional explanations emphasize learning as a process in which the learner internalizes a ready-formed body of objective knowledge with the transmission of knowledge being separate from its generation, the concepts of embodied mind, embodied practice and situated cognition stress that learning is most accurately understood as 'a process of apprenticeship' and as an integral part of 'generative social practice in the lived in world'. The ownership and distribution of knowledge engendering practices thus become crucial considerations for quality of life. Issues of participation, citizenship, sociality and justice become central concerns.

An understanding of how people respond to change is also crucial in this area. The 'agency' model of unemployment (Fryer and Payne, 1984) argues that the negative consequences of unemployment are due to stress engendered when individuals are hindered in planning and organizing their lives. In contrast, Jahoda (1982) emphasizes the crucial importance for well-being of institutional support, the removal of which, as in unemployment, gives rise to negative consequences. Csikszentmihalyi and Larson (1984) argue that life themes are conducive to well-being and that while conscious thought is important in the process by which life goals are adopted, unconscious factors are also significant. Central to this debate are the views of Merleau-Ponty (1962) that our perceptions of the world, our commitment to activity and our response to change are all influenced by our past history, and that our past experiences and perceptions help to create, largely unconsciously, an 'intentional arc' (or life trajectory) which helps to trace out in advance our path, or style, of what is to come. On this thesis the negative consequences of unemployment shown by some people could be a result of interference with the subconscious development of a satisfactory life trajectory and style of being, rather than by primarily frustrating conscious planning, as Fryer and Payne's agency account seems to emphasize. Merleau-Ponty's thesis would also help in explaining why some individuals find it so difficult to develop new meaningful activity, quickly, even in conducive social situations, which in this respect would appear contrary to aspects of Jahoda's model.

If human beings are best seen as temporal creatures embedded in changing social relationships, then organizing the appropriate social institutions to accommodate change, and providing the necessary time for change to be assimilated, is essential.

Finally, it appears that a significant feature of what it is to be a human being in the world is enjoyment. Rather than enjoyment being the 'icing on the cake' of successful survival activity, it could be a crucial factor which helps to underpin successful survival, as Csikszentmihalyi has cogently argued (Csikszentmihalyi and Csikszentmihalyi, 1988). Research has shown that for many people enjoyable flow experiences are most likely to come from work (e.g. Csikszentmihalyi and Le Fevre, 1989; Haworth and Hill, 1992). Arguably, enjoyment may enhance inherence in situations with a concomitant increase in perception and understanding of the working process which may be recovered by reflection. If such is the case, it would seem important that enjoyment is not designed out of work, either consciously or inadvertently, in the quest for greater short-term efficiency.

Equally, enjoyment is often obtained in leisure and this can be a major contributor to well-being and quality of life. As indicated in Chapter 6 enjoyment in leisure can also enhance locus of control dispositions which can influence satisfaction and performance at work. This may be indicative of the totality of human experience, amply illustrated in the embodiment theory and associated new conceptions of what it is to be a human being in the world.

REFERENCES

Anderson, R.J. and Sharrock, W.W. (1991) *Can Organisations Afford Knowledge?*, Cambridge: Rank Xerox Ltd.

Bargh, J.A. (1989) 'Conditional automaticity: varieties of automatic influence in social perception and cognition', in J.S. Uleman and J.A. Bargh (eds), *Unintended Thought*, New York: The Guilford Press.

Berry, D.C. and Dienes, Z. (1993) *Implicit Learning*, Hove: Lawrence Erlbaum.

Bourdieu, P. (1990) *The Logic of Practice*, Oxford: Polity Press.

Commission on Social Justice (1994) *Strategies for National Renewal*, London: Vintage.

Csikszentmihalyi, M. (1975) *Beyond Boredom and Anxiety*, San Francisco: Jossey-Bass.

Csikszentmihalyi, M. (1991) *Flow: The Psychology of Optimal Experience*, New York: Harper & Row.

Csikszentmihalyi, M. and Csikszentmihalyi, I.S. (1988) *Optimal Experience. Psychological Studies of Flow in Consciousness*, Cambridge: Cambridge University Press.

Csikszentmihalyi, M. and Larson, R. (1984) *Being Adolescent*, New York: Basic Books.

Csikszentmihalyi, M. and Le Fevre (1989) 'Optimal experience in work and leisure', *Journal of Personality and Social Psychology* 56, 815–22.

Fiske, S.T. (1993) 'Social cognition and perception', *Annual Review of Psychology* 44, 155–94.

Fischer, M. (1994) 'Work process knowledge in skilled production and maintenance work', unpublished paper in Work Process Knowledge Seminar Papers, University of Manchester.

Fryer, D. and Payne, R. (1984) 'Proactive behaviour in unemployment: findings and implications', *Leisure Studies* 3, 273–95.

Gergen, K.J. (1982) *Toward Transformation in Social Knowledge*, London: Sage.

Gergen, K.J. (1994) *Toward Transformation in Social Knowledge* (2nd edn), London: Sage.

Gibson, J.J. (1979) *The Ecological Approach to Visual Perception*, Boston: Houghton Mifflin.

Haworth, J.T. (1996) 'Contemporary psychological research: visions from positional standpoints', in J.T. Haworth (ed.), *Psychological Research: Innovative Methods and Strategies*, London: Routledge.

Haworth, J.T. and Evans, S. (1995) 'Challenge, skill and positive subjective states in the daily life of a sample of YTS students', *Journal of Occupational and Organisational Psychology* 68, 109–21.

Haworth, J.T. and Hill, S. (1992) 'Work, leisure and psychological well-being in a sample of young adults', *Journal of Community and Applied Psychology* 2, 147–60.

Ingold, I. (1992) 'Culture and the perception of the environment', in E. Cron and D. Parkin (eds), *Bushbase: Forestfarm. Culture, Environment and Development*, London: Routledge, 39–56.

Ingold, T. (1995) 'Work, time and industry', *Time and Society* 4: 1, 5–28.

Ingold, T. (1996) 'Culture, perception and cognition', in J.T. Haworth (ed.), *Psychological Research: Innovative Methods and Strategies*, London: Routledge.

Jahoda, M. (1982) *Employment and Unemployment: A Social Psychological Analysis*, Cambridge: Cambridge University Press.

Jahoda, M. (1984) 'Social institutions and human needs: a comment on Fryer and Payne', *Leisure Studies* 3, 297–9.

Jahoda, M. (1986) 'In defence of a non-reductionist social psychology', *Social Behaviour* 1, 25–9.

Jahoda, M. (1987) 'Unemployed men at work', in D. Fryer and P. Ullah (eds), *Unemployed People*, Milton Keynes: Open University Press.

Kohn, M.L. and Slomczynski, K.M. (1990) *Social Structure and Self-direction: A Comparative Analysis of the United States and Poland*, London: Blackwell.

Lave, J. (1988) *Cognition in Practice*, Cambridge: Cambridge University Press.

Levine, J.M., Resnick, L.B. and Higgins, E.T. (1993) 'Social foundations of cognition', *Annual Review of Psychology* 44, 585–612.

LeWontin, R. (1989) 'A natural selection: review of J.M. Smith's *Evolutionary Genetics*', *Nature* 339, 107.

Maguire, M., Maguire, S. and Felstead, A. (1993) 'Factors influencing individual commitment to lifetime learning', Research Series No. 20, Sheffield: Department of Employment.

Merleau-Ponty, M. (1962) *Phenomenology of Perception*, London: Routledge & Kegan Paul.

Merleau-Ponty, M. (1964a) 'The primacy of perception', in J.M. Eddie (ed.), *The Primacy of Perception*, Evanston: North Western University Press.

Merleau-Ponty, M. (1964b) 'Eye and mind', in J.M. Eddie (ed.), *The Primacy of Perception*, Evanston: North Western University Press.

Merleau-Ponty, M. (1968) 'Working notes', in Claud Lefort (ed.), *The Visible and the Invisible*, Evanston: North Western University Press.

Mowday, R.T. and Sutton, R.I. (1993) 'Organisational behaviour: linking individuals and groups to organisational contexts', *Annual Review of Psychology* 44, 159–229.

Posner, M.I. and Rothbart, M.K. (1989) 'Intentional chapters on unintentional thoughts', in J.S. Uleman and J.A. Bargh (eds), *Unintended Thought*, London: The Guilford Press.

Uleman, J.S. and Bargh, J.A. (eds) (1989) *Unintended Thought*, London: The Guilford Press.

Varela, F.J., Thompson, E. and Rosch, E. (1991) *The Embodied Mind: Cognitive Science and Human Experience*, Cambridge, MA: MIT Press.

Warr, P. (1987) *Work, Unemployment and Mental Health*, Oxford: Clarendon Press.

Chapter 8

Serious leisure and well-being

Robert A. Stebbins

Following on the intellectual foundation laid by Josef Pieper, Sabastian de Grazia and Max Kaplan, among others, the term 'serious leisure' made its debut in leisure studies circles in 1982. The initial statement (Stebbins, 1982) and several more recent ones have centred on the nature of serious leisure, a concept now reasonably well elucidated in what seems to have become its standard short definition: serious leisure is the systematic pursuit of an amateur, hobbyist, or volunteer activity that participants find so substantial and interesting that, in the typical case, they launch themselves on a career centred on acquiring and expressing its special skills, knowledge and experience (Stebbins, 1992a: 3).[1] This is probably as good a depiction of this form of leisure as any single-sentence definition can provide. Serious leisure is commonly contrasted with 'casual' or 'unserious' leisure, which is considerably less substantial and offers no career of the sort just described. Casual leisure can also be defined residually as all leisure falling outside the three basic types of serious leisure.

The goal of this chapter is to present an overview of several basic elements of serious leisure theory and research. Except where noted otherwise, this overview is based on my longitudinal research project consisting of eight groups of amateurs, which is summarized and elaborated theoretically in Stebbins (1992a), as well as on a study of a hobbyist group, which is reported in Stebbins (1996a). The amateur groups were examined sequentially over a fifteen-year period, starting with those in classical music and continuing with those in theatre, archaeology, baseball, astronomy, Canadian football, entertainment magic, and stand-up comedy. Upon completion of the longitudinal project, I entered the world of hobbies to study several chapters of barbershop singers. I am currently engaged in research using the serious leisure perspective to examine francophone volunteers working in Canadian cities outside Quebec.[2] I will also refer to this study from time to time where appropriate.

THE NATURE OF SERIOUS LEISURE

We can further explore the nature of serious leisure by going beyond our convenient, albeit limited, one-sentence definition to describe its three basic types. Amateurs are found in art, science, sport and entertainment, where they are invariably linked in a variety of ways with their professional counterparts. For their part, the professionals are identified and defined according to theory developed in the social scientific study of professions, a subtantially more exact procedure than one relying on the simplistic and not infrequently commercially shaped commonsense images of these workers. In other words, when studying amateurs and professionals it is not enough to define these two categories descriptively, such as by noting that the activity in question constitutes a livelihood for the second but not the first and that the second works full time at it whereas the first pursues it part time. As we shall see later in this section, the two are locked in and therefore defined by a relationship of far greater complexity than this.

Hobbyists lack this professional alter ego, even if they sometimes have commercial equivalents and often have small publics who take an interest in what they do. Hobbyists can be classified according to one of five categories: (1) collectors, (2) makers and tinkerers, (3) activity participants (in non-competitive, rule-based pursuits); (4) players of sports and games (where no professional counterparts exist); and (5) enthusiasts in one of the liberal arts. Fishing (Bryan, 1977), bird-watching (Kellert, 1985) and barbershop singing (Stebbins, 1996a) exemplify the activity participants, whereas field hockey (Bishop and Hoggett, 1986), long-distance running (Yair, 1990) and competitive swimming (Hastings *et al.* 1989) exemplify the players. The liberal arts hobbyists are enamoured of the systematic acquisition of knowledge for its own sake. This is typically accomplished by reading voraciously in a field of art, sport, cuisine, language, culture, history, science, philosophy, politics or literature (Stebbins, 1994).

Volunteers – the third basic type – engage in volunteering, which Jon Van Til (1988, p. 6) defines and describes as

> a helping action of an individual that is valued by him or her, and yet is not aimed directly at material gain or mandated or coerced by others. Thus, in the broadest sense, *volunteering* is an uncoerced helping activity that is engaged in not primarily for financial gain and not by coercion or mandate. It is thereby different in definition from work, slavery, or conscription. (his emphasis)

It is important to note, however, that the field of career volunteering is narrower than this, even if it does cover considerable ground. The taxonomy prepared by Statistics Canada (1980) lists seven types of organizations, within which different services are provided by career volunteers: health (physical and non-physical health care for all ages), educational (service inside and outside the formal school system), social/welfare (child care, family counselling, correctional services), leisure (service in athletic and non-athletic associations), religious (service in religious organizations, civic/community action (advocacy, service in professional and labour organizations, and political (service in political organizations). Although much of career volunteering appears to be connected in one way or another with an organization of some sort, the scope of this leisure is possibly even broader, perhaps including the kinds of helping devoted individuals do for social movements or for neighbours and family.[3] Still, the definition of serious leisure restricts attention everywhere to volunteering in which the participant can find a career, in which he or she offers more or less continuous and substantial help, rather than a one-time donation of money, organs, services, etc.

Serious leisure is further defined by six distinctive qualities, qualities found among amateurs, hobbyists and volunteers alike. One is the occasional need to *persevere*, as seen in confronting danger (e.g. eating wild mushrooms: Fine, 1988, p. 181), managing stage fright (e.g. participating in theatre and sport: Stebbins, 1981) or handling embarrassment (e.g. doing volunteer work: Floro, 1978, p. 198). Yet, it is clear that positive feelings about the activity come, to some extent, from sticking with it through thick and thin, from conquering adversity. A second quality is, as indicated earlier, that of finding a *career* in the endeavour, shaped as it is by its own special contingencies, turning points and stages of achievement and involvement.

Most, if not all, careers in serious leisure owe their existence to its third quality: serious leisure participants make a significant personal *effort* based on specially acquired *knowledge*, *training* or *skill* and, indeed at times, all three. Examples include such achievements as showmanship, athletic prowess, scientific knowledge and long experience in a role. Fourth, a number of *durable benefits*, or *rewards*, of serious leisure have so far been identified, mostly from research on amateurs and hobbyists. They are self-actualization, self-enrichment, self-expression, regeneration or renewal of self, feelings of accomplishment, enhancement of self-image, social interaction and belonging-ness and lasting physical products of the activity (e.g. a painting, a scientific paper, a piece of furniture). A further benefit – self-gratification, or pure fun, which is by far the most evanescent benefit in this list – is the only one of the eight also enjoyed by casual leisure participants. We shall return to the rewards of serious leisure in a later section.

The fifth quality – that participants in serious leisure tend to *identify* strongly with their chosen pursuits – springs from the presence of the other five. In contrast, casual leisure, although hardly humiliating or despicable, is none the less too fleeting, mundane, and commonplace for most people to find a distinctive identity there. I should imagine that this was the quality Cicero had in mind when he coined his famous slogan: *Otium cum dignitate*, or 'Leisure with dignity'.

The sixth quality of serious leisure is the *unique ethos* that develops in connection with each expression of it. A central component of this ethos is the special social world that begins to take shape when enthusiasts in a particular field pursue their interests there over many years. David Unruh (1979, p. 115) defines the social world as a unit of social organization which is diffuse and amorphous . . . . Generally larger than groups or organizations, social worlds are not necessarily defined by formal boundaries, membership lists, or spatial territory . . . . A social world must be seen as an internally recognizable constellation of actors, organizations, events, and practices which have coalesced into a perceived sphere of interest and involvement for participants. Characteristically, a social world lacks a powerful centralized authority structure and is delimited by . . . effective communication and not territory nor formal group membership.

In a later paper, Unruh (1980) added that social worlds are characterized by voluntary identification, by a freedom to enter into and depart from them. Moreover, because they are so diffuse, it is common for their members to be only partly involved in all the activities these formations have to offer. After all, a social world may be local, regional, multi-regional, national, even international. Third, people in complex societies are often members of several social worlds, only some of which are related to leisure. Finally, social worlds are held together, to an important degree, by semi-formal, or 'mediated communication'. In the typical case they are neither heavily bureaucratized nor, due to their diffuseness, substantially organized through intense face-to-face interaction. Rather, communication is commonly mediated by newsletters, posted notices, telephone messages, mass mailings, radio and television announcements and similar means.

Every social world contains four types of members: strangers, tourists, regulars and insiders (Unruh, 1979, p. 1980). The strangers are intermediaries who normally participate little in the leisure activity itself, but who none the less do something important to make it possible, for example, by managing municipal parks (in amateur baseball), minting coins (in hobbyist coin collecting), and organizing the work of teachers' aids (in career volunteering). Tourists are temporary participants in a social world; they have come on the scene momentarily for profit, advantage or entertainment. Most amateur and hobbyist activities have publics of some kind which, in the language of the present discussion, can be said to consist of tourists. The clients of many volunteers can be similarly classified. The regulars routinely participate in the social world; in serious leisure, they are the amateurs, hobbyists and volunteers themselves. The insiders are those among them who show exceptional devotion to the social world they share, to maintaining it, to advancing it. In the studies of amateurs and hobbyists, such people have often been analysed as 'devotees' and contrasted with 'participants', who are the regulars in Unruh's scheme (more on this distinction later).

Missing from Unruh's conceptualization of the social world, but vitally important for the study of serious leisure, is the proposition that a rich subculture is found there as well, one function of which is to interrelate the 'diffuse and amorphous constellations'. Consequently, I wish to add that we find associated with each social world a set of special norms, values, beliefs, styles, moral principles, performance standards and similar shared representations. These elements help to explain social stratification in social worlds, for example, a process underlying Unruh's distinction between insiders and regulars and my own that separates devotees from participants.

DEFINING AMATEURS

Of the three types of serious leisure participants, the amateurs have so far been the object of the greatest theoretical elaboration, an elaboration that has been carried out on both the macroanalytic and the microanalytic levels. With reference to the first, amateurs are further defined by their complicated link to professionals, with the two groups coalescing, along with the public they share, into a three-way constellation of relations and relationships known as the professional–amateur–public, or PAP, system. Thus, when seen in relationship to their fans, amateur and professional baseball players constitute a distinctive PAP system.

The microanalytic definition of amateurs centres on the attitudinal differences separating them and their professional counterparts. Five of these have been identified to date. When compared with the professionals, the amateurs have less *confidence* in their skills and knowledge which, in performance fields, often manifests itself as severe, uncontrollable stage fright. Professionals must also *persevere* more than amateurs if, for no other reason, than they must earn their living in the activity. Further, the greater perseverance of professionals is fostered, in part, by their greater *commitment* to continuing in the activity. Professionals and amateurs are differentiated, then, by their degree of 'continuance commitment', but not by their degree of 'value commitment' to the activity (Stebbins, 1970), or their attachment to and identification with that activity (see also Buchanan, 1985; Shamir, 1988; Tomlinson, 1993), an attitude that both types tend to hold with the same intensity. Fourth, professionals evince a greater *preparedness* than amateurs, a greater readiness to perform the activity to the best of their ability at the appointed time and place (e.g. being punctual, being sufficiently rested, having equipment in good repair). Finally, with reference to *self-conception*, amateurs and professionals conceive of themselves in these very terms, as amateurs and professionals.

THE MOTIVATIONAL BASIS OF SERIOUS LEISURE

Many people are inclined to look on serious leisure as a good thing. Yet, paradoxical as it may seem, given the commonsense belief that all leisure is casual and sought primarily as pure enjoyment, there is no denying that those who engage in serious leisure encounter costs *and* rewards, both of which can be sharply felt. It is precisely this paradox, however – realizing important values in the face of adversity – that speaks most directly and consistently to the motivational question of why some people take up forms of leisure at which they 'must work'.

The costs of serious leisure can be so poignant that many practitioners ask themselves from time to time why they do it. It follows that researchers in this area must consider these costs in any analysis of the durable benefits of serious leisure mentioned earlier in this chapter. The costs offset the durable benefits to some extent, while combining with them to form patterns of costs and rewards unique to each pursuit. These patterns may turn out, upon further research, to be generalizable in certain ways. For the present, however, one effective way to explore them in a given amateur, hobbyist or career volunteer field is to proceed from the perspective provided by the following simple proposition taken from the social exchange theory of George Homans (1974, p. 31): the main costs and rewards of an activity, when psychologically weighed against each other, result in a personal sense of 'profit' or 'loss'.

The rewards of a pursuit are the more or less routine values attracting and holding its practitioners. Working from a list of nine possible rewards, the amateurs and hobbyists in eight of my nine studies were asked first to select those that applied to them and then to rank their selections according to their degree of rewardingness.[4] I developed this list inductively during my early studies of amateurs, refining it in the later ones centred on other amateurs and on hobbyist barbershop singers. Of note is the fact that some of these rewards (e.g. self-actualization) are discussed in the social psychology of leisure as generalized benefits of leisure. Nevertheless, here, as elsewhere in my research, these rewards were also used as probes to encourage discussion of the ways each general reward is more particularly expressed in the leisure pursuit under study.[5]

The nine rewards were presented to the respondents in the following format, although in a different order and without classification as personal or social. I created a special set of parenthetic statements for each study, with each set being designed to adapt these rewards to the leisure activity under consideration.

Personal rewards
- Personal enrichment (gained while pursuing the activity);
- Self-actualization (developing skills and abilities);
- Self-expression (expressing skills and abilities already developed);
- Self-image (known to others as a certain kind of amateur, hobbyist, or volunteer);
- Enjoyable, fun (sense of play, hedonistic pleasure);
- Recreate oneself, regenerate oneself through the activity after a day's work;
- Financial return from the activity.

Social rewards
- Social attraction (associating with like-minded leisure enthusiasts);
- Group accomplishment (collective effort in creating a leisure product such as a show, concert or play in sport).

After discussing in detail with each respondent the rewards and their ranking, I encouraged him or her, in line with the exploratory mission of the fifteen-year project and the barbershop study, to add other rewards to the list. The later studies produced no additional suggestions. These nine rewards were found in every serious leisure activity studied, although the pattern of ranks for the rewards varied from activity to activity. As the foregoing list shows, the rewards of the amateur and hobbyist pursuits are mostly personal. Still this may not be true for career volunteering, a question that will be addressed in the interview part of the previously mentioned study of francophone volunteers.

Let us examine the personal rewards more closely. Self-actualization, or self-realization, refers to the opportunity participants find in their leisure activities to develop their talents, skills and knowledge; to realize an important part of their potential as human beings. Moreover, the expression of such talents, skills and knowledge, to the extent that they have already been developed, is rewarding in itself. Enhanced self-conception results from the favourable social identity associated with participation in a particular field. Self-gratification refers to the pure enjoyment people experience from time to time in a serious leisure pursuit. It is the only essentially hedonistic reward in this list. The unusual, memorable experiences found in the activity contribute to self-enrichment by endowing the person with moral, cultural or intellectual resources. Re-creation, or regeneration, denotes the capacity of the activity to divert the leisure practitioner's mind from work or from any event or problem in life commanding substantial attention. Finally, a few amateurs, hobbyists and career volunteers even find financial rewards in their serious leisure, although given that leisure is not work, these rewards cannot constitute a livelihood.

Both social rewards – social attraction and group accomplishment – can be described, in part, as 'fun', or the sense of participating with others in an attractive activity (Podilchak, 1991). Social attraction denotes the camaraderie that develops around a pursuit, the appeal of talking about it, and the exhilaration of being part of the scene. With respect to group accomplishment, it is possible only in collective undertakings, such as those found in the team sports and the concerted arts. This reward flows from doing one's part in a collaborative project.

But there are also costs to be endured; they have been found to occur in three broad types: dislikes, tensions and disappointments. Some of them can be extremely poignant. All are highly specific to particular serious leisure pursuits. In general, the dislikes revolve around more substantial issues than life's omnipresent pet peeves. Examples include coaches who favour certain players on the team, barbershop singers who talk excessively during rehearsals, and stand-up comics who steal lines from their colleagues. Among the tensions in serious leisure are try-outs (e.g. auditions), stage fright, interpersonal friction and the questionable calls referees occasionally make during athletic contests. Disappointments are the absence of expected rewards and their manifestations. They are born in the failure of high hopes, for instance, losing a championship game in football, failing to master one's part in the community orchestra and missing a lunar occultation in astronomy because the sky clouded over at the last minute.

In accordance with Homans' proposition, then, it has been possible to conclude in every one of these studies that, after weighing its costs against its rewards, the interviewees invariably saw a 'profit' in their serious leisure activity. This profit and the level of intensity with which it is felt help account for the differential levels of seriousness found among serious leisure practitioners. Those who are highly involved and dedicated to their pursuits have been classified in the serious leisure perspective as *devotees*. Those who are moderately involved and dedicated, but significantly more so than the dabblers and dilettantes of casual leisure, have been classified as *participants*. Empirically, these two types are distinguished, among other ways, by the different amounts of time each devotes to doing the activity and preparing for it.

SERIOUS LEISURE AND MARGINALITY

I have argued over the years that amateurs and the activities they pursue are marginal in society, for amateurs are neither dabblers nor professionals (see also Stebbins, 1979). Several properties of amateurism give substance to this hypothesis. One, although seemingly illogical at the level of theory, amateur leisure was said earlier to be characterized empirically by an important degree of continuance commitment to a pursuit. This commitment is measured, among other ways, by the sizeable investment of time and energy in the leisure made by its devotees and participants.[6]

Two, amateurism is pursued with noticeable seriousness (i.e. as a type of serious leisure), with such passion that Erving Goffman (1963) once qualified amateurs and similar enthusiasts as the 'quietly disaffiliated'.[7]

Three, amateurism tends to be uncontrollable; it engenders in its practitioners a desire to engage in the activity beyond the time and money available for it. Whereas some casual leisure can also be uncontrollable, our marginality hypothesis implies that this proclivity is significantly stronger among amateurs.

Four, amateurs occupy the status of peripheral members of the profession on which they model their activities, while nevertheless being judged in their execution of those activities by the standards of that profession. The studies of barbershop singers and francophone volunteers suggest that the first three properties are also found in hobbyist activities and career volunteering.

As it is used here the idea of marginality is different from the marginality afflicting the 'marginal man', a conception sociologists have used for many years to describe the lifestyles of immigrants. The latter are marginal because, typically, they are caught between two cultures, such that their marginality becomes a way of life, a condition touching nearly every corner of their existence. Although this ethnic marginality and the leisure marginality on which the present chapter focuses are both centred on peripheral and ambiguous social statuses, the second kind of marginality is hardly as pervasive as the first. Rather, leisure marginality is a segmented and hence limited marginality associated with certain uncommon or unusual statuses.[8]

In leisure marginality, as in ethnic marginality, we find among the status incumbents themselves as well as in the wider community an *ambiguity*, or a lack of clarity, as to who these incumbents, these marginal people, really are and what they really do. The studies I conducted on amateurs and hobbyists revealed the multifaceted nature of this ambiguity. On the cultural side, ambiguity is manifested narrowly as a conflict of expectations and broadly as a conflict of values (e.g. on commitment to special interests and rewards: Stebbins, 1992a, Chapter 7). On the relational side, incongruent status arrangements develop, such as when amateurs in pursuit of their leisure goals help professionals to reach their work goals. On the psychological side, practitioners may become ambivalent towards their serious leisure as they confront their own marginality during the many and diverse expressions of this ambiguity in everyday life. The following episode taken from the baseball study exemplifies the psychological ambiguity inherent in serious leisure:

> One father arrived at a late Sunday afternoon practice with his two young boys: 'My wife had to be away this afternoon,' he commented. 'She said you watch them or stay home.' He had to leave the field several times during the workout to break up a fight between them or soothe a minor injury incurred while scampering around the bleachers or surrounding area.
>
> (Stebbins, 1979, p. 220)

In summing up these ideas about ambiguity, it is evident that both practitioners of a serious leisure activity and the larger society are inclined to see it as marginal to the main problems around which the social institutions of work, family and leisure have developed and to the principal ways in which people try to solve those problems.

My research in all three types of serious leisure demonstrates that family and work and even other leisure activities pull the serious leisure practitioners in two, if not three, directions at once, making time demands that together often exceed the total available hours. In addition, unlike family and work activities where institutional supports sustain serious involvement, such support for equivalent activities in leisure is absent. For example, such widely accepted values as providing for one's family, working hard on the job, or being family centred – all of which help to justify our efforts in these spheres – are simply lacking in most serious leisure.[9] Moreover, their very existence in the institutions of family and work threatens amateur involvement elsewhere by reducing the importance of the latter while enhancing that of the former.

Most critical, however, is the observation that serious leisure practitioners are marginal even to the institution of leisure itself. That is, they implicitly or explicitly reject a number of the values, attitudes and patterns of behaviour constituting the very core of modern leisure. For instance, many an interviewee told me about his or her feeble interest in television or in such passive leisure as frivolous talk and people watching. Like marginal people everywhere, then, those who go in for serious leisure lack key institutional supports for their goals as well as for their personal and collective ways of reaching them.

Marginal statuses are common in industrial societies, where rapid social change gives birth to new forms of work and leisure. Still, as time passes in these societies, certain forms do become less, sometimes even much less, ambiguous and marginal.[10] A few of them may even become central. Nevertheless, according to the studies referred to in this chapter, such a transformation has failed to occur in the field of serious leisure. Furthermore, it is unlikely to occur there for some time, it appears.

CONTRIBUTIONS TO THE COMMUNITY

Yet, notwithstanding its marginality, serious leisure does make many significant contributions to the community. We shall consider four of them here. First, through the great variety of social worlds it generates, serious leisure offers a sense of belonging and participation for the four different types of members. This sense stood out in relief in every study discussed in this chapter. It is also evident in Mittelstaedt's (1995) detailed description of the four types of members inhabiting the social world of American Civil War reenactments. Here each type enjoys its own special involvements.

Second, serious leisure can stand as evidence, for the millions of people in this world who do not pursue it, that leisure can be more than pure hedonism and something other than a wretched malady of contemporary Western civilization – Glasser's (1970, pp. 190–2) bitter indictment. Still, whether serious leisure will be able to 'dignify' the entire field of leisure studies (a transfiguration some of my colleagues tell me they are hoping for) remains to be seen. In any case, knowledge of the former is still confined too much to intellectual circles for that to happen very soon.

Third, to the extent that it is pursued with other people, serious leisure can contribute signficantly to communal and even societal integration. Thus Thompson (1992) found that the members of a women's tennis association in Australia, who meet weekly for matches, came from a range of different social classes and age groups. In a similar vein, as part of my participant observation for the francophone volunteer project, I sat on the board of directors of a community organization composed of a real estate agent, teacher, banker, homemaker, data analyst, business executive, high school student, and myself, a sociologist and university professor. There was an almost equal representation of the two sexes who, together, ranged in age from 16 to around 65. Likewise, gun collectors from the city and its rural hinterland rub elbows periodically at various 'shows' where they display their collections for, and discuss them with, the general public and no small number of dealers (Olmsted, 1988).

Four, serious leisure has a far-reaching salutary effect on the general welfare of the community. Put more concisely, it benefits its publics in important ways, as when a community orchestra gives a performance or the local astronomical society hosts a 'star night'. The latter is open to anyone interested in observing the evening sky through the portable telescopes of the society's members. Ruth

Finnegan (1989) describes for a single community the complex, positive effect on the different music publics of an entire local amateur-professional-hobbyist music scene. She studied the English 'new' town of Milton Keynes.

SERIOUS LEISURE AND WELL-BEING

The first question to pose in this conclusion is whether an activity, even though freely chosen, can engender well-being when encumbered with significant costs and a marginal status *vis-à-vis* three major social institutions. The answer is that it can. For, to the extent that well-being is fostered by enjoyment of and satisfaction with the activities of everyday life, research evidence suggests that it is an important by-product of serious leisure (Haworth, 1986; Haworth and Hill, 1992; Mannell, 1994). Furthermore, when interviewed, the respondents in the studies of serious leisure discussed in this chapter invariably described in detail and with great enthusiasm the satisfaction and enjoyment they get from their amateur and hobbyist activities. I would expect to find the same reaction in the study of volunteers.

All this evidence is correlational, however. No one has yet carried out a study expressly designed to ascertain whether long-term involvement in a form of serious leisure leads to significant enduring increases in feelings of well-being. The extent to which serious leisure can generate major interpersonal role conflict for some practitioners – it led to two divorces among the twenty-five respondents in the theatre study (Stebbins, 1979, pp. 81–3) – should be sufficient warning to avoid postulating an automatic link between this kind of leisure and well-being. I also have anecdotal evidence that serious leisure activities can generate intrapersonal conflict, such as when people fail to establish priorities among their many and varied leisure interests. Even an approach–approach conflict between two cherished leisure activities can possibly affect well-being unfavourably. Hamilton-Smith (1995, pp. 6–7) says our lack of knowledge about the link between serious leisure and well-being is a major lacuna in contemporary leisure research.

Finally, are we being realistic when we argue that serious leisure is a primary source of personal well-being in life? There is probably no sphere in life where well-being can take root and grow in pure, undiluted form. In other words, I suspect that when we are filled with feelings of well-being, whether at work, during leisure or while performing non-work obligations, we are, in effect, experiencing those feelings as a significant profit of rewards against costs. Moreover, what is noteworthy about the theoretical link between any kind of leisure and well-being is that, in commonsense, we seldom expect costs in the former, whereas we routinely expect them at work and during the execution of obligatory tasks. That we expect to find pure enjoyment everywhere in our leisure, however unrealistic, may be shown some day to have a powerful effect on how much we enjoy, or are satisfied with or happy about, the serious leisure we pursue. And when a sense of well-being does emerge here – as it surely will –

this expectation will influence the level of intensity with which the well-being is felt. Certainly, we can be mildly *or* highly satisfied with a serious pursuit or activity, enjoy it somewhat *or* enjoy it immensely.

Serious leisure and well-being would seem to make a perfect couple, but their relationship appears destined to be far more complicated than current levels of theory and research would suggest.

NOTES

1 I use the term 'career' broadly in this definition, following Goffman's (1961, pp. 127– 8) elaboration of the idea of 'moral career'. Such careers are available in all substantial, complicated roles, including especially those in work, leisure, deviance, politics, religion and interpersonal relationships (see also Lindesmith *et al.*, 1991, p. 277; Hewitt, 1991, p. 246).

2 I have completed the participant observation for a Canada-wide study of career volunteering in five Canadian urban francophone communities outside Quebec. Pending the availability of funding, I will carry out a series of personal interviews with a sample of these serious leisure practitioners in Vancouver, Calgary, Hamilton, Toronto and Halifax, five predominantly anglophone cities where francophones live in minority circumstances.

3 I am indebted to Stanley Parker (private correspondence) for calling my attention to this possibility.

4 To my knowledge, no other research has examined the costs and rewards of serious leisure using the procedures described here.

5 We might question whether exploration is justified in this area of sociology and psychology where a great deal of research has already been conducted on leisure motives and rewards. Exploration is justified, however, because the theory and data in this area are much too general to inform us about the particular nature of the motives involved in and the rewards gained from the pursuit of a given form of leisure as an everyday life activity. For an illustration of the difference between general and particular motives and rewards, see Stebbins (1992b).

6 On commitment see also Buchanan (1985) and Shamir (1988). On the investment of time and energy in leisure, see Kelly (1983, pp. 195–6).

7 As good a description as this is, Goffman's (1963, pp. 143–5) decision to classify the quietly disaffiliated as deviant fails to square with the amateurs' views of themselves and, for that matter, with the canons of deviance theory (e.g. Stebbins, 1996b, pp. 2–7).

8 Chiropractors were once described in these terms (see Wardwell, 1952). For a recent discussion of marginal professions, see Ritzer and Walczak (1986, Chapter 9).

9 Some fields of career volunteering, rooted as they are in altrustic ideals, may be shown in future research to be blessed with a higher degree of community-wide support than is available for amateur and hobbyist activities.

10 Rosenthal's (1981) study of chiropractors exemplifies this possibility.

REFERENCES

Bishop, J. and Hoggett, P. (1986) *Organizing around Enthusiasms: Mutual Aid in Leisure*, London: Comedia Publishing Group.

Bryan, H. (1977) 'Leisure value systems and recreational specialization: the case of trout fishermen', *Journal of Leisure Research* 9, 174–87.

Buchanan, T. (1985) 'Commitment and leisure behavior', *Leisure Sciences* 7, 401–20.

Fine, G.A. (1988) 'Dying for a laugh', *Western Folklore* 47, 177–94.

Finnegan, R. (1989) *The Hidden Musicians: Music-Making in an English Town*, Cambridge: Cambridge University Press.

Floro, G.K. (1978) 'What to look for in a study of the volunteer in the work world', in R.P. Wolensky and E.J. Miller (eds), *The Small City and Regional Community*, Stevens Point, Wisc.: Foundation Press.

Glasser, R. (1970) *Leisure: Penalty or Prize?*, London: Macmillan.

Goffman, E. (1961) *Asylums: Essays on the Social Situation of Mental Patients and Other Inmates*, Garden City, NY: Doubleday.

Goffman, E. (1963) *Stigma: Notes on the Management of Spoiled Identity*, Englewood Cliffs, NJ: Prentice-Hall.

Hamilton-Smith, E. (1995) 'The connexions of scholarship', *Newsletter* (official newsletter of Research Committee 13 of the International Sociological Association), March, 4–9.

Hastings, D.W., Kurth, S. and Meyer, J. (1989) 'Competitive swimming careers through the life course', *Sociology of Sport Journal* 6, 278–84.

Haworth, J.T. (1986) 'Meaningful activity and psychological models of non-employment', *Leisure Studies* 5, 281–97.

Haworth, J.T. and Hill, S. (1992) 'Work, leisure, and psychological well-being in a sample of young adults', *Journal of Community and Applied Social Psychology* 2, 147–60.

Hewitt, J.P. (1991) *Self and Society* (5th edn), Boston: Allyn & Bacon.

Homans, G.C. (1974) *Social Behavior* (rev. edn), New York: Harcourt Brace Jovanovich.

Kellert, S.R. (1985) 'Birdwatching in American society', *Leisure Sciences* 7, 343–60.

Kelly, J.R. (1983) *Leisure Identities and Interactions*, Boston: George Allen & Unwin.

Lindesmith, A.R., Strauss, A.L. and Denzin, N.K. (1991) *Social Psychology* (7th edn), Englewood Cliffs, NJ: Prentice-Hall.

Mannell, R.C. (1994) 'High investment activity and life satisfaction among older adults: committed, serious leisure, and flow activities', in J.R. Kelly (ed.), *Activity and Aging: Staying involved in Later life*, Newbury Park, CA: Sage.

Mittelstaedt, R.D. (1995) 'Reenacting the American Civil War: a unique form of serious leisure for adults', *World Leisure & Recreation* 37: 1, 23–7.

Olmsted, A.D. (1988) 'Morally controversial leisure: the social world of gun collectors', *Symbolic Interaction* 11, 277–88.

Podilchak, W. (1991) 'Establishing the fun in leisure', *Leisure Sciences* 13, 123–46.

Ritzer, G. and Walczak, D. (1986) *Working: Conflict and Change* (3rd edn), Englewood Cliffs, NJ: Prentice-Hall.

Rosenthal, S.F. (1981) 'Marginal or Mainstream? Two Studies of Contemporary Chiropractic', *Sociological Focus* 14, 271–85.

Shamir, B. (1988) 'Commitment and leisure', *Sociological Perspectives* 31, 238–58.

Statistics Canada (1980) *An Overview of Volunteer Workers in Canada*, cat. no. 71–530. Ottawa: Supply and Services Canada.

Stebbins, R.A. (1970) 'On misunderstanding the concept of commitment: a theoretical clarification', *Social Forces* 48, 526–9.

Stebbins, R.A. (1979) *Amateurs: On the Margin Between Work and Leisure*, Beverly Hills, CA: Sage.

Stebbins, R.A. (1981) Toward a social psychology of stage fright', in M. Hart and S. Birrell (eds), *Sport in the Sociocultural Process*, Dubuque, Iowa: W.C. Brown.

Stebbins, R.A. (1982) 'Serious leisure: a conceptual statement', *Pacific Sociological Review* 25, 251–72.

Stebbins, R.A. (1992a) *Amateurs, Professionals, and Serious Leisure*, Montreal and Kingston: McGill-Queen's University Press.

Stebbins, R.A. (1992b) 'Costs and rewards in barbershop singing', *Leisure Studies* 11, 123–33.

Stebbins, R.A. (1994) 'The liberal arts hobbies: a neglected subtype of serious leisure', *Loisir et Société/Society and Leisure* 17, 173–86.

Stebbins, R.A. (1996a) *The Barbershop Singer: Inside the Social World of a Musical Hobby*, Toronto: University of Toronto Press.

Stebbins, R.A. (1996b) *Tolerable Differences: Living with Deviance*, Toronto, Ont.: McGraw-Hill Ryerson.

Thompson, S. (1992) '"Mum's tennis day": the gendered definition of older women's leisure', *Loisir et Société/Society and Leisure* 15, 323–43.

Tomlinson, A. (1993) 'Culture of commitment in leisure: notes towards the understanding of a serious legacy', *World Leisure and Recreation* 35 (Spring), 6–9.

Unruh, D.R. (1979) 'Characteristics and types of participation in social worlds', *Symbolic Interaction* 2, 115–30.

Unruh, D.R. (1980) 'The nature of social worlds', *Pacific Sociological Review* 23, 271–96.

Van Til, J. (1988) *Mapping the Third Sector: Voluntarism in a Changing Political Economy*, New York: The Foundation Center.

Wardwell, W.I. (1952) 'A marginal professional role: the chiropractor', *Social Forces* 30, 339–48.

Yair, G. (1990) 'The commitment to long-distance running and level of activities', *Journal of Leisure Research* 22, 213–27.

Chapter 9

A psychological analysis of leisure and health

Seppo E. Iso-Ahola

INTRODUCTION

To understand the relationship between leisure and health, one has to consider first the meaning of these two constructs. Health is a general concept that refers to the absence of illness, but it also covers the more positive aspects: physical, mental and social well-being. Similarly, leisure is a global construct that refers to the state of being, rather than time, money or activity. Thus, seeing somebody in a presumably pleasant leisure context (e.g. restaurant) does not mean that a person is having leisure or engaging in a leisure activity. As Csikszentmihalyi and Graef (1979) reported, when wives had to go to restaurants to please their husband's boss, they felt more irritated there than in their everyday work. For leisure to exist, one has to be in control of one's behaviours and have a sense of freedom to pursue willingly a given activity. Thus, perceived freedom and intrinsic motivation are the most important defining characteristics of leisure (Iso-Ahola, 1980).

Both leisure and health vary on a continuum. Some leisure experiences are better than others. Similarly, even in the absence of illnesses, some people are healthier than others. In a scientific sense, then, a major question is: does health covary with leisure experiences? In other words, when people's reported leisure experiences increase, what happens to their health status? Or, when the reported illness symptoms increase, does leisure involvement decrease? It is obvious that if there is a causal relationship between the two constructs, it has to be bidirectional: leisure participation affects health and health affects leisure involvement. Scientifically, then, it becomes important to determine the conditions under which leisure activity is a cause of health and the conditions under which health (or lack of it) is a cause of leisure involvement (Iso-Ahola, 1994).

The idea of reciprocal causation is difficult for science because one cannot categorically and exclusively establish that one factor is the cause of the other. What this means here is that it takes some degree, or perhaps a considerable degree, of health to be able to participate in leisure activity. In this sense, health is always a cause of leisure. But, once people have become able to choose to participate in a leisure activity, then leisure experiences may contribute significantly to health. Increased health or well-being may in turn encourage additional leisure involvement. Which, then, is a cause of which?

Although it is not possible to answer this question in the strictest sense of causality, nevertheless it is logical to argue that in certain cases, the relationship is likely to be a one-way street. For example, if it is shown that people with relatively low levels of self-esteem or a negative self-concept improve significantly on this variable after having been made to participate in an Outward Bound Program (Marsh *et al.*, 1986), it is difficult to argue that self-esteem would have caused their participation in the programme. Rather, it has to be the other way, assuming, of course, that effects of other intervening variables have been controlled for methodologically. Thus, for logical and conceptual reasons, the present review seeks answers to the question about the effects of leisure on health, not vice versa, and possible psychological mechanisms underlying these effects.

DISCOVERY OF LEISURE

Leisure can influence health in two principal ways. First, in and of itself, leisure is conducive to health. The mere existence of leisure in a person's everyday life has consequences for health. The fact that an individual acknowledges, values and engages in leisure for its own sake, for its inherent characteristics, is one way in which leisure contributes to health. Another way is where leisure is used as a tool to achieve certain health outcomes. An example of this is a person who takes time to exercise regularly: leisure provides time for him or her to exercise.

Whether used as an end in itself or as a tool, leisure has to be discovered. This discovery occurs at the cognitive, affective and behavioural levels. Cognitively, people have to acquire information about leisure and become aware of its potential in their lives. Affectively, discovery refers to development of liking for leisure in general and for certain leisure experiences. Finally, people may discover that they are capable of participating in actual leisure behaviours. Unfortunately, such discovery is not easy for many people. Lack of information and attitudes can become major constraints to leisure (Iso-Ahola and Mannell, 1985). These and other constraints may be the biggest reason why many people are not able to use leisure for health purposes. For example, it is well documented that women are afraid of asking the question, 'What about my leisure?' (Shank, 1986), and consequently have relatively little leisure. Either because of, or in spite of, this major psychological barrier, women do more of the household chores than men in dual-career families (Starrels, 1994), with the net result of less leisure for them, especially at weekends (Shaw, 1985). On the other hand, research suggests that women value leisure for its own sake (intrinsic motivation) more than men do (Iso-Ahola, 1979), which helps them to compensate for the fewer hours of actual free time. Intrinsic leisure motivation, in turn, is positively correlated with psychological health (Iso-Ahola, 1980; Graef *et al.*, 1983).

Does society promote discovery of leisure? In the countries where the Puritan work ethic is glorified, as in the US, leisure and work do not go hand-in-hand, but rather are expected to be negatively related. That is, if one values work, one is expected to devalue leisure. Hunnicut (1988) has shown that in this kind of society, people are not able to reconcile work and family, have little time for cultivating hobbies, and find it difficult to engage in civic activities that would nourish a democratic society. As a result, leisure becomes a slave to work, to be used for recuperation from it. Long hours of work are good for economy because people can then spend more money in consumer goods, and the more they spend, the harder they have to work (Schor, 1991). In this work-spend-work-spend mentality, leisure becomes trivial and the opposition of leisure to work promotes escapism in leisure. Escapism in leisure leads to passive lifestyle, as evidenced by the fact that people spend more of their free time in watching television than in any other activity. It also leads to 'cheap thrills' (e.g. 'demolition derby') becoming important leisure activities for many people (Csikszentmihalyi, 1982). If leisure were promoted for human growth and development, people would use it for finding optimal experiences, in which they would seek challenges and would try to match them with their skills. Such optimal experiences correlate positively with mental health (Csikszentmihalyi, 1990; Clarke and Haworth, 1994; Haworth, 1993, 1995; Haworth and Evans, 1995).

Glorification of the work ethic also leads to proliferation of 'workaholic' individuals. These are people who not only cannot stand leisure but actually dread it. They tend to be rigid people, terrified of unstructured time. Their universal worry is lack of time; they are afraid of wasting time and, as a consequence, never learn to play (Machlowitz, 1980). Psychiatrists view workaholics as obsessive-compulsive personalities and the accompanying lifestyle takes heavy toll on these individuals by way of broken marriages, physical ailments (e.g. high blood pressure, ulcers and migraines) and emotional costs for their children (Machlowitz, 1980). Psychologically, workaholics suffer from heightened stress and anxiety and guilt feelings: 'Excessive pumping of adrenalin will eventually result in chronic fatigue' (Killinger, 1991, p. 134). Chronic fatigue is a symptom of helplessness which in turn feeds into depression. To fight their guilt feelings, many workaholics take up physical exercise. But in doing so, unfortunately, they work at their play or game. They feel they must master a game, accomplish tasks, reach goals, and win. Play, for its own sake, is alien to their views. They may exercise for health reasons, but they do not really enjoy it. Thus exercise does not become play for them. Playfulness, according to Killinger (1991), should be experienced as joyful, amusing fun and an effortless celebration of life.

The fact that society does not promote or encourage the personal discovery of leisure leads to a sedentary lifestyle. People do not seek meaningful leisure activities for their own growth and development but, instead, resort to passive activities to escape their everyday problems. It is well established that an average American adult spends about four hours a day watching television and that only

22 per cent of the American population is considered physically active (US Department of Health and Human Services, 1991). Sadly, even teenagers are sedentary and spend, on average, about 30 hours per week watching television (Tangney and Feshbach, 1988). Such escapism is not conducive to mental health, nor, needless to say, does it promote physical health. Csikszentmihalyi *et al.* (1977) reported that while teenagers spend most of their time watching television, they rated sports and games psychologically best. In contrast, television watching was the activity associated with least positive overall mood, offering virtually no challenge, requiring a very low level of skills and providing the least amount of personal control. Sports and games were considered desirable because they were perceived to provide the greatest amount of challenge, required a relatively high level of skills and offered a strong feeling of control over the participant's behaviours. Similarly, a more recent study by Thorlindsson *et al.* (1990) showed that adolescents who were active participants in sports tended to experience less anxiety and depression, have fewer psychophysiological symptoms, and rate their health better than those who were not active in sports.

Thus evidence supports the idea that escapism in and through passive leisure is not conducive to physical and mental health. Rather, it is the seeking of intrinsic rewards through leisure that is psychologically, and even physically, more rewarding. Intrinsic motivation correlates positively with psychological health, and the main components of intrinsic motivation (i.e. perceived freedom and control) have been linked to physical health as well (Deci and Ryan, 1987; Rodin *et al.*, 1985; Wallston *et al.*, 1987). Seeking and escaping are the two fundamental dimensions of motivation for leisure (Iso-Ahola, 1989). While participation in any leisure activity is motivated by these two forces, an important issue is which dimension dominates one's overall leisure involvement: that is, can a person's leisure be characterized mainly by the seeking of personal and interpersonal rewards or by escaping one's personal or interpersonal world through leisure? Evidence suggests that people who are predominantly seeking-oriented motivationally in their leisure are healthier than those who are predominantly escapists in their leisure (Iso-Ahola, 1994; Iso-Ahola and Weissinger, 1984).

Escapism through passive leisure is psychologically troublesome because it leads to boredom, which in turn feeds into apathy and depression. It has been found that lack of awareness of leisure and its potential in one's life is the single most important factor contributing to boredom in leisure (Iso-Ahola and Weissinger, 1987). In other words, failure cognitively to realize or personally discover leisure is a significant antecedent to leisure boredom. Other factors significantly contributing to it are: poor leisure attitude or ethic, high work ethic, lack of leisure skills, barriers to leisure participation and poor self-motivation in general (as a personality trait). These findings are important for two reasons. First, they demonstrate that leisure in itself is a negative thing for many people, because it (or, at least, a failure to discover leisure) leads to boredom and subsequently to depression. Second, the fact that lack of awareness, concurrently coupled with poor leisure attitude and a high work ethic, is the most significant contributor to leisure boredom reflects the extent to which leisure's influence on health is psychological. How can one use leisure for health maintenance and improvement if one does not value it in the first place and is not aware of what to do with it?

So, lack of awareness (especially in combination with leisure and work attitudes) undermines mental health through increased leisure boredom and by serving as a major barrier to active leisure lifestyle. In support of this reasoning, Weissinger (1995) found that people who were high in leisure boredom reported lower physical and mental health than persons with relatively low leisure boredom. Dupuis and Smale (1995) found that older adults' participation in various forms of active leisure (i.e. hobbies/crafts, visiting friends and swimming) was negatively associated with depression and positively correlated to psychological well-being. Caldwell *et al.* (1992) reported that life satisfaction was higher among those who were active in their leisure and that active participation in specific types of leisure activities was associated with higher perceived physical, mental and social health.

EFFECTS OF LEISURE ON HEALTH

It is clear from the above that one cannot gain health benefits from leisure if one has not discovered leisure or uses it negatively, either by maintaining a sedentary lifestyle and/or by resorting to such health-damaging behaviours as drug use. Active leisure lifestyle, on the other hand, promotes health because participation in various leisure activities is geared towards seeking intrinsic rewards through use of one's cognitive, physical or social skills. It is based upon the principle of 'use it or lose it'. For example, dendrites that connect nerve cells in the brain stay extended with use, but begin shrinking without use. 'Some people like to do crossword puzzles. Some go back to school. Some like to visit neighbors. The main factor is stimulation. The nerve cells are designed to receive stimulation. And I think curiosity is a key factor. If one maintains curiosity for a lifetime, that will surely stimulate neural tissue and the cortex may in turn respond' (Diamond, 1984, p. 70).

If intellectual activity has such profound effects on human physiology (i.e. nerve cells), the same can be said about the effects of physical activity on physiological indicators of health and mortality (Blair, 1993; Blair *et al.*, 1995). As a result, lack of exercise was recently promoted to the same level with smoking, obesity, hypertension and cholesterol as a primary risk factor for coronary heart disease (McGinnis, 1991). Research has convincingly shown that physical activeness or exercise decreases significantly one's likelihood of having heart disease and even some forms of cancer and increases one's chances of living longer. It appears that while sports participation in general makes 'remarkably specific, positive and widespread contributions' to participants' health status, some activities are clearly better than others in this respect (e.g. martial arts versus bowling) (Lamb *et al.*, 1988).

As for the influence of physical activity on mental health, several main effects have been reported in the literature. First, there is tentative evidence to suggest that physical exercise improves cognitive functioning in humans, especially the elderly (e.g. Tomporowski and Ellis, 1986; Emery and Blumenthal, 1991; Pierce *et al.*, 1993). Second, physical exercise reduces depression and anxiety and produces positive moods (e.g. Holmes, 1993; Byrne and Byrne, 1993; Tuson and Sinyor, 1993); exercise has been found beneficial even in prevention and treatment of psychopathology (Plante, 1993). Third, physically active leisure and challenging leisure, such as rock climbing, has been reported significantly to improve participants' self-esteem and self-concept (Iso-Ahola *et al.*, 1989; Marsh *et al.*, 1986; Plante and Rodin, 1990). Fourth, social interaction is both a motivator and a benefit of physical activity involvement. People describe the best leisure experiences as those that lead to positive feelings about doing things and meeting with friends (Crandall, 1979; Larson, *et al.*, 1986). Exercising with friends, meeting friends at the health club and socializing outside the club with people met there, etc. improve exercise adherence and consequently provide social benefits (Unger and Johnson, 1995). Social interaction, in turn, is positively related to mental health and psychological well-being (Argyle, 1987, 1992). Finally, physical activity involvement or exercise has a significant positive relationship with general psychological well-being and life satisfaction (Stephens, 1988; Ross and Hayes, 1988; Hayes and Ross, 1986; Wankel and Berger, 1990).

All of these effects of physical activity participation on various aspects of mental health have been reported along with the positive effects of general leisure participation as well. In other words, active leisure lifestyle correlates with increased psychological well-being, self-esteem and positive self-concept, social interaction, life satisfaction and happiness, and with reduced depression (Iso-Ahola, 1994). There is also evidence that play activity improves children's cognitive functioning (i.e. creativity and problem-solving ability) and that older adults age more successfully from the cognitive standpoint if they have been active in leisure (for a review, see Iso-Ahola, 1980). The finding that the same benefits for mental health can be obtained from physical exercise and non-physical leisure activities alike is an important one: it demonstrates that the positive effects of exercise on mental health do not depend on significant increases in aerobic or anaerobic fitness and other physiological changes.

If active leisure lifestyle is positively related to mental health, what about its relationship with physical health? Can activeness in leisure, other than in physically demanding activities, improve physical health? Knowing that mental health affects physical health (Hayes and Ross, 1986), the indirect effect of active leisure on physical health through increased mental health is evident. There is also more direct evidence that doing some leisure activity is more health-promoting than doing little or nothing at all (Roberts *et al.*, 1989). These researchers found that people with 'impoverished leisure' were the least healthy of all the respondents; they also found that people with a 'rich leisure' pattern (i.e. a more varied and frequent involvement than the average for the sample) were the healthiest group. The rich leisure pattern, however, included sport participation in its definition. The importance of sports was further underscored by the fact that people with sports-centred leisure were the healthiest unemployed group. Another line of research suggests that physiological tolerance and recovery from stress are faster and more complete when people are exposed to natural environments and outdoor recreation activities (Ulrich *et al.*, 1990). Taken together, it appears that active leisure lifestyle is good for physical health, especially if it includes sports participation.

By way of summary, Figure 9.1 shows the relationship between leisure and health. The solid arrows are reflective of the well-established empirical links between the variables and the dotted arrow indicates tentative evidence. There is good scientific evidence that physical and psychological well-being are strongly correlated. Physical health affects psychological health (Hayes and Ross, 1986) and psychological health affects physical health. The latter relationship is attested by the well-documented effects of perceived control, for example, on physical health (e.g. Rodin, 1986; Deci and Ryan, 1987). Similarly, it has been shown that perceived self-efficacy to exercise control over stressors is a modulator of the immunological system status (Wiedenfeld *et al.*, 1990) and that the self-reported mood changes lead to changes in the secretory immune system, specifically such that the immune system is stronger during times of positive moods than negative moods (Stone *et al.*, 1987). There is, of course, abundant evidence in the literature that leisure experiences induce positive moods (e.g. Forgas and Moylan, 1987; Hull, 1990; Mannell, 1980). It is, then, logical to conclude that frequent, positive leisure experiences contribute to physical health, especially the immune system. As discussed, effects of leisure on psychological or mental health have, of course, been well documented.

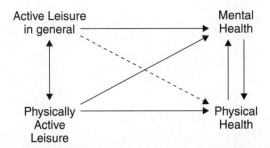

Figure 9.1 Empirically documented relationships among leisure and health variables

STRESS AND LEISURE

Stress is one of the main culprits of physical and mental illness in modern society. But not everyone even under prolonged stress becomes ill: some people are able to cope better than others because of their resistance resources. There are potentially numerous resources that can be employed to buffer the deleterious effects of stress. Wheeler and Frank (1988) identified twenty-two such possible buffers and found four of them to be 'true' buffers between stress and well-being: a sense of competence, nature and extent of exercise, sense of purpose and leisure activity. When considering that a sense of competence is one of the main intrinsic rewards people seek from leisure activities and that exercise is a form of leisure, it is clear from this study that leisure is indeed a central factor in the alleviation of the effects of stress. Thus it is not surprising to find studies in the literature showing that people report fewer physical and psychological illness symptoms when engaging in stress-reducing outdoor-active sports (e.g. Caltabiano, 1995).

Figure 9.2 illustrates the buffering hypothesis of leisure (Iso-Ahola, 1994). Accordingly, active leisure lifestyle protects against physical and mental illness when stress increases, whereas passive leisure lifestyle fails to do so with increasing stress. Leisure can be used on both a short-term and long-term basis in coping with stress. The former refers to emotion-focused and the latter to problem-focused coping (Folkman and Lazarus, 1980). In general, people use both forms of coping in virtually every type of stressful situation. Passive leisure lifestyle is symptomatic of emotion-focused coping, while active leisure participation is consistent with problem-focused coping. Television watching

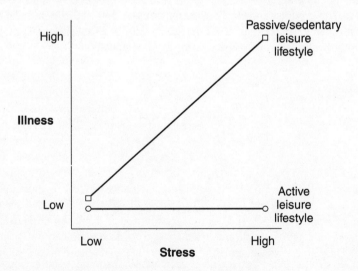

Figure 9.2 The buffering effect of active leisure lifestyle

and drinking are good examples of activities that are used for hiding from problems and stress. At best, these types of leisure activities provide temporary escape and relief from stress and represent negative leisure coping, but they do not promote health in the long run. It is even questionable how successful such behaviours are in the short run because perceived control over emotional reactions is effective in reducing stress (Wallston *et al.*, 1987). Yet, these activities are known to reduce feelings of personal control (Csikszentmihalyi *et al.*, 1977).

Active leisure lifestyle can also be used for regulating emotions and thereby escaping stress and daily problems on a temporary basis. In doing so, however, a person uses leisure in a *health-promoting* manner. But, perhaps a more important stress-buffering function of active leisure lifestyle is the fact that active leisure is based on use of personal physical, mental or social skills and is personally caused. Such leisure builds the self-determination predisposition, which is a major resistance resource for stress (Coleman and Iso-Ahola, 1993). People high in the self-determination predisposition take problems as challenges rather than as threats, feel competent about themselves and feel they are in control of their lives and behaviours. This general approach helps in solving problems and thus in coping with stress.

Two different lines of research are consistent with this reasoning. First, Kobasa and her associates' studies (1979, 1982, 1985) suggest that a 'hardy' personality buffers stress by helping people transform events into less stressful forms. Because of their general orientation towards challenge, control and commitment, 'hardy' persons are able to appraise stress and strain as manageable. Second, Dienstbier's (1989) work suggests that certain physically challenging activities (e.g. exercise and rock climbing) build 'toughness' that is relevant to either physical or mental challenge-threat situations. Supposedly, this toughening correlates with challenge and positive emotions and provides energy needed to cope with stressful situations. So, an active leisure lifestyle buffers stress because it enables people to feel self-determined and reinforces or builds the predisposition towards self-determination. A considerable amount of empirical research supports this theorizing (e.g. Coleman, 1993, 1996; Reich and Zautra, 1981).

Another dimension of active leisure lifestyle that buffers stress is social support (Coleman and Iso-Ahola, 1993). A huge volume of research in general social psychology has confirmed the idea that various forms of social support buffer the adverse effects of stress on health (Cohen and Wills, 1985; Sarason and Sarason, 1985). Also, several recent studies have reported that leisure-related social support moderates the stress–illness relationship (Caltabiano, 1995; Iso-Ahola and Park, 1996; Rook, 1987). One study went further and showed that only discretionary forms of social contact (i.e. leisure-related social contacts) buffered stress; obligatory contacts at work and school failed to do so (Bolger and Eckenrode, 1991). This should not be surprising, however, as social leisure plays a central role in motivation for leisure (Iso-Ahola, 1989). Leisure provides an unmatched opportunity for the regulation and achievement of an optimum level of daily social interaction. It is used for development and maintenance of companionships and friendships. Chalip *et al.* (1993) found that social contacts and networks built through leisure and sports participation were critical for immigrants' efforts to assimilate into their new culture and community. Leisure friends also serve as major resources for perceived social support to which people can resort at times of emergency and crisis. For most people it is easier to rely on leisure friends' support than that of workmates because leisure friends have been chosen and workmates more or less forced upon them. So, leisure-related social support buffers stress either through social interaction in leisure activities or through social support provided by leisure friends.

CONCLUDING REMARKS

It is clear from the above review of the literature that the effect of leisure on health is mainly a psychological problem. Obviously, leisure cannot protect or enhance health if people think leisure is not important or that they have very little of it. This 'discovery' problem of leisure, however, cannot be solved by increasing leisure time alone. If it were a time problem, there would not be a leisure problem today. People have plenty of free time; in fact, the amount of free time has steadily increased since 1965, by nearly five hours a week (Spayd, 1995). A part of the problem is people's tendency to overestimate the amount of time worked. Spayd reported that people who actually worked 55 hours a week estimated they spent 80 hours on the job. Overestimation of working hours means underestimation of leisure time. As the social environment emphasizes the puritan work ethic, it is socially desirable to engage in such an overestimation and underestimation of work and leisure hours, respectively. Thus, people begin to believe that they do not have much leisure time or enough time to do anything. The resultant sedentary lifestyle, in turn, reinforces their belief, as Bem's (1967) self-perception theory would predict, that because I am sedentary in my leisure, I must not have much free time. It is as Lord Chesterfield, the British author, observed: 'The less one has to do, the less time one finds to do it in'.

So, the problem of leisure is twofold. On the one hand, many people fail to discover leisure in the first place and therefore are unable to use it for their health. On the other hand, many of those who have realized the potential of leisure fail to use it for health-promoting behaviours. 'Cheap thrills' occupy most of their free time. Such use of free time serves the escape or distraction function, but this diversion value of leisure, from the health promotion standpoint, is temporary at best. While emotion-focused coping is important because of temporary regulation of emotions, it is shortlived and better serviced through participation in the activities that promote perceived control. Cheap thrills and passive forms of leisure, however, tend to undermine perceived control. Thus the distraction hypothesis to explain the effects of leisure on health does not seem to be particularly viable.

What psychological mechanisms, then, explain the health-promoting effects of leisure? All the evidence points to the idea that the use of personal skills and competencies in challenging situations, when done on the self-determined basis, is psychologically most beneficial. When people participate in self-chosen leisure activities that challenge them physically and mentally, a sense of self-determination is experienced and developed; that is, they feel competent about themselves in general and about their skills in particular. They feel they are in control of their behaviours and lives, their actions emanating from themselves. This sense of self-determination is invariably accompanied by positive affect and mood states. The sense of personal competence and control is further enhanced by social reinforcement and support often associated with leisure participation. When people learn that leisure environments support self-determination more than other environments do, then health benefits can be expected. As Deci and Ryan concluded (1987, p. 1030), 'It is only when people learn to experience their environment as supporting self-determination, only when they become more autonomous, that there will be long-term positive benefits on their health'.

REFERENCES

Argyle, M. (1987) *The Psychology of Happiness*, London: Methuen.

Argyle, M. (1992) *The Social Psychology of Everyday Life*, London: Routledge.

Bem, D.J. (1967) 'Self-perception: an alternative interpretation of cognitive dissonance phenomena', *Psychological Review* 74, 183–200.

Blair, S. (1993) 'Physical activity, physical fitness, and health', *Research Quarterly for Exercise and Sport* 64, 365–76.

Blair, S., Kohl, H., Barlow, C., Paffenbarger, R., Gibbons, L. and Macera, C. (1995) 'Changes in physical fitness and all-cause mortality', *Journal of American Medical Association* 273, 1093–8.

Bolger, N. and Eckenrode, J. (1991) 'Social relationships, personality, and anxiety during a major stressful event', *Journal of Personality and Social Psychology* 61, 440–9.

Byrne, A. and Byrne, D. (1993) 'The effect of exercise on depression, anxiety and other mood states: a review', *Journal of Psychomatic Research* 37, 565–74.

Caldwell, L., Smith, E. and Weissinger, E. (1992) 'The relationship of leisure activities and perceived health of college students', *Society and Leisure* 15, 545–56.

Caltabiano, M. (1995) 'Main and stress-moderating health benefits of leisure', *Society and Leisure* 18, 33–52.

Chalip, L., Thomas, D. and Voyle, J. (1992) 'Sport, recreation and well-being', in D. Thomas and A. Veno (eds), *Psychology and Social Change*, Palmerston North, New Zealand: Dunmore Press, 132–56.

Clarke, S. and Haworth, J. (1994) '"Flow" experience in the daily lives of sixth form college students', *British Journal of Psychology* 85, 511–23.

Cohen, S. and Wills, T., (1985) 'Stress, support, and the buffering hypothesis', *Psychological Bulletin* 98, 310–57.

Coleman, D. (1993) 'Leisure based social support, leisure dispositions and health', *Journal of Leisure Research* 25, 350–61.

Coleman, D. (1996) 'Potential of intrinsic leisure motivation to moderate the impact of stress on health', *Journal of Leisure Research*, unpublished manuscript.

Coleman, D. and Iso-Ahola, S. (1993) 'Leisure and health: the role of social support and self-determination', *Journal of Leisure Research* 25, 111–28.

Crandall, R. (1979) 'Social interaction, affect and leisure', *Journal of Leisure Research* 11, 165–81.

Csikszentmihalyi, M. (1982) 'Towards a psychology of optimal experience', *Review of Personality and Social Psychology* 3, 13–36.

Csikszentmihalyi, M. (1990) *Flow*, New York: Harper & Row.

Csikszentmihalyi, M. and Graef, R. (1979, December) 'Feeling free', *Psychology Today* 13, 84–90, 98–9.

Csikszentmihalyi, M., Larson, R. and Prescott, S. (1977) 'The ecology of adolescent activity and experiences', *Journal of Youth and Adolescence* 6, 281–94.

Deci, E. and Ryan, R. (1987) 'The support of autonomy and the control of behavior', *Journal of Personality and Social Psychology* 53, 1024–37.

Diamond, M. (1984, November) 'A love affair with the brain', *Psychology Today*, 62–73.

Dienstbier, R. (1989) 'Arousal and physiological toughness: implications for mental and physical health', *Psychological Review* 96, 84–100.

Dupuis, S. and Smale, B. (1995) 'An examination of the relationship between psychological well-being and depression and leisure activity participation among older adults', *Society and Leisure* 18, 67–92.

Emery, E. and Blumenthal, J. (1991) 'Effect of physical exercise on psychological and cognitive functioning of older adults', *Annals of Behavioral Medicine* 13, 99–107.

Folkman, S. and Lazarus, R. (1980) 'An analysis of coping in a middle-aged community sample', *Journal of Health and Social Behavior* 21, 219–39.

Forgas, J. and Moylan, S. (1987) 'After the movies: transient mood and social judgments', *Personality and Social Psychology Bulletin* 13, 467–77.

Graef, R., Csikszentmihalyi, M. and Gianinno, S. (1983) 'Measuring intrinsic motivation in everyday life', *Leisure Studies* 2, 155–68.

Haworth, J. (1993) 'Skill–challenge relationships and psychological well-being in everyday life', *Society and Leisure* 16, 115–28.

Haworth, J. (1995) 'Leisure and categorial models of mental health', *Society and Leisure* 18, 53–66.

Haworth, J. and Evans, S. (1995) 'Challenge, skill and positive subjective states in the daily life of a sample of YTS students', *Journal of Occupational and Organisational Psychology* 68, 109–21.

Hayes, D. and Ross, C. (1986) 'Body and mind: the effect of exercise, overweight, and physical health on psychological well-being', *Journal of Health and Social Behaviour* 27, 387–400.

Holmes, D. (1993) 'Aerobic fitness and the response to psychological stress', in P. Seraganian (ed.), *Exercise Psychology*, New York: John Wiley, 39–63.

Hull, R. (1990) 'Mood as a product of leisure: causes and consequences', *Journal of Leisure Research* 22, 99–111.

Hunnicut, B. (1988) *Work Without End: Abandoning of Shorter Hours for the Right to Work*, Philadelphia, PA: Temple University Press.

Iso-Ahola, S. (1979) 'Some social psychological determinants of perceptions of leisure: preliminary evidence', *Leisure Sciences* 2, 305–14.

Iso-Ahola, S. (1980) *The Social Psychology of Leisure and Recreation*, Dubuque, IA: W.C. Brown.

Iso-Ahola, S. (1989) 'Motivation for leisure', in E. Jackson and T. Burton (eds), *Understanding Leisure and Recreation: Mapping the Past, Charting the Future*, State College, PA: Venture, 245–79.

Iso-Ahola, S. (1994) Leisure lifestyle and health', in D. Compton and S. Iso-Ahola (eds), *Leisure and Mental Health*, Park City, UT: Family Development Resources, Inc., 42–60.

Iso-Ahola, S. and Mannell, R. (1985) 'Social and psychological constraints on leisure', in M.G. Wade (ed.), *Constraints on Leisure*, Springfield, IL: Charles C. Thomas, 111–51.

Iso-Ahola, S. and Park, C. (1996) 'Leisure-related social support and self-determination as buffers of stress–illness relationship', *Journal of Leisure Research*, 28, 38–56.

Iso-Ahola, S. and Weissinger, E. (1984, June) 'Leisure and well-being: is there a connection?', *Parks and Recreation* 19, 40–4.

Iso-Ahola, S. and Weissinger, E. (1987) 'Leisure and boredom', *Journal of Social and Clinical Psychology* 5, 356–64.

Iso-Ahola, S., Laverde, D. and Graefe, A. (1989) 'Perceived competence as a mediator of the relationship between high risk sports participation and self-esteem', *Journal of Leisure Research* 21, 32–9.

Killinger, B. (1991) *Workaholics*, New York: Simon & Schuster.

Kobasa, S. (1979) 'Stressful life events, personality, and health: an inquiry into hardiness', *Journal of Personality and Social Psychology* 37, 1–11.

Kobasa, S., Maddi, S. and Kahn, S. (1982) 'Hardiness and health: a prospective study', *Journal of Personality and Social Psychology* 42, 168–77.

Kobasa, S., Maddi, S., Puccetti, M. and Zola, M. (1985) 'Effectiveness of hardiness, exercise and social support as resources against illness', *Journal of Psychosomatic Research* 29, 525–33.

Lamb, K., Dench, S., Brodie, D. and Roberts, K. (1988) 'Sports participation and health status: a preliminary evidence', *Social Science and Medicine* 27, 1309–16.

Larson, R., Mannell, R. and Zuzanek, J. (1986) 'Daily well-being of older adults with friends and family', *Journal of Psychology and Aging* 1, 117–26.

Machlowitz, M. (1980) *Workaholics: Living with Them, Working with Them*, New York: New American Library.

Mannell, R. (1980) 'Social psychological techniques and strategies for studying leisure experiences', in S. Iso-Ahola (ed.), *Social Psychological Perspectives on Leisure and Recreation*, Springfield, IL: Charles C. Thomas, 62–88.

Mannell, R. and Bradley, W. (1986) 'Does greater freedom always lead to greater leisure? Testing a person x environment model of freedom and leisure', *Journal of Leisure Research* 18, 215–30.

Marsh, H., Richards, G. and Barnes, J. (1986) 'Multidimensional self-concepts: the effect of participation in an Outward Bound Program', *Journal of Personality and Social Psychology* 50, 195–204.

McGinnis, J. (1991) 'Health objectives for the nation', *American Psychologist* 46, 520–4.

Pierce, T., Madden, D., Siegel, W. and Blumenthal, J. (1993) 'Effects of aerobic exercise on cognitive and psychosocial functioning in patients with mild hypertension', *Health Psychology* 12, 286–91.

Plante, T. (1993) 'Aerobic exercise in prevention and treatment of psychopathology', in P. Seraganian (ed.), *Exercise Psychology*, New York: John Wiley, 358–79.

Plante, T. and Rodin, J. (1990) 'Physical fitness and enhanced psychological health', *Current Psychology: Research and Reviews* 9, 1–22.

Reich, J. and Zautra, A. (1981) 'Life events and personal causation: some relationships with satisfaction and distress', *Journal of Personality and Social Psychology* 41, 1002–12.

Roberts, K., Lamb, K., Dench, S. and Brodie, D. (1989) 'Leisure patterns, health status and employment status', *Leisure Studies* 8, 229–35.

Rodin, J. (1986) 'Aging and health: effects of the sense of control', *Science* 233, 1271–6.

Rodin, J., Timko, C. and Harris, S. (1985) 'The construct of control: biological and psychological correlates', *Annual Review of Gerontology and Geriatrics* 5, 3–55, New York: Springer.

Rook, S. (1987) 'Social support versus companionship: effects on life stress, loneliness, and evaluations by others', *Journal of Personality and Social Psychology* 52, 1132–47.

Ross, C. and Hayes, D. (1988) 'Exercise and psychologic well-being in the community', *American Journal of Epidemiology* 127, 762–71.

Sarason, I. and Sarason, B. (eds) (1985) *Social Support: Theory, Research and Applications*, The Hague: Kluwer.

Schor, J. (1991) *The Overworked American: The Unexpected Decline of Leisure*, New York: Basic Books.

Shaw, S. (1985) 'Gender and leisure: inequality in the distribution of leisure time', *Journal of Leisure Research* 17, 266–82.

Shank, J. (1986) 'An exploration of leisure in the lives of dual career women', *Journal of Leisure Research* 18, 300–19.

Spayd, L. (1995) 'How time lies', *Washington Post*, 26 November, C1–C4.

Starrels, M. (1994) 'Husbands' involvement in female gender-typed household chores', *Sex Roles* 31, 473–90.

Stephens, T. (1988) 'Physical activity and mental health in the United States and Canada: evidence from four population surveys', *Preventive Medicine* 17, 35–47.

Stone, A., Cox, D., Valdimarsdottir, H., Jandorf, L. and Neal, J. (1987) 'Evidence that secretory IgA antibody is associated with daily mood', *Journal of Personality and Social Psychology* 52, 988–93.

Tangney, J. and Feshbach, S. (1988) 'Children's television viewing frequency: individual and demographic correlates', *Personality and Social Psychology Bulletin* 14, 145–58.

Thorlindsson, T., Vilhjalmsson, R. and Valgeirsson, G. (1990) 'Sport participation and perceived health status: a study of adolescents', *Social Science and Medicine* 31, 551–6.

Tomporowski, P. and Ellis, N. (1986) 'Effects of exercise on cognitive processes: a review', *Psychological Bulletin* 99, 338–46.

Tuson, K. and Sinyor, D. (1993) 'On the affective benefits of acute aerobic exercise: taking stock after twenty years of research', in P. Seraganian (ed.), *Exercise Psychology*, New York: John Wiley, 80–121.

Ulrich, R., Dimberg, V. and Driver, B. (1990) 'Psychophysiological indicators of leisure consequences', *Journal of Leisure Research* 22, 154–66.

Unger, J. and Johnson, C. (1995) 'Social relationships and physical activity in health club members', *American Journal of Health Promotion* 9, 340–3.

US Department of Health and Human Services, Public Health Service (1991) *Healthy People 2000: National Health Promotion and Disease Prevention Objectives*, DHHS Publication No. 91–50212: Washington, DC.

Wankel, L. and Berger, B. (1990) 'The psychological and social benefits of sport and physical activity', *Journal of Leisure Research* 22, 167–82.

Wallston, K., Wallston, B., Smith, S. and Dobbins, C. (1987) 'Perceived control and health', *Current Psychological Research and Reviews* 6, 5–25.

Weissinger, E. (1995) 'Effects of boredom on self-reported health', *Society and Leisure* 18, 21–32.

Wheeler, R. and Frank, M. (1988) 'Identification of stress buffers', *Behavioral Medicine* 14, 78–89.

Wiedenfeld, S., O'Leary, A., Bandura, A., Brown, S., Levine, S. and Raska, K. (1990) 'Impact of perceived self-efficacy in coping with stressors on components of the immune system', *Journal of Personality and Social Psychology* 59, 1082–94.

Chapter 10

Work and leisure in young people's lives

Ken Roberts

INTRODUCTION

This chapter examines young people's changing experiences of work and leisure and identifies typical problems that are likely to ensue. The focus is on how broad, but fairly short-term trends are changing young people's situations and experiences.

Recent trends alert us to the hazards of trying to gaze even into the medium-term future. In the 1970s there were few pundits in Britain who predicted that the final two decades of the century would prove worse than the inter-war years in terms of the level of unemployment. Even in the mid-1980s few experts on the communist world predicted the early disappearance of their subject. It seems safe to predict that the twenty-first century will contain similar surprises. Yet, despite the real senses in which we live in rapidly changing times, some features of modernity have retained their pivotal positions for the last hundred years: the role of science and technology in economic change; paid occupations in governing individuals' social levels; and educational qualifications in distributing labour-market chances, for example. This chapter is not written in the conviction that we are currently in transit to a postmodern era, experiencing a historical break as momentous as the earlier passage from traditional to modern society. It is likely, though not absolutely certain, that many landmarks of modernity will survive well into and possibly beond the next century. Social forms and processes that have survived the last hundred years will probably display greater future staying power than the recent, relatively short-term trends on which this chapter concentrates. The justification for this concentration is that the recent changes are important for young people and their families, even if their historical impact is unlikely to be as persistent as the Industrial Revolution.

A final scene-setting point is that this chapter is about young people in Europe. The chapter is not a report from any specific piece of research but its arguments have been developed during a series of my enquiries since the mid-1980s. First, there was the Economic and Social Research Council's 16–19 Initiative, a set of longitudinal enquiries among representative samples of young people in four parts of Britain – Kirkcaldy, Liverpool, Sheffield and Swindon (see Banks *et al.*, 1992; Bates and Riseborough, 1993). Second, there were the Anglo-German comparative projects which were linked to the 16–19 Initiative (see Bynner and Roberts, 1991; Evans and Heinz, 1994; Roberts *et al.*, 1994). Third, there is a series of enquiries that began in 1992 about the impact of 'the reforms' among young people in former communist countries – Poland, Ukraine, Georgia and Armenia (see Roberts and Jung, 1995). The UK is possibly the most insular country in Europe, which makes it particularly important to stress that some of the main recent changes affecting its young people have not been due to the economic condition of Britain alone or its government's policies but have been affecting young people throughout Western Europe since the 1970s, while the situations of young people in the European parts of the former Soviet 'empire' have changed rapidly to resemble those of their Western counterparts since the reforms were set in motion. So, although this chapter's material is mainly from Britain, the arguments are meant to apply across Europe and in some other parts of the world such as Australasia, which, up to now, have been European in economic, social and cultural senses though not geographically. However, a North American sociologist would have been unlikely to write a similar chapter. The analysis is meant to apply across Europe but not throughout the entire Western world. North America is different because the vast majority of its young people have been receiving full secondary education, and mass higher education has existed, for over a generation. Another way in which North America is different is that the European practice of providing young school leavers with systematic work-based training leading to skilled status has never become embedded to the same extent across the Atlantic. A consequence is that some recent trends in young people's situations in Europe have been considered normal in North America for over a generation and are therefore provoking less concern among young people themselves, and the scholars who research and write about them. Some of the arguments in this chapter will no doubt apply to some young people in the new industrial and less developed countries but the extent to which the analysis holds in these parts of the world must be left for others to judge.

TRENDS IN WORK, EDUCATION AND LEISURE

The decline of youth employment

Young people today (meaning for these purposes 15- to 25-year-olds) are doing less paid work than their counterparts in the 1950s and 1960s. At that time the majority of Britain's young people completed their full-time education at the earliest opportunity, at age 15 up to 1972, and most obtained full-time jobs immediately. Levels of youth employment have subsequently declined steeply and this trend is continuing. Economic restructuring has eliminated many 'entry jobs' into which school-leavers used to be recruited. Employment in manufacturing industries has declined, and there has been a particularly steep decline in manual jobs in manufacturing. Hence the disappearance of most of the apprentice training that some young people, mostly males, used to receive, and the non-skilled jobs that were entered by others. Economic restructuring has affected the entire working population, not just young people. Its consequences have included higher levels of unemployment than were experienced during the so-called 'thirty glorious years' that followed 1945. However, young people have proved particularly vulnerable. In virtually all European countries, whatever the general level of unemployment, the rates have been higher among young people. School-leavers have been vulnerable when firms have downsized through 'natural wastage' which usually means a block on recruitment. Young people have also suffered from competition from older displaced, experienced workers. Female school-leavers have been exposed to labour-market competition from the married women who have been seeking work in growing numbers. Youth employment declined throughout Western Europe in the 1970s and 1980s. In most former communist countries the implementation of market reforms immediately transformed endemic labour shortages into surpluses. The future working lives that would have awaited school-leavers often vanished abruptly. The vanishing youth labour market has not been a peculiarly British phenomenon, but the trend has been especially dramatic in those European countries, which include Britain, where levels of youth employment were relatively high in the recent past. Until lately Britain retained a relatively low proportion of 16- to 20-year-olds in formal education and training.

The decline of youth employment has left persistent youth unemployment across Europe. As already explained, official figures in virtually all countries record higher levels of unemployment among young people than throughout the workforces in general. However, the official figures invariably underestimate the real scale of youth unemployment. Much of this age group's unemployment is concealed because those affected continue in education or enter training schemes. Moreover, since young people's welfare entitlements, if any, are invariably inferior to those of adults, this reduces their incentive to register as unemployed. In Britain it has been estimated that, at any point, approximately one in seven 16- and 17-year-olds are 'status zero', meaning that they are not in education, training or employment (Istance et al., 1994), and since 1988 most 'status zero' young people aged under 18 have not been eligible for social security payments. For the majority, 'status zero' is a temporary situation but a 'hardcore' appears to be 'out of the system' on a long-term basis. Actually, the individuals concerned are often in contact with other parts of 'the system'; many are well known to the police, courts, probation and Social Services departments.

The vanishing youth labour market has not left young people with oceans of leisure time. As we will see, the majority have found other forms of work to occupy themselves. Equally noteworthy, there has been no sea change in young people's values away from the work ethic and towards a post-materialist leisure ethic. Getting employment, and preparing themselves for employment, remain extremely important priorities for most young people. Nowadays, this applies equally to males and females. Their difficulties in obtaining paid work have not led young people to question the desirability of employment. Work values are actually strongest among the groups most at risk of unemployment, the least qualified (Banks *et al.*, 1992). The experience of unemployment does not erode young people's desire to work, only their confidence when job searching (Furlong, 1992). The decline of youth employment has not stoked a demand for education either as or for leisure. Young people seem to regard educational qualifications, the type that unlock job opportunities, as more important than ever before. A common view is that, in tight labour-markets, one needs to become as well qualified as possible in order to stand any realistic chance of obtaining a decent job. Courses and qualifications that promise to strengthen young people's labour market chances are invariably popular (Brown, 1987). It is young people and their parents as well as government policies that have pressured schools to pay greater attention to preparing school-leavers for the labour market. Hence the paradox: the more distant full-time employment has become, the greater the schools' efforts to prepare young people for it. There has been increasing emphasis on work experience, vocational skills and competencies.

The expansion of education and training

Young people's time that has become surplus to productive requirements has mostly been absorbed by other forms of work, in education and training, and rather more of the former than the latter. This work is typically unpaid, but it is still work. When remunerated the rewards are grants or allowances that fall well short of normal wage levels.

Some young people who enrol in post-compulsory education and training are discouraged workers who would be in employment if jobs were available. However, the vanishing youth labour market is not the sole reason for the upward extension of education. This trend has been in process throughout the twentieth century. There has been a generation rachet effect: every generation of parents wants its children at least to equal and preferably exceed its own educational attainments. Hence the progressively rising levels of educational aspiration and expectation which, in recent years, have interacted with the decline in job opportunities.

It is often said that present-day high-tech economies need more skilled and less unskilled labour than before, and that Britain's and Europe's competitiveness depend on educating and training their young people to rising world standards. This pull from the economy has certainly been one of the forces behind the expansion of education, but it has been exceeded by the push from beneath. The pace at which more young people have been gaining qualifications at all levels, from GCSEs to degrees, has outpaced the growth in the number of jobs for which these qualifications were formerly required. Hence the devaluation of qualifications in terms of their labour-market returns. This has affected young people at all levels in the qualification hierarchy, from 16-year-old job seekers to university graduates. A-levels can now be demanded for jobs to which young people with O-levels and CSEs were once recruited, and the majority of recent university graduates have been unable to enter the levels of employment hitherto considered suitable for the highly educated. Governments and business leaders continue to proclaim the need for more highly educated, qualified and skilled young people. For most young people, however, the main labour market problem has been the shortage of jobs in which they can use their certified abilities. So many young people have acted on the message that better qualifications lead to better jobs that many have found their ambitions frustrated. Up to now, rather than leading to disillusion with education, a more widespread consequence of the devaluation of credentials has been to fuel parents' and young people's appetites for qualifications to still higher levels (Dore, 1976).

The recent growth in post-16 education and training has been remarkable. In the early 1970s two-thirds of Britain's young people quit full-time education at age 16, whereas by the early 1990s, 70 per cent were staying on and it was only by age 19 to 20 that the majority of a cohort were in full-time employment (Banks *et al.*, 1992). When the Robbins Committee (which was appointed by the government to consider the future of higher education, and reported in 1963) recommended an expansion of higher education in 1963 only one young person in twenty was entering Britain's universities. By the mid-1990s higher education had expanded to be able to accommodate one-third of the age group. The numbers of young people gaining academic qualifications at all levels have risen steeply. Grades A to C in the 16-plus examinations used to be considered a sign of exceptional academic ability but nowadays nearly a half of young people reach this level in at least five subjects. The numbers of young people on long-established academic routes have expanded, and there has been a parallel growth in the numbers on courses leading to vocational qualifications, usually NVQs and GNVQs. Somewhat smaller numbers of 16- and 17-year-olds pursue skills and qualifications within government programmes such as Youth Training and Youth Credits.

Educational participation in the 16-plus age group has risen in all European nations but the rise has been especially pronounced in Britain where, up to the 1980s, participation rates lagged well behind those of most economically advanced countries. This expansion has brought some particular difficulties in Britain. Some of these stem from a culturally ingrained assumption that high levels of academic attainment are possible only for an intellectual elite. So when more young people gain a given level of qualification there are suspicions that standards must have been relaxed. It is different in Scandinavia and North America where the assumption has been that, with appropriate teaching, virtually all young people should be able to meet the prescribed standards in secondary, and even higher, education. The more exclusive view of academic attainment has been less of an obstacle in the European countries that have developed well-regarded technical and vocational routes through their secondary, further and higher education systems. In Germany, for example, technical and vocational education are seen as developing different kinds, not simply inferior levels of talent to those that flourish on academic courses. Britain has never developed a similar regard for vocational qualifications which have therefore suffered a persistent low status problem. Up to now, Britain's alternative routes have never taken firm root – hence the successive versions of Youth Training and the constant revisions of vocational qualifications as existing schemes and courses lose credibility.

Many young people are distinctly unenthusiastic about their new enlarged opportunities in post-compulsory education and training. Some fear, with justification, that their qualifications will prove worthless, 'not worth the paper', when taken into the labour market. Others fear, again with justification, that their qualifications will not lead to the deferred gratifications that they were hoping for (less is heard about deferred gratifications these days than in the 1960s). Youth researchers, and young people themselves, realize that returns on post-compulsory education may fail to materialise even in the long term. There is the related phenomenon of young people remaining in education simply because they feel that they have no alternative. They are motivated less by the intrinsic interest or the prospect of long-term rewards than the fear of dropping out. This situation is familiar in North America where successive generations of high school students have known that financial independence is many years away and often view their years in upper high school and college as 'serving time' (Larkin, 1979).

It is necessary to draw attention to the fact that some young people have not been part of the trend towards a better qualified population. Approximately one in ten young people in Britain leaves school with no qualifications whatsoever, and this figure has not declined since the early 1980s. The crucial change has been that until the 1960s the young people who became well qualified were the minority. When the grandparents of today's pupils were in education the vast majority left with no qualifications at all. The expansion of education has blurred the division between high achievers and the rest and created a more visible gulf between the majority and a tail-end of unqualified school-leavers from whom the 'status zero' hardcore tends to be recruited.

Part-time and other precarious jobs

The trends described above have not denied teenagers all experience of paid work. The full-time jobs sought by school-leavers have become scarcer, but there has been sustained growth of part-time and other forms of precarious employment. Married women and students have been among the groups that have filled these positions. Britain's new part-time jobs have been mostly in retailing and other consumer sectors where the services have to be produced and delivered at the time of demand. Unlike manufacturing, businesses such as shops, restaurants and banks cannot build up stock for periods of peak demand. They need additional labour during evenings, weekends and holidays, and students are among the groups who have responded. The part-time employment of secondary school pupils and students in higher education is more prevalent in Britain than in most other European countries largely because employment in Britain is less regulated by the state, and students (and married women) can be hired often without any restrictions as regards rates of pay and, in some cases, their hours of employment.

The number of students holding part-time jobs varies from place to place depending mainly on the availability of this type of work. Typically, however, around one-half of pupils in their final year of compulsory education have Saturday jobs or other part-time occupations (see Roberts, 1995a). The percentage working part time is somewhat higher among students in sixth forms and further education but, up to now, it has been lower, though rising rapidly, among nominally full-time higher education students. Part-time employment used to be considered undesirable by teachers and parents who were keen for their children to gain the best possible results in education. Up to the 1970s the secondary school pupils with part-time jobs, typically delivering newspapers and milk, tended to be in the non-examination streams. This is no longer the case. Britain's middle classes have changed their attitudes in the direction long customary in North America. Nowadays, parents in all social strata, and many teachers, regard part-time employment as a sensible way of enabling students to gain some financial independence, perhaps contribute to their upkeep and to obtain experience of 'real work'. Universities that retain regulations that officially require full-time students to be *de facto* full time are now turning a blind eye to breaches.

In most cases the part-time and temporary jobs that students take are unrelated to their long-term career intentions, but the experience is still likely to be a significant form of occupational socialisation. Part-time and temporary employees learn to respond to business authority and incentives, and to work hard and reliably without identifying closely with their occupations. This is the way in which some eventually adjust during their adult working lives. They combine strong work values with low levels of psychological commitment to their own jobs.

One consequence of the prevalence of part-time employment is that many students' lives are time pressured rather than leisurely. Their progress towards the full-time labour market may be slower than in the past but their pace of life from day-to-day and week-to-week can be hectic. Teachers have become accustomed to students missing classes, appearing tired and inattentive and failing to complete homework as a result of the competing demands on their time (see Bates and Riseborough, 1993). The decline of youth employment has not left most young people with time on their hands. The opposite problem has become more common; coping with studies, paid employment, maintaining leisure interests and social relationships, and still finding some time to be with families and simply relax.

Dependence on families

Despite their own incomes from part-time jobs, it is mainly young people's families that have taken the financial strain as full-time youth employment has declined. The overall costs of child-rearing have risen. Until the 1970s it was normal in working-class households for young people to be earning from age 16. Their contributions to household expenses were often nominal. Many parents did, and continue to, 'spoil' their teenage children and ensure that they have enough spending money to enjoy a 'brief flowering period' (Leonard, 1980), but up to the 1970s, after age 16, the majority of parents ceased to be responsible for buying all their children's clothes, paying for their holidays, and providing weekly spending money. This no longer applies and, to aggravate parents' problems, as young people have become less able to earn their own livelihoods the state has become less generous in its support (see Coles, 1995; Jones and Wallace, 1992). Since 1988 most unemployed 16- and 17-year-olds have been unable to claim either Unemployment Benefit (which was replaced in 1996 by the Job Seekers' Allowance) or Income Support. Discretionary educational awards have become harder to obtain. Maintenance grants for higher education students have been reduced in value and supplemented by loans which, even in combination, do not cover students' full living costs. The head of an Oxford college attracted national publicity in 1995 when she warned intending students' families to be prepared to meet some of their children's expenses. It is not that Oxford and Cambridge are particularly expensive for students; residential costs are often higher at less generously endowed new universities. Needless to say, families differ in their ability to take the financial strain, but the evidence shows that even non-affluent households will go to enormous lengths to try to do so (Hutson and Jenkins, 1989). Parents will increase their mortgages, sacrifice holidays and take additional jobs rather than deny their children the chance to become as well educated as possible.

Many families in Britain have felt that the financial burden that they are now expected to bear is morally wrong (Allatt and Yeandle, 1991). There is a prevalent feeling that, in failing to maintain young people's right to work, then refusing to support them when unemployed and failing to maintain 'free' education for all who are qualified and wish to continue, governments have broken their side of a long-running understanding with their citizens. The cost of supporting children beyond age 16 has been a culture shock in many British families. Most European and North American families shoulder these responsibilities without the same sense of outrage. Outside Britain it has been normal for over a generation for parents in all social strata to support their children financially while they continue in education or training until age 20 or beyond. Also, other Western countries have never introduced the mandatory, albeit means-tested, maintenance grants which until recently in Britain were supposed to cover higher education students' costs. The customary responsibilities of parents in most countries include supporting their children until they later achieve independence, no matter at what age this might be. Maybe it will take a generation, until the young people in Britain who have completed their education since the 1970s become the parents of teenagers, before popular attitudes in Britain reflect the new reality.

Leisure preserved

The decline of youth employment has not been accompanied by the disappearance of youth cultures. Young people's leisure has been maintained through their own earnings, their parents' generosity, the incomes some receive from Social Security and educational grants and, perhaps most significant of all, the ability of the non-employed to do virtually as much while spending far less than contemporaries with jobs and wages. Since the affluent young worker became a rare species we have become aware of the layers of commercial flab that garnished post-war youth cultures. Today as ever, there are huge income and spending inequalities among young people but these are not faithfully mirrored in their rates of leisure participation. Young wage-earners can often afford to purchase cars, holidays and clothes that are beyond the means of students and the unemployed, but the latter still manage to go out and about, to take holidays away from home, model their looks on the fashions that they fancy and follow trends in popular music. The main differences between the leisure of young wage-earners and the unemployed are that the latter reduce not so much the range as their frequency of participation in activities such as evenings in pubs and clubs and, even more so, the unemployed do these things at lower cost. Young people in the post-communist countries have much lower spending power than their Western counterparts but they wear the same fashions and listen to the same music. It is not immediately self-evident that their leisure is relatively impoverished (Roberts, 1995b).

Full-time students in Britain are not the richest, but they are the most active members of their age group in most leisure activities. This is possible partly on account of the free or subsidised recreational facilities that are available in educational institutions, but mainly through students' capacity to do things cheaply. They not only have the highest levels of interest and rates of participation in politics and high culture which are traditionally associated with Britain's educational and social elites, but manage to equal or exceed contemporaries' levels of interest and activity in sport, playing and listening to popular music and visiting pubs and clubs (Roberts and Parsell, 1994).

There has been no overall decline in young people's levels of leisure activity since the 1970s. The former growth in alcohol consumption has levelled off, but sports participation has risen considerably (Roberts, 1995c). Young people's typically broad leisure interests contribute to their generally busy lives. Compared with all other age groups, young people's leisure is distinguished by the wide range of activities in which they manage to participate. Some display high levels of time-management skills. Yet most young people's lives are still not so congested that they are unable to take up something new without dropping an existing activity. The leisure multiplier continues to operate among young people, as among adults. Those who are active in any one type of out-of-home recreation are the most likely to be active in virtually all others (Department for Education, 1995). People find the time by spending fewer hours doing nothing in particular, at home, with television, CD players or cassettes providing background noise.

There are certain functions that leisure performs for all sections of the population. For example, it performs cathartic functions, giving vent to otherwise suppressed desires and feelings. It also enables individuals to express and sometimes to obtain confirmation of their preferred social identities. Among young people leisure is also important for age-specific reasons. It is normally in leisure that young people first learn to operate independently of adult carers and to treat, and be treated, as equals by other actors without external surveillance. It is also in leisure activities and relationships that young people learn to play sexualized roles, nurture corresponding feelings and acquire the associated identities. It is these functions that make young people's leisure different: adults may participate in much the same activities but these usually have a different significance within youth cultures. This is one reason why youth cultures are unlikely to be obliterated by the spread of consumer cultures throughout all age groups. In any case, age *per se* remains a powerful basis for social discrimination in many settings. These include employment and, perhaps most of all, during leisure. Young people are acutely age sensitive. 'Mature' 18-year-olds avoid scenes that are attended by 15-year-old 'kids'.

The maintenance of their leisure enables young people to grow up and experience adult status despite lacking employment. Unemployment reduces self-esteem in all age groups and, among young people, slows down personal and social development, but the majority of young people who are not in employment are not simply unemployed but occupy other positions; most are trainees or students. It may be the case that lack of employment excludes individuals from many areas of social life, but adulthood is not among them. Upper-class youth have a long record of commanding adult treatment despite their lack of gainful employment. Other young people, whose futures are less dependent on their families, are now following suit.

YOUTH'S NEW CONDITION

A life stage between childhood and adulthood, generally known as youth, is not a recent development. The terminological continuity is not wholly misleading but may conceal how the life stage is not just the same today as in the recent past. The trends described above, in combination, have created a 'new social condition' for young people. Hence the current experiments with terms such as 'post-adolescence' and 'young adulthood', but as yet none has been adopted in popular culture.

Prolonged adolescence

One obvious change is that youth lasts longer than in the recent past. This is indicated by the typical ages when individuals establish themselves in continuous full-time employment. These ages have risen, and likewise the ages at which other thresholds are usually crossed. There has been no upward movement in Britain since 1972 in the age at which young people become legally entitled to terminate their formal education. Nor have the ages at which individuals can legally vote, marry and engage in consensual sex been raised. However, the typical ages when couples do, in fact, marry and become parents have risen. There are fewer teenage brides and grooms, and parents, than in the 1960s. New social practices have developed to fill the life space created by the prolonging of transitions to full adulthood. One of the better known is cohabitation. Up to the 1960s leaving the parental home and getting married occurred simultaneously for most young people, whereas now marrying couples are most likely to be already living at the same address.

Youth's new condition has not been marked by an upward movement in the ages at which teenagers begin to establish independence from their parents, and develop tastes and lives of their own. The age of first full sexual intercourse (typically 16) is probably as good as any single indicator of young people's independence, and this age has not risen. Youth starts sufficiently early, and lasts long enough nowadays to be more prolonged than childhood. Pre-teenagers dress in teenage fashions, acquire their own tastes in popular music and help to decide which performers become stars and whose recordings are hits. The majority begin consuming alcohol regularly long before they are legally able to purchase and consume intoxicants in licensed premises, and their precocity is normally with parental knowledge and acquiescence if not active approval. The strength of the youth market has been consolidated rather than threatened by the demise of the affluent young worker through individuals retaining the lifestyles, tastes and spending patterns until they are well into their twenties. Today many young 'singles scenes' are dominated by the 20-somethings rather than teenagers.

Individualization

This is not a new trend. It began during the breakdown of traditional ways of life and the birth of modern societies. Industrial employment has always been of individuals who have been paid personal wages and salaries. Likewise in modern times the vote has always been in the hands of individual electors. However, in recent years the trend has taken several giant strides. A crude but reasonable way of measuring individualization is through the number of non-kin in people's current social networks who lived as children in the same neighbourhoods and attended the same schools.

There was never a time or place where every single boy in the village went down the pit or every girl into the cotton mill, but there used to be many parts of

Britain where biographies were shared by many members of the communities. Of course, there were always people who broke out, but this notion has become less relevant as the former dominant patterns have disintegrated. This has been due to the contraction of the large firms and industries that once dominated many local labour markets, the weakening of neighbourhood and religious communities, higher rates of geographical mobility, the spread of private transport which has widened personal labour markets and firms' catchment areas, and, especially relevant when discussing young people, the variety of experiences in post-compulsory education and training, part- and full-time jobs and spells of unemployment, through which many move rapidly between age 16 and their early twenties. Whereas earlier cohorts used to travel towards adulthood as if in public transport vehicles, now young people make their journeys as if in private motorcars. Needless to say, the 'cars' have differently powered engines. Some young people have already accumulated what will be decisive advantages.

Individualization does not necessarily diminish the differences associated with social backgrounds, gender or anything else, but means more variety within all social categories. This variety blurs what used to be clearer social divisions. It has become more difficult than in the past to sketch a typical male or female biography. To repeat, this is not to claim that there are no longer any important differences between the sexes. The situation is rather that there is more variety within each. Fewer males than in the past are experiencing sole breadwinner status for a substantial part of their working lives. There are fewer housewives with no paid employment, and more women who pursue uninterrupted full-time labour-market careers. It is no longer possible to identify one life course that is typically feminine or masculine. Young women are taking more varied courses in education, they are more diverse in terms of their levels of educational attainment, they are entering a wider variety of occupations, and the 'greater variety' applies also to their leisure patterns. Smoking, drinking lager regularly, and playing sport do not unite all young women, but it is no longer only the males who drink, smoke, play sport and congregate in same-sex groups in public places.

There has been a similar trend towards greater variety, and more overlapping, between the social classes. Young people who are destined for different kinds of employment are no longer educated in different kinds of secondary schools. Post-compulsory education no longer distinguishes a minority, mostly from privileged backgrounds, and nearly all destined for high occupational levels. The same applies to leisure patterns. There are no longer tastes in dress or music that typify middle-class and working-class youth. Again, this is not to say that class differences have ceased to exist, but the greater variety of experience among those on all social class trajectories, and the degree of overlap that results, have blurred the former boundaries. Middle-class youth have taken to popular music and the related fashions, while working-class youth nowadays play the range of sports that was once regarded as distinctly middle class.

Individualization has reduced the value of traditional youth ethnography. It used to be possible for fieldworkers to make contact with young people in particular districts, on the streets or wherever the subjects congregated, to become participants in the young people's ways of life and, with the knowledge gained, to construct a picture of their typical backgrounds, situations, activities, attitudes and prospects. This kind of research does not yield such a rich pay off anymore. The old neighbourhood communities have disintegrated. Young people who are brought up in particular districts are no longer nearly all educated to exactly the same levels in the same local schools, in the same subjects, and they no longer progress into similar kinds of employment. It is hardly surprising, therefore, that they do not all 'hang about' and spend time in the same places or have the same leisure interests. The sports centres and discos where young people gather tend to draw clients from many residential districts, family and educational backgrounds; many of the individuals attend the places only for weeks or months, then disperse into different futures.

Individualization should be distinguished from egocentric individualism and privatism. The trend has not been towards young people's lives becoming home centred and their social participation declining, and they engage in far more 'good deeds' than acts of delinquency. Most young people lead busy leisure lives and have wide social networks. Very few are isolates. The point is that each individual nowadays tends to have an individualized network and the youth population is linked through interlocking webs rather than clearly divided into groups, all with distinctive subcultures, between which there is little contact.

Young people at leisure constantly form themselves into groups. Indeed, much of their leisure can be construed as a search for community. For today's young people group membership is not simply 'given' but needs to be sought and created, at sports events or raves for example. In these milieux the participants can experience intense feelings of belonging, but only temporarily in most cases. The groups do not arise from, or give rise to, enduring social categories. According to one school of thought, these 'new tribes' (Maffesoli, 1994) or *bunde* (Hetherington, 1994) to which individuals feel strong attachments but often only fleetingly, are a distinctive feature of late modernity.

There are objective and subjective dimensions to individualization. Objective individualization is linked, partly as cause and partly as effect, to individuals feeling that their opportunities, achievements and problems are personal rather than shared by large numbers of peers. Individualization means that young people are likely to regard themselves as responsible for their past biographies and current circumstances, and for constructing their futures. People are less likely to perceive close links between their personal worries and prospects and those of any wider social category. This, of course, has potential political significance. It becomes more difficult for parties to build stable and secure support through identification with the interests of any specific sections of the population. Young political activists today are less likely to be in traditional parties than 'new social movements' which campaign for animal rights or the environment rather than the interests of specific sections of the population. The young people who are politically active, and who eventually become professional politicians, are increasingly just that, practising politics as a profession rather than articulating the concerns of the social constituencies from which they are drawn and in which they retain firm roots.

Uncertainty and risk

Another feature of youth's new condition is that their futures are less predictable than in the past. It is impossible for today's teenagers to know the types of adults that they will become. This is not primarily because adulthood itself has become more fluid, though it is true that the pace of scientific, technological and occupational change means that fewer careers than in the past can be relied on to last until retirement, and that there is less reason than in the past to assume that one's first marriage will be for life. It is sometimes argued that it has become more difficult to know when transitions have ended; that stable employment and marriage are no longer satisfactory benchmarks because many marriages are unstable and some adults may never experience stable employment. However, the most common terminator of marriage is still death despite the rise in rates of divorce and separation, and many adults are still experiencing main lifetime occupations. Young people's prospects have become less certain mainly because the links between their routes onwards from compulsory education, and types of eventual adult employment, have weakened. This is because the increased numbers of young people on traditional routes, in higher education for example, mean that they cannot all expect what would once have been regarded as graduate jobs, and because recently introduced training schemes and educational programmes have no track records. The steps forward that young people take continue to affect their longer term futures, but at the time the effects cannot be known with sufficient certainty to inspire confidence. This is very different from the days when by age 20 the majority of young people knew what their main kinds of adult employment would be, if not the specific occupations, and, in many instances, to whom they would be married for the rest of their lives and where they would live.

Today's young people cannot avoid taking risks. Without higher education professional-level employment may be out of the question but successful completion of university will not guarantee such a career. The entrants have to gamble. The same applies to those who are trained by employers for specific occupations: these young people may be retained by the firms, and the occupations may endure, or the careers may prove extremely short lived. In the 1960s some young people rebelled and dropped out (albeit temporarily in most cases) from the predictable careers for which their society appeared to have them destined. In the 1990s young people's overriding preoccupation has been to 'get in'.

The spread of uncertainty has been most dramatic in the former communist countries. Prior to the reforms their young people were mostly educated and trained for specific types of employment in state enterprises and departments.

Labour shortages were endemic, so employment in which the individuals were expected to remain was virtually guaranteed. As soon as market reforms were implemented all this changed: many state sector careers disappeared; former links between schools and employment were shattered. Young people were released from, but also lost the security of the old systems. Their new condition has become a base for boundless optimism or chronic worry depending largely upon individuals' confidence in themselves (see Roberts and Jung, 1995). In individualized societies it is individuals who have to take the decisive steps, and the risks, and the stakes are their own future lives.

THREATS TO WELL-BEING

The new balances between study, training, paid work and leisure in young people's lives, and their more prolonged, individualized and uncertain states, do not in themselves pose fundamental threats to the age group's well-being. The recent moral outrage in Britain at teenagers' inability to obtain 'proper jobs' and parents' shock at the costs of their children 'winning' places in higher education, are likely to prove an extreme but temporary case of culture shock. After all, 26 is no less natural an age than 16 for commencing employment and ceasing to be financially dependent on one's parents. As explained earlier, the culture shock is largely a UK peculiarity. There are few other European countries in which most present-day parents of teenagers commenced employment at age 16 and moved rapidly towards adult wages. British parents are no less able to afford to support young people through prolonged transitions than their counterparts in most other European countries. In the relatively poor communist countries young people did not normally commence employment until age 18 or 19. In other countries parents regard it as their normal duty to feed, clothe and house children who are continuing in education or training and expect to receive neither board payments nor state support. Parents' responsibilities sometimes include ensuring that their children obtain independent housing. Needless to say, there is usually an expectation that the children will contribute if they are able to do so, but this is normally regarded as the children assisting their families to fulfil the group's obligations rather than vice versa. The chances are that within a generation these norms will have taken root in Britain.

Many present-day parents feel that their own transitions to adulthood were far less complicated and much easier than the conditions facing young people in the 1990s. Popular common sense in the UK, and in most parts of the Western world, says that transitions have become more difficult. Young people themselves, however, attach less significance than their parents to comparisons with the 1960s. In judging their personal well-being young people's main reference points are their own circumstances earlier in their own lives, and how other members of their own age group are faring. Prolonged transitions, uncertain prospects and individualized predicaments are normal facts of life for young people in the 1990s. These circumstances pose problems with which they need, and expect, to cope. The situation was comparable in the 1950s and 1960s when some commentators deplored the stresses of the abrupt transitions when 15-year-olds were plunged straight from school into employment where they became the most junior players, with much longer hours of work, more routine working lives and fewer opportunities to play than during their school days. However, young people themselves accepted the abrupt entry into employment as a challenge which they had to meet, and in the 1990s most young people are responding similarly to their new social state. This has been normalized, accepted as simply a fact of life, by young people more rapidly than by their elders. All young people need to recognize is that their own uncertain prospects and so on are shared with most contemporaries in order to realize that their own lives are not in a hopeless mess due to their own inadequacies.

Individualization and uncertainty are simultaneously liberating and threatening. Throughout post-communist East-Central Europe most young people have felt that the new opportunities greatly outweigh the new problems. Most have felt that their own adult lives will be better than would have been possible under the old systems. There is a problem in the old Western world which is not so much a direct product of young people's new social state as the absence of inspirational visions of a better future which individuals can endeavour to achieve for themselves. Such visions are undoubtedly easier to construct in the post-communist countries; their people need only to look West and filter the images transmitted by satellite television.

Young people's new social condition does not of itself threaten the age group's short-term or long-term well-being, but it gives rise to typical problems.

The need for prolonged family support

One set of the problems arises from young people's prolonged dependence on their families. Young adults today have less opportunity to support themselves by obtaining jobs paying adult wages than their parents did when they were teenagers. The jobs that young people can obtain today are typically part time or temporary and pay only 'component wages', insufficient to support independent adult lifestyles. State provisions – the grants available to students, levels of Unemployment Benefit and training allowances – assume that these will be supplemented by family support.

Families differ in their ability and willingness to take the strain during young people's prolonged transitions. The majority of families do in fact cope. As we have seen, most parents are prepared to make sacrifices for the sake of their children: they take second jobs, bank loans, second mortgages and miss holidays to ensure that their children's futures do not suffer. However, there are some young people who do not have families on which they are able, or on which they wish, to depend. This is an inevitable consequence of rising divorce and separation rates, which are signs of the instability of the modern family. A generation ago teenagers who left home almost always did so for their education, employment or to live with an opposite-sexed partner. These are still important reasons for teenagers leaving their parents' homes, but a growing minority have been leaving on account of unsatisfactory relationships (Jones, 1995). The UK has been faced with a visible problem of young people sleeping rough (see Hutson and Liddiard, 1994). Young people with local authority care backgrounds have an appallingly high rate of failed transitions (Coles, 1995). Social Services departments know that some children are exposed to danger if left in the care of their parents, but are equally aware of the problems inherent in long-term statutory care. Nevertheless, for the under-16s there are alternatives to the family, albeit less than entirely satisfactory alternatives. For the over-16s there is really no alternative and this is among the main current challenges for social policy *vis-à-vis* young people.

Economic conditions

Another threat to young people's well-being stems from the blunt fact of contemporary economic life that it is impossible for them all to end their transitions in positions that others respect, and which therefore allow the individuals concerned to respect themselves. Despite the talk of adulthood itself being less stable than in the past, young people who are able to do so are still equipping themselves for main lifetime occupations. The vast majority of males and females are still marrying in the hope that their relationships will last for life, which remains the reality in most cases. And more young people are purchasing their own dwellings which, they can still reasonably hope, will guarantee some security for the remainder of their lives. However, there are simply not enough good jobs to make this possible for all young people and this applies in every modern Western country, and in all the post-communist societies.

In the 'thirty glorious years' that followed 1945 there was full employment and plenty of jobs for young people. Britain, like all other Western countries, began this era with a small 'service class' of professionals and managers which grew rapidly; in fact, it had doubled in size, and accounted for nearly one-third of all males, by the 1980s. Most present-day adult members of this class have therefore experienced social ascent. Throughout the 'thirty glorious years' there was expanding room at the top and a leading social policy issue was how to promote more young people and widen their horizons.

Since the 1970s the rate of economic growth has slowed throughout the Western world. Mass unemployment, including youth unemployment, has been a persistent problem. Britain, like other Western countries, now has a relatively mature 'service class' that is no longer expanding at its former rate. More young people than before are starting their lives in the middle to higher levels rather than at the base of the class structure. Their preoccupation, and interest, is to 'hang on'. This increasingly requires economic and cultural capital that young people from less privileged backgrounds are unable to accumulate (see Brown,

1995). Hence the polarization between those who feel that their success is down to their own efforts and see little reason to share the benefits, and 'socially excluded groups' whose only strategies for maintaining self-respect set them apart, and keep them apart, from the remainder of the population.

Identity construction and maintenance

A third typical threat to well-being arises through adult identity construction and maintenance being more complicated than in the past. This is not to say that these processes were ever problem free. Establishing an independent lifestyle and identity has always been among young people's principal developmental tasks. In modern societies individuals' main social roles, and therefore their social identities, are primarily achieved rather than ascribed. This has applied even though males and females have achieved in somewhat different social arenas; in different segments of the labour market, for example. Likewise, different ethnic groups have had different advantages and disadvantages, and social class origins have always been influential, but within all these groups there has been scope for individuals to achieve. During youth, individuals have been expected to relinquish identities derived from their particular backgrounds and make their own ways, which used to be a fairly rapid process. Young people in higher education and those who were training for skilled occupations could confidently internalize the roles that they expected to enter.

The chances are that for the foreseeable future individuals' occupations will continue to act as major foundations of their social identities. Ascribed statuses (based on sex, ethnicity and locality, for example) can be useful complements but are usually unsatisfactory substitutes in societies that value achievement. Leisure interests, achievements and group affiliations are often too temporary, and are typically regarded as too ephemeral by the participants themselves, to be useful for more than expressing and adding fine detail to identities with other bases. Intimate personal relationships in which the actors reinforce each others' preferred self-concepts are too private, and often too temporary, to be of lasting value.

This means that young people will need to base their adult self-concepts on what they hope to become, the careers that they want to pursue, but before they can be confident that they will ever reach the occupations in question. Identity construction has become risky. It requires more social and psychological skill, and judgement, than hitherto. The best strategy may often be to base one's identity on what one feels qualified for and capable of, and to be prepared to defend such a self-concept for life if necessary even if one is denied the opportunity to practise the occupation, or to reach the level that one feels capable of. An alternative strategy is to negotiate changes of identity. Adult identities have never been set in concrete: they have always changed with age. Self-concepts and social identities are adaptable. But young people will need to be more sensitive and circumspect than in the past in the hopes and ambitions with which they become identified, and more adept at managing change. Some commentators have contrasted active and passive individualization (Evans and Heinz, 1994). Active individualizers realize pre-formulated plans, while the passive group adapt to opportunities. However, most people's lives are likely to fall somewhere between the two extremes where the risks of injury are likely to be greatest. Over-confident egoists and those who dare not express or even formulate any goals for themselves are both likely to suffer.

IMPLICATIONS

Suicide and psychiatric referral rates are poor indicators of the numbers who are dissatisfied with their lives and themselves, but the trends in these statistics are probably as sensitive as any other indicators of changes in the socio-psychological health of the population, and the recent trends among young people have been upwards. There is cause for concern, though not about young people's new social condition *per se*. In any case, this condition has been created by broader social and economic trends that it will be impossible to reverse merely for young people's sake. In the next century their well-being is likely to depend on their society's ability and willingness to address, or to assist young people in addressing, the typical problems that their new condition poses. They will need strong family support or an effective substitute. There will have to be enough decent jobs for everyone to complete their transitions to their own satisfaction. Perhaps most crucially, young people will need the social and psychological competence to manage their identities and social relationships in conditions where only the actors themselves can diagnose and solve their own problems, and will need to do so with a flexibility to match their uncertain and risky situations.

REFERENCES

Allat, P. and Yeandle, S.M. (1991) *Youth Unemployment and the Family: Voices of Disordered Times*, London: Routledge.

Banks, M., Bates, I., Breakwell, G., Bynner, J., Emler, N., Jamieson, L. and Roberts, K. (1992) *Careers and Identities*, Milton Keynes: Open University Press.

Bates, I. and Riseborough, G. (eds) (1993) *Youth and Inequality*, Milton Keynes: Open University Press.

Brown, P. (1987) *Schooling Ordinary Kids*, London: Tavistock.

Brown, P. (1995) 'Cultural capital and social exclusion: some observations on recent trends in education, employment and the labour market', *Work, Employment and Society* 9, 29–51.

Bynner, J. and Roberts, K. (1991) *Youth and Work*, London: Anglo–German Foundation.

Coles, B. (1995) *Youth and Social Policy*, London: UCL Press.

Department for Education (1995) *Young People's Participation in the Youth Service*, Statistical Bulletin 1/95, London.

Dore, R. (1976) *The Diploma Disease*, London: Allen & Unwin.

Evans, K. and Heinz, W.R. (eds) (1994) *Becoming Adults in England and Germany*, London: Anglo–German Foundation.

Furlong, A. (1992) *Growing Up in a Classless Society?* Edinburgh: Edinburgh University Press.

Hetherington, K. (1994) 'The contemporary significance of Schmalenbach's concept of the Bund', *Sociological Review* 42, 1–25.

Hutson, S. and Jenkins, R. (1989) *Taking the Strain*, Milton Keynes: Open University Press.

Hutson, S. and Liddiard, M. (1994) *Youth Homelessness*, Basingstoke: Macmillan.

Istance, D., Rees, G. and Williamson, H. (1994) *Young People not in Education, Training or Employment in South Glamorgan*, Cardiff: South Glamorgan Training and Enterprise Council.

Jones, G. (1995) *Family Support for Young People*, London: Family Policy Studies Centre.

Jones, G. and Wallace, C. (1992) *Youth, Family and Citizenship*, Milton Keynes: Open University Press.

Larkin, R.W. (1979) *Suburban Youth in Cultural Crisis*, New York: Oxford University Press.

Leonard, D. (1980) *Sex and Generation*, London: Tavistock.

Maffesoli, M. (1994) *The Time of the Tribes*, London: Sage.

Robbins Report (1963) *Higher Education*, Report of the Committee on Higher Education, London: HMSO.

Roberts, K. (1995a) *Youth and Employment in Modern Britain*, Oxford: Oxford University Press.

Roberts, K. (1995b) 'Young people's leisure in post communist Poland', in D. Leslie (ed.), *Tourism and Leisure: Culture, Heritage and Participation*, Eastbourne: Leisure Studies Association, 11–30.

Roberts, K. (1995c) 'School-children and sport', paper presented to the Leisure Studies Association conference, Eastbourne.

Roberts, K. and Jung, B. (1995) *Poland's First Post-Communist Generation*, Aldershot: Avebury Press.

Roberts, K. and Parsell, G. (1992) 'Entering the labour market in Britain: the survival of traditional opportunity structures', *Sociological Review* 30, 727–53.

Roberts, K. and Parsell, G. (1994) 'Youth cultures in Britain: the middle class takeover', *Leisure Studies* 13, 33–48.

Roberts, K., Clark, S.C. and Wallace, C. (1994) 'Flexibility and individualisation: a comparison of transitions into employment in England and Germany', *Sociology* 28, 31–54.

Chapter 11

Activity and ageing: challenge in retirement

John R. Kelly

'Retirement' has different meanings in the current developed economies. Changing economic structures of production and markets are encouraging corporations to buy out workers once considered in mid-career or even forcing them out of the paid workforce. Unemployment and retirement now overlap in meaning. At the same time, in the first three decades of the twenty-first century, the number of those in traditional retirement age will nearly double. Many issues of this new retirement are economic, matters of income and health care; others are social and psychological. What becomes of the quality of life when traditional work roles have been left behind?

The common canard is that those in retirement have no valued social roles. Those who don't die from the shock of being a non-person with no productive position or schedule face a life of emptiness. Time is a measureless void, both frightening and shapeless. Except for some seasonal gardening, retirement can become a kind of vegetative state without goals or meaning. In cold climates a few sad souls sit around tables in senior centres crocheting doilies and exchanging tales of 'the good old days'. In the American sunbelt they sit around the pool exchanging the same tales augmented by tales of sun damage and the sport of insect swatting.

A summary of this drab picture is that retired persons have *nothing worthwhile to do*. The assumption is that in a production-oriented society dominated by a work ethic, retirement is little more than a prelude to death. Further, in order to mitigate this sad state, it is necessary to provide a special set of time-filling activities in segregated places to fill the void. Note the assumptions of this view. First, most adults centred the meaning as well as the timetables of their lives around their jobs. Second, they have no other significant commitments or relationships. Third, they have been forced out of the gracious environments of employment. And fourth, they lack the flexibility to adapt to change.

ACTIVITY IN ORDINARY RETIREMENT

Fortunately, relatively few retired men and women would recognize themselves in this sad tale. Almost everyone has seen or read of the marvellous 'old folks' who

are organizing multi-cultural festivals, starting innovative pollution-free businesses and snowshoeing across the Himalayan tundra at age 84. Few retired adults
recognize anything relevant to their lives in those tales either. Nor do most retirees
find that upscale retirement resorts in glamorous locales are a remote possibility
for their budgets. In between the few who can afford expensive options and those
who are severely limited by poverty are the ordinary folk for whom retirement is
one more phase in the self-propelled journey of life in which most have already
had to cope with a series of transitions and traumas (Kelly, 1987). Retirement is
one more change, generally foreseen and usually anticipated.

Retired adults often comment on how busy they are. 'I don't know how I had
time for work' is a common reflection. What do they do, these ordinary people in
retirement? An interview study of twenty-five men and women who had retired
from a food-processing plant in the American Midwest focused on their own
accounts of activity as well as their resources and relationships (Kelly and
Westcott, 1991). These women and men had left routine jobs and were without
the special resources of higher education or financial affluence. Except for the
few who had health problems or had recently suffered the loss of a spouse, they
were getting along reasonably well. Life was full and viable, if not spectacular.
For most, a common story emerged from the interviews, a general profile of
ordinary retirement for unexceptional people.

A PROFILE OF ORDINARY RETIREMENT

What do ordinary people do in retirement? A profile from the same study (Kelly
and Westcott, 1991) begins with a decision to retire several years before the age
of 65. They are 'ageing in place', in the community and home that were their
pre-retirement physical and social environments. The overall image is one of
continuity – in relationships, values and patterns of activity. The blocks of time
opened by retirement afforded the opportunity for a planned car trip or two and
the completion of a couple of projects. 'At first I did a lot of work around the
house' was a common description of the first months. After the completion of
that initial agenda, individuals settled into routines built around the relationships, interests and commitments that had paralleled work for years, often for
most of the adult life course.

Positive elements include a sense of freedom, blocks of time for travel and
other activity, not having to get up early in the morning and reduced pressure.
One man specified relief from 'setting the clock at 5.30'. Another asserted that
'It's good just not to be so tired so much of the time'. A relatively active man
summarized the freedom when he said, 'I can do what I want to do when I want
to do it'.

For the retired workers in this case study, there was not quite as much
travelling as anticipated. Plans for becoming active in one or more community
organizations did not materialize. The activity picture is one of continuity, doing
the kinds of things done before retirement with the addition of days and weeks

free for things that take a chunk of time. There are not many plans unfulfilled because most plans were rather vague to begin with.

For those with only a secondary education, the range of leisure interests seldom extends far beyond the immediate. For those with intact marriages and other family members accessible, the family is the centre of the social world. This is reflected in their value priorities. Family and home in some combination are first in importance. Men are more likely to be engaged in projects around the residence; women spend more time in family interaction. Both, however, are generally 'family-focused' in their orientations and values. Trips are usually family visits. Family celebrations punctuate the yearly schedule. For those who are married, the husband or wife is the usual companion for most activities as well as the main confidant. Other kin are also important. A recently widowed woman referred to her 'precious grandchildren' just one state away. If nearby, children and grandchildren are a regular part of the social routine and the most common destinations for trips if distant. Distance is the main factor in patterns of extended family interaction.

Financial conditions are neither lavish nor extremely limited. For those who have lived their entire lives on modest incomes, a modest retirement is not a great change. For those in reasonable health, satisfaction with retirement tends to be fairly high. For most, life is as good as it has ever been, if not quite all that had been hoped. Unlike many whose work has greater elements of autonomy and variety or who are forced out of high-status positions, for these retired factory hands leaving the workplace is final with no desire for part-time employment, even for those who left the plant in their mid-50s. Their jobs were routine and demanding and defined instrumentally, primarily as a source of necessary income.

Activity patterns revolved around a core of relatively accessible and low-cost engagements. The ordinary retired watch television, regularly if not always intensively. They talk to others in their household and get together with immediate family as well as friends. They do some entertaining, usually informally. Get-togethers with friends may involve card games, eating out inexpensively, or just spending the evening together. As one man said, 'I just do what comes along'.

Around the home, most do some reading, at least newspapers and magazines. Gardening is common in the summer, sometimes as a satisfying commitment and sometimes as a chore. Men usually have some little project in the offing. Women more often seek out conversation with family and friends. Religious activity is the most common organizational activity outside the home and is significant for a minority of the retired. Most women have a hobby, usually a traditional women's handicraft. Almost half the men go fishing regularly in season, although several admitted they did less fishing than they had anticipated. Special engagements for a half-dozen include regular square dancing or bingo. Men are somewhat more likely to head out in the car and women to talk on the telephone. Going shopping is common for all. And *none* participate in any age-designated 'senior' activity. Why not? They report that their lives seem fairly full.

So what takes the place of the structuring of work schedules and the 'everydayness' of work associates? For the most part, new routines are constructed around a core of companions and activities. The regularities are punctuated or highlighted by occasional special events, often involving some travel. Routines, however, are synchronized with television schedules, regular involvement with other family contacts and the simple, everyday tasks of living. Ordinary retirement seems rather predictable, with few surprises or idiosyncratic patterns. Of course there are exceptions: three blue-collar men play golf regularly in season; one woman is involved in a special volunteer programme in a nursing home and one man in prison tutoring; a man with a college education is working on a crossword puzzle book; another builds radio-controlled aeroplanes but does not fly them himself. No two retirees are exactly alike, but the similarities seem to overshadow the differences. The stories told by this small number of retired workers are consistent with other research (Kelly, 1987). For those with intact families and viable health, their core of activities is focused on home and family, even when the quality of the relationships is less than perfect.

These men and women are in early retirement. As each year passes, more will experience losses in their social networks and in their own abilities. The 'active old' will enter a period of transition that requires more and more adaptation to limits. Nevertheless, any approach to activity in retirement begins with the fact that most men and women are at least relatively engaged, satisfied and going on with most of the things they did before retirement. Whatever the losses related to leaving their work roles, they seem to be more than compensated by the release from routines and demands.

CONTINUITIES OF RETIREMENT

There are individuals so invested in their work that life loses meaning without it. There are some who have to reinvest in activity that resembles work to cope with retirement (Ekerdt, 1986). Maintaining a sense of worth and even productivity is a central theme of satisfying retirement, even when the context of activity yielding such a self-definition shifts away from the work place. The old image of the trauma of retirement has given way to one that stresses the normal transition that is expected and taken in company with cohort companions. The new image is that of the 'active old' who have to make time in their schedules for anything new or extraordinary. 'Continuity theory' (Atchley, 1989) has replaced models of disengagement as well as those that focus on activity itself. Continuity encompasses who people are as well as what they do.

For the retired person the journey of life has had its zigzags. Some directions have been blocked, some surprising opportunities opened, and some lines of action diverted. Through that journey, however, there are the continuities of the self who has learned a variety of skills, social repertoires and self-definitions that carry over from one situation and time to another. As social actors, we become largely consistent in who we are and how we act, in our identities and styles of behaviour.

In the same way, there is consistency over time in our relationships and activities. Death, divorce, geographical moves and other events disrupt our social tapestries. We add and subtract activities as resources, opportunities, associations and interests change. Nevertheless, there are commitments – to others and to activity investments – that persist through the years. Especially in relationships and activities in which there is a sustained commitment, we tend to manage our lives towards continuity. When a skill-based activity such as fishing or chamber music is central to a sense of life's meaning, then the retired usually sustain involvement. Further, such activities continue as the basis for companionship and friendship.

Any perspective that assumes that at some magical or cataclysmic time, age 65 or any other, we become different persons is quite false. For the most part, even when recognizing incremental and inevitable change, we see ourselves as the same person who was 55 a few years ago and 45 only a decade before. We do not categorize ourselves by age, but know ourselves in the continuity of an 'ageless self' (Kaufman, 1986, 1993).

The implications of this continuity of selfhood for leisure and recreation are threefold. First, there is the likelihood that most older adults will go on doing most of the things they have done before with most of the same associates. Second, while revised activities are not precluded, the likelihood is that changes will build on previous satisfactions, associations and skills rather than require leaping into something entirely new. Third, any opportunities that need a radical redefinition of the self are unlikely to attract much interest. This is especially true when the redefinition involves a category with negative connotations such as 'old' or 'senior'. The self that is getting older, especially in the relatively active early retirement years, is the same person as before, more 'ageless' than primarily defined by age.

IS THERE 'EXTRAORDINARY RETIREMENT'?

People, however, are characterized by their diversity. The error of accepting negative stereotypes about 'retirees' should not lead to the inverse mistake of defining almost everyone as 'ordinary'. Economically, there are the up-market affluent as well as the disinherited marginal and poor. Culturally, there are those bound into prescriptive lifestyles as well as those who are experimental, the conventional and the risk takers. There are even a few whose lives revolve primarily around their work or their leisure.

There are extraordinary retirees who have the financial means and initiative to travel and even own second homes in friendly climates. At the up-scale end of the market are those with the wealth to purchase condominiums or homes in richly appointed communities that are usually on water and offer private golf courses and other recreational facilities. More common are those who develop retirement lives on a budget. They usually remain in place and continue many familiar patterns of engagement, minus the constraints of an employment schedule.

At the other extreme are the retirees who struggle to survive due to histories of irregular or low-income employment. They have no pensions or savings, only the limited income of low-level state support. Their lives are dominated by the problems of the bills already on the table and the devastation that can be wrought by acute health costs. Their lives also demonstrate continuity in their day-to-day strategies of survival.

The affluent are important markets for upscale provisions. The poor are significant targets for life-sustaining programmes. Most retirees, however, stay in the communities and neighbourhoods where they have lived before. Further, their values and routines reflect their histories despite some reorientations related to preparation for retirement. In a study of pre-retirement and retired older adults in the prototypical community of Peoria, Illinois (Kelly, 1987), two lifestyles were found to be far and away the most common.

The first type was composed of 'balanced investors' who found significant meaning in a combination of family, work and leisure. They found at least two of the three aspects of life important enough to take some priority in the allocation of resources. Their identities were not limited to a single role, but took on a balanced configuration appropriate to their period in the life course. The second common lifestyle pattern was the 'family focused', who tended to organize their lives around the central commitment of family roles. Usually with less educational background, they defined their lives primarily in terms of home and family. Work and leisure were valued in terms of their contribution to the expression and strengthening of family bonds.

The retired replace work demands and opportunities by expanding their other commitments, especially those of the family. Retirees with a balanced investor-type lifestyle characterize those whose lives include somewhat greater resources and variety than the 'ordinary' retired factory workers. They are more likely to allocate financial and time resources based on an articulated set of values. Further, although their lives are seldom spectacular in 'unusual' commitments, they have made decisions about activities and relationships that are worth maintaining, cultivating or renewing. When they achieve a balance of caring and sharing relationships and meaningful activity, they are most satisfied with their later years.

However striking is later-life continuity, it does not preclude shifts in emphasis or even a resocialization into new roles and commitments. There are radical changes in the life course of many adults, but life tends to be more a matter of building on foundations and composing with familiar themes than turning to the utterly new. As a consequence, those with the fullest and most diverse base on which to build are best able to respond to the opportunities of retirement.

Retirement is a significant change, all emphasis on continuity notwithstanding. This is especially the case for those forced out of employment before they are financially or emotionally prepared. The most obvious change is in the structure of time. The week is no longer dominated by employment obligations, which opens blocks of time to be reallocated for new routines or special events. While travel is the most obvious possibility, new commitments of meeting friends, caring for grandchildren or neighbours, or redeveloping a demanding skill are not unusual. Also, there is a flexibility in timetables that permits more spontaneous response to unplanned opportunities.

For leisure, two parallel possibilities may be developed. The first is to utilize leisure to reconstitute a fundamental structure for time. Freedom from incessant demand does not imply a total lack of regularity: most retirees rebuild some structure in their timetables. Complete voids are no more satisfying than demand saturation. New commitments to leisure activity and groups may be combined with a re-engagement with former skills and identities. The second possibility is to retain enough openness that it is possible to respond to the immediacy of a lovely afternoon, an unexpected invitation or a random impulse.

As a consequence, extraordinary retirement is partly a matter of recognizing the opportunities that are released by the new life situation. Further, if ordinary retirees tend to be relatively satisfied with their lives, then what is special about being more than ordinary? The answer may be surprising.

REQUISITES AND PREREQUISITES OF SATISFYING RETIREMENT

What characterizes those who are doing more than getting along reasonably well in their later years? Are there marks of extraordinary retirement?

The 'prerequisites' are almost self-evident: functional health and economic viability (Palmore, 1979). Without these fundamental conditions, everything else is difficult or impossible. No community programme, service, support or association can replace such prerequisites. The issue is what is most significant when these two conditions are met. In a longitudinal study, group and physical activity for both men and women and solitary activity for women were the most salient factors distinguishing those with a high level of satisfaction in later life (Palmore, 1979). A causal model of analysis identified health, socio-economic status and activity as the three primary factors (Markides and Martin, 1979). In a review of thirty years of research, Larson (1978) found that, following health conditions, social activity accounts for between 1 and 9 per cent of the variance in life satisfaction.

Other research has identified some refinements in the importance of activity. Especially among older persons, the quality rather than quantity of relationships is most significant (Tobin and Neugarten, 1961; Conner, Powers and Bultena, 1979; Kelly, Steinkamp and Kelly, 1986, 1987). One issue is the extent to which leisure and social activity make a direct contribution to life satisfaction rather than as a context for social interaction and integration. This question was addressed directly in a study of women who were retired from employment or had always been homemakers (Riddick and Daniel, 1984). Leisure activity was found to have the strongest direct effect on life satisfaction, followed by income and health. In a different study, leisure activity level accounted for 6.2 per cent of the remaining variance in life satisfaction after the 11.8 per cent of health, occupational status, education level, age, gender and marital status were entered (Kelly, Steinkamp and Kelly, 1987).

A number of explanations has been offered for the consistent finding that social and leisure activity make an independent contribution to well-being in later life. One holds that engagement in activity is itself important to a balanced and satisfying life (Cutler and Hendricks, 1990; Longino and Kart, 1982). Lemon, Bengtson and Peterson (1972) suggest that informal leisure provides a context for significant social interaction. They further argue that frequent participation in fewer salient activities contributes more than does a wide range of activities. Atchley (1993) proposes that leisure enables retired persons to continue roles that they have valued earlier. This approach of engagement in meaningful activity defines leisure as an arena for the development and expression of valued identities in which some competence, achievement and recognition may be gained (Havighurst, 1961; Rapoport and Rapoport, 1975; Gordon, Gaitz and Scott, 1976; Kelly, 1983).

In summary, there seems to be ample evidence to suggest that leisure and recreation are important elements of the quality of life in retirement. Further, there are indications that some kinds of activities contribute more than others and that quality is more important than quantity. A summary of the early findings of the Yale Health and Aging Project (Elder, 1991) points to the importance of genetic endowment and then adds: 'But if staying involved with other people and keeping up your tennis game turns out to be even part of the answer, it just may be the closest humankind will ever get to the fountain of youth'.

ALTERNATIVE THEORIES OF ACTIVITY

In the 1961 volume edited by Robert Kleemeier, *Aging and Leisure*, a number of authors went beyond presentations of what older people did to analyse the relationship of changes in economic and family roles in retirement to the meanings of non-work activity. In particular, the chapter by Robert Havighurst on 'The nature and value of meaningful free-time activity' examined the dimensions of values found in a range of leisure engagements. He and others in the Kansas City Study of Adult Life found that leisure is multi-dimensional in meanings, varied in forms and interwoven with family and community roles. Lifestyles of 'balance' and 'home-centred' at high, medium and low levels of activity were in part indexed by social status measures.

The reduction model

From the same study, Cumming and Henry (1961) proposed their 'disengagement theory' that has usually been placed in opposition to views of ageing that stress activity and continuity. Disengagement is based on the dual findings that older people tend to be less involved than younger in activity outside the home and that both tend to be relatively satisfied with this situation. The argument was then developed that some withdrawal from activity is functional for older people who need to concentrate their resources and energies on activity that is appropriate and satisfying for their stage in life.

It is certainly true that advancing age is correlated with lower rates of activity and even a constriction of interests (Havighurst, 1961). In a more recent study, lower rates of participation were found for each older age category in travel, outdoor recreation and exercise and sport (Kelly, Steinkamp and Kelly, 1986). For those over 74, the rates were lower also for participation in community organizations, cultural activity and even home-based activity. There appears to be a constriction process that narrows the range of activities in spatial location as well as number in later life. However, two kinds of activities – social activities and family leisure – remain relatively high in participation. Continuity is demonstrated in the 'core' of relatively accessible and informal leisure that makes up the ongoing, day-to-day centre of activity.

This constriction in the range of activity was also reported in a time-diary study (Lawton, 1987). Increasing age was associated with more time spent alone eating, resting and relaxing and engaging in at-home religious activity rather than in more active engagement outside the home. In a Houston area study, the pattern of constriction associated with age held for such activities as dancing, film-going, sports and exercise, outdoor recreation, travel, reading, cultural production, and spectator sports to a greater degree than for social interaction, entertaining, voluntary organizations and cultural consumption (Gordon, Gaitz and Scott, 1976).

The engagement model

Constriction, however, may be an adaptation to conditions rather than a preference. Gordon, Gaitz and Scott (1976), for example, suggest that energy reductions and the relinquishing of some social roles lead to some constriction in frequency and range of activity participation, but that the 'meaningful integration' of sharing and interaction remain central for those in retirement years. Further, self-definitions with valued identities are significant and often supported by leisure engagement.

Maddox (1968) reports on a longitudinal study in which declining health reduces capacity to engage in many kinds of activity. The decline, however, tends to be gradual for those without traumatic loss in ability. Further, the declines are more gradual for activities such as reading, cultural activities, entertaining, conversation, home enhancement and other in-home and social activity than for events that are physically demanding (Gordon, Gaitz and Scott, 1976; Kelly, Steinkamp and Kelly, 1986). Even travel and community organization participation are markedly lower only for those in age categories associated with frailty. Older people continue to engage in activity that brings them together with valued other persons and in which they feel comfortable with their abilities. The stability of golfing rates suggests that even outdoor activity can continue to attract those with developed skills, resources and companions.

The reduction model, then, is supported when the sole measure is frequency of participation by activity type. A life-course approach that is based on continuity, however, suggests an engagement model of adaptation and choice. With activity associated with perceived quality of life, older persons are more likely to focus on those activities and relationships that they believe contribute most to their lives. Those most satisfied with their lives in later years are those who have maintained engagement with meaningful activities and associations. Overall age-related lower rates of participation in many kinds of recreational activities obscure the relative stability in rates for activities that are appropriate, possible and satisfying. Activities are selected rather than simply reduced, at least until the time when frailty severely limits the possibilities.

LEISURE THAT MAKES A DIFFERENCE

The approach towards leisure in retirement being developed here has the following theses:

1 The activity patterns of retired men and women are characterized by considerable continuity with the activities and relationships that have been meaningful to them in their pre-retirement years.
2 Retirement, then, involves a reconstruction of patterns of involvement based in previously established competence and associations to accommodate the new freedom from demand.
3 The image of the 'active old' is more accurate than one of voids of time and commitment, despite a pattern of age-related constriction in activity.
4 Retired adults are social actors who are selecting valued engagements that have proven satisfying rather than disengaged pawns sliding into voids of meaninglessness and low life satisfaction.

A primary issue, then, is that of resources and opportunity. What do retired men and women need in order to develop a satisfying lifestyle with adequate levels of engagement? What are the factors that really make a difference?

In general, the two complementary elements of satisfying retirement, beyond the prerequisites, are activity and community. They are regular and meaningful engagement with doing things that are satisfying and sharing life with people through interaction and involvement. For most older persons, both the activity and the relationships are an extension of histories that have been developed through the life course.

Retirement activity

Does it make any difference what kinds of activity older adults do? Is bingo as satisfying as volunteer service, television as golf or gardening as travel? One approach would be that almost any pattern of regular action and interaction that provides a sense of meaning and brings retirees into association with friends and family would fulfil the requirements. Some research, however, indicates that for those with the highest levels of satisfaction, certain kinds of activity have a place in the spectrum of participation. In the Peoria study, there were significant age differences (Kelly, Steinkamp and Kelly, 1986). For those aged 40 to 64, regular travel and participation in the arts and other cultural activities distinguished those with the highest level of perceived quality of life. Social and travel activities marked those aged 65 to 74 with the highest satisfaction. For those aged 75 and older, family and home-based activities were most salient. What is suggested is that the activity should be whatever provides the greatest stimulation and social involvement within the pattern of constriction that develops in later years.

In the longitudinal Duke study (Palmore, 1979), activity outside the home, social and physical, marked the retirement-aged men and women highest in life satisfaction. The two dimensions necessary for life satisfaction seem to be challenge and social integration. In addition for women, who are more likely to live alone, solitary activity that is involving is significant. Another approach identified the kind of activity often referred to as 'serious leisure' (Stebbins, 1979). This is activity that is demanding of skill, attention and commitment. Serious leisure has a career of inauguration, development and demonstrated competence. It usually involves its devotees, 'amateurs', in regular interaction with groups in which association is built around common action. Those engaged in serious leisure make this commitment a central element of their identities. In retirement, these identities may claim even greater centrality. A Canadian study of time use and associations in later life found that those who were extraordinarily satisfied with their lives were those engaged in serious leisure (Mannell, 1993). They experienced both the sense of community with their companions and the sense of competence produced by meeting the challenge of the activity (Csikszentmihalyi, 1990).

Again, the two critical elements seem to be challenge and community. Challenge is stimulating, involving and even exciting. Facing a challenge – physical, mental or social – requires concentration and effort; meeting the challenge requires a demonstration of skill. The outcome is twofold: the immediate involvement and the consequent sense of ability and worth. Community is commonly developed in the process of such engagement. Bonds are formed not by mere proximity or being entertained, but in common action; especially activities that require exchange and reciprocity to form relationships of communication, sharing and trust.

The forms of activity that combine the two elements are almost infinite and may focus on physical, mental, aesthetic or social tasks and challenges (Csikszentmihalyi, 1990). They may involve outcomes that can be seen and appreciated, that are shared or more individual, that are of recognized social value or more private. They are commitments that become central to life's meaning over time. They are the 'extra' that may lift retirement above the ordinary. Thus retirees run, dance, fish, play golf, produce plays, counsel, teach, write, experiment, explore, learn and organize; they sculpt in metal or wood, throw pots or create stained glass, rebuild old cars or train dogs, landscape or decorate, coach or provide care. The keys are that the engagement is regular, demanding and involves some kind of community. It calls for continued learning and development, for assessment and commitment. And usually it has some connection with previously valued identities.

Such 'serious leisure' is not the whole story of anyone's retirement activity. In the balance of a leisure style there is also disengagement and relaxation, low-intensity as well as demanding activity, appreciation as well as creation, being alone as well as sharing. The ordinary patterns of living are there as well, especially in the day-to-day associations of home, family, neighbourhood and friends. But the extraordinary is the 'something more' that highlights the ordinary, that makes the self someone special – a person of ability sharing with others. And it is the highlights that produce extraordinary enjoyment in the routines of retirement.

IMPLICATIONS FOR PROGRAMMES AND RESOURCES

It is evident that the world of retirees is not waiting around out there for just about anything to fill their time. In an analysis of 13,000 people over age 60 in the 1984 US National Health Interviews, the proportion participating regularly in 'senior centre' programmes was quite low (Kelly and Reis, 1991). The percentage never going to senior centres was 86.9 and never eating at centres 92.7. In general, the percentage of those over 60 who are regularly engaged in any specific type of age-designated programme is about 1 per cent. If there was ever an accepted myth that desperate retirees would flock to just about any programme, that presumption has been exploded. The issue to be resolved concerning such programmes is the extent to which they serve and support those most bereft of economic and social resources rather than the more resourceful 'active old'.

The negative image is related to the requirement of a redefinition of the self. Even though they recognize the reality of age and loss, in general older people do not reclassify themselves as 'old', 'senior' or 'golden'. They are the same persons who guided and taught children, improved a home, fulfilled the demands of a job and shared life with friends. Any programme that requires the negative redefinition of age runs counter to continuities of identity. When such a programme also requires entering an age-segregated and unfamiliar environment, the psychological price of admission is too high. This resistance also reflects a common confusion between service and activity programmes that is intensified by locating them in the same place.

One community response to all this would be to recognize that retirees are still people who will direct their lives in a balance of engagement that is at least relatively satisfying. Why not just accept ordinary retirement as it is? The problem is that 'ordinary' is not all that it might be. Those who are more than doing OK are those involved in communities of challenging activity: they have more than routines that fill the day; they have commitments that yield a sense of competence and community. They have that 'something more' that transforms the ordinary into the extraordinary. The process of constriction that characterizes later life may at least be delayed by opportunities that are both possible and satisfying. The analysis developed up to this point provides some guidelines for age-designated programmes:

1 Build on continuities. Older persons have built up their own repertoires of abilities, histories of meaningful engagements and orienting priorities. Useful provisions of opportunities will build on previous histories of significant and satisfying activity. The activities, locales and associations should be familiar rather than require going to different age-designated places with different age-segregated people. Programmes should build on the continuities of the 'ageless self' rather than the discontinuities of being 'old'.
2 Emphasize quality. The premise would be that retirees allocate resources, including time, much as they have before. Any commitment has to be seen as worth it. Programmes for older adults should have leadership recognized as the best, be in locales associated with quality, and gain a reputation for challenging abilities rather than accommodating to the lowest levels.
3 In most situations, there is no need to designate programmes by age at all. Scheduling alone will tend to attract those now free from usual work timetables. Since there is no reliable correlation between age and ability in most activities, there is no inherent reason why skill-based activities need to be strictly age segregated anyway.
4 This does not mean that opportunities may not take into account limitations in mobility, communication and social ties that come to many with age. The decremental process leading towards frailty may call for activity contexts that are brought closer to the life conditions of ordinary people in the transition from being active towards frailty. Nevertheless, quality and continuity remain principles that support dignity as well as ability.

SUMMARY

In the life course studies of leisure, two main dimensions of motivation have been found. The first embraces the more individual: action contexts that offer the opportunity to develop, build and demonstrate competence. People want to relax, rest, escape and withdraw at times. But the engagement they find most central and valued offers the challenge of action. The second theme of motivation that draws consistent engagement is social – the expression of community. To be able and to be related to others, these are the elements that most often draw people of any age into consistent activity. And it is such activity that makes the difference between ordinary and extraordinary leisure in later life.

REFERENCES

Atchley, R. (1989) 'A continuity theory of normal aging', *The Gerontologist*, 29: 2, 183–9.
Atchley, R. (1993) 'Continuity theory and the evolution of activity in later adulthood', in J. Kelly (ed.), *Activity and Aging*, Newbury Park, CA: Sage.
Csikszentmihalyi, M. (1990) *Flow: The Psychology of Optimal Experience*, New York: Harper and Row.
Conner, K., Powers, E. and Bultena, G. (1969) 'Social interaction and life satisfaction: an empirical assessment of later life patterns', *Journal of Gerontology* 34, 116–21.
Cumming, E. and Henry, W. (1961) *Growing Old: The Process of Disengagement*, New York: Basic Books.
Cutler, S. and Hendricks, J. (1990) 'Leisure and time use across the life course', in R. Binstock and L. George (eds), *Handbook of Aging and the Social Sciences* (3rd edn), New York: Academic Press.
Ekerdt, D. (1986) 'The busy ethic: moral continuity between work and retirement', *The Gerontologist* 26, 239–44.
Elder, S. (1991) 'The secrets of (successful) aging', *Yale Alumni Magazine*, April, 24–9.
Gordon, C., Gaitz, C. and Scott, J. (1976) 'Leisure and lives: personal expressivity across the life span', in R. Binstock and E. Shanas (eds), *Handbook of Aging and the Social Sciences*, New York: Van Nostrand Reinhold.
Havighurst, R. (1961) 'The nature and value of meaningful free time activity', in R. Kleemeier (ed.) *Aging and Leisure*, New York: Oxford University Press.
Kaufman, S. (1986) *The Ageless Self: Sources of Meaning in Later Life*, New York: New American Library.
Kaufman, S. (1993) 'Values as sources of the ageless self', in J. Kelly (ed.), *Activity and Aging*, Newbury Park, CA: Sage.
Kelly, J.R. (1983) *Leisure Identities and Interactions*, London: Allen and Unwin.
Kelly, J.R. (1987) *Peoria Winter: Styles and Resources in Later Life*, Lexington, MA: Lexington Books.
Kelly, J.R. (ed.) (1993) *Activity and Aging*, Newbury Park, CA: Sage.
Kelly, J.R. and Reis, J. (1991) 'Identifying senior program participants', *Journal of Park and Recreation Administration* 9, 55–64.
Kelly, J.R., Steinkamp, M. and Kelly, J. (1986) 'Later life leisure: how they play in Peoria', *The Gerontologist* 26, 531–7.
Kelly, J.R., Steinkamp, M. and Kelly, J. (1987) 'Later life satisfaction: does leisure contribute?', *Leisure Sciences* 9, 189–200.
Kelly, J.R. and Westcott, G. (1991) 'Ordinary retirement: commonalities and continuity', *International Journal of Aging and Human Development* 32, 81–9.
Kleemeier, R. (1961) *Aging and Leisure*, New York: Oxford University Press.
Larson, R. (1978) 'Thirty years of research on the subjective well-being of older adults', *Journal of Gerontology* 16, 134–43.
Lawton, M.P. (1987) 'Activities and leisure', in M. Lawton and G. Maddox (eds), *Annual Review of Gerontology and Geriatrics*, New York: Springer.
Lemon, B.W., Bengtson, V. and Peterson, J. (1972) 'An exploration of the activity theory of aging', *Journal of Gerontology* 27, 511–23.

Longino, C. and Kart, C. (1982) 'Explicating activity theory: a formal replication', *Journal of Gerontology* 37, 713–22.

Maddox, G. (1968) 'Persistence of life style among the elderly: a longitudinal study of life patterns of social activity in relation to life satisfaction', in B. Neugarten (ed.), *Middle Age and Aging*, Chicago: University of Chicago Press.

Mannell, R. (1993) 'High investment activity and life satisfaction: commitment, serious leisure, and flow in the daily lives of older people', in J. Kelly (ed.) *Activity and Aging*, Newbury Park, CA: Sage.

Markides, K. and Martin, H. (1979) 'A causal model of life satisfaction among the elderly', *Journal of Gerontology* 34, 86–93.

Palmore, E. (1979) 'Predictors of successful aging', *The Gerontologist* 19, 427–31.

Rapoport, R. and Rapoport, R. (1975) *Leisure and the Family Life Cycle*, London: Routledge & Kegan Paul.

Riddick, C. and Daniel, S. (1984) 'The relative contributions of leisure activity and other factors to the mental health of older women', *Journal of Leisure Research* 16, 136–48.

Stebbins, R. (1979) *Amateurs: On the Margins between Work and Leisure*, Newbury Park, CA: Sage.

Tobin, S. and Neugarten, B. (1961) 'Life satisfaction and social interaction of the aged', *Journal of Gerontology*, 16, 344–6.

Chapter 12

Work and leisure futures: trends and scenarios

Stanley Parker

The future of work and leisure can take four broad forms, based on four types of human understanding and social interaction. We can stay more or less as we are, we can go back to an earlier state of affairs, we can change a bit or we can change a lot. This, of course, is very much to over-simplify the choices, and we need to ask some additional questions. Is there a real difference between staying more or less as we are and changing a bit? When is a change a small one and when is it a large one? Are we talking of the near future (say, the next five years), the medium term (twenty-five years) or the long term (a century or more)?

At the outset a warning note should be sounded about why people try to predict the future. As Dubin (1990) points out, governments and businesses pay handsomely for prognostications which attempt to provide information on which they can make decisions. They are, in effect, attempting to determine the future as much as to predict it. Predictions create expectations, and people tend to act on those expectations. Academics who write about the future, even by selecting the writings of others to report dispassionately, are not exempt from this motivation, although their concerns may be seen generally as less influenced by special pleading than those of government or business (except where such academics are working for the government or business).

It may help, for the purposes of this discussion, to put labels on the four types of possible futures, as long as we recognize that these are only labels of convenience, not of precise or adequate definition. Using 'isms', they are conservatism, reactionism, reformism and revolutionism (the last isn't in my dictionary but its meaning is reasonably clear). Let us look at each of these futures in turn, first in terms of work, then leisure, then the relationship between the two.

CONSERVATISM

If the future is going to be more or less the same as today, then we are looking at a continuation or perhaps slowing down of recent trends: not a reversal (that would be reactionism), not a speeding up (reformism) and not something qualitatively new (revolutionism). The conservative concern about the future is that, put positively, it should be in safe pairs of hands or, more negatively, it is the devil we know rather than the devil we don't. Either way, work for most people in the foreseeable future will continue to mean mainly employment. If you have enough capital you don't need to do it, if you are unemployed you are looking for it, if you are a dependant you rely on someone else doing it, and if you are retired from it then society allows you a life of leisure, providing your pension is adequate, or a life of free time if it isn't.

The conservative view of leisure is that it is first and foremost an industry. With the decline of manufacturing industries in the economically advanced countries, services of various kinds have grown, including those connected with leisure: tourism, entertainment, hotel and catering, gambling, spectator sport, electronic games and so on. Leisure is said mostly to need some kind of market provider, if not profit-seeking enterprises then the local council or the government. Non-market leisure – what we do for ourselves, collectively or individually – is recognized as existing, but it does not play a central role in the conservative view of leisure.

Today the work–leisure relationship can take three forms. First, we can let work (what we do for a living) extend into our leisure time; second, we can see the one as the opposite of the other; or third, we can order the work and leisure aspects of our lives in two different worlds (Parker, 1983). The 'extension' pattern is experienced most often by people, like artists and social workers, who are deeply involved in their work. The 'opposition' pattern, typical of miners and oil-rig workers, is that of a minority who often have to recuperate from their work before they can enjoy leisure. Many, perhaps most, of us have employment that is neither particularly creative nor damaging, so we tend to keep work and leisure separate.

Martin and Mason (1982) posit four alternative work and leisure scenarios up to the year 2001, one of which they call 'frustration'. The two variables they consider are the level of economic growth and stability or change in social attitudes. The 'frustration' scenario combines low economic growth with no change in prevailing attitudes to work and leisure and is essentially conservative. The other three scenarios (to be considered below) are reforms of different kinds in the present system of employment and leisure provision.

REACTIONISM

Reactionist views of work and leisure are based on the perception of a past 'golden age' to which it is thought desirable to return. With regard to work, this is often taken to be the Renaissance period in Europe around the fifteenth century – a time when religious views of work as a curse or a punishment for original sin were beginning to be challenged by more humanistic views.

Reactionist approaches to work, seeking to restore in the future an attitude to and experience of work that is seen to be threatened by modern and impersonal mass production methods, are to be found in de Man's *Joy in Work* (1929). More recently, Applebaum (1992) has expressed the view that 'The advance of technology now provides industrial cultures with the possibilities of choice – choice of work and choice of what useful things to make, so as to restore work to its human dimensions and meanings'. Even the contemporary demand in some quarters for a return to 'full employment' may be interpreted as an essentially reactionist desire to return to the conditions of the past.

The reactionist view of leisure was expressed by de Grazia (1962), in a book that has been much discussed in the last three decades. That approach looks back to ancient Greece for the leisure ideal, as expressed by Aristotle and quoted by de Grazia: 'Leisure is a state of being in which activity is performed for its own sake or as its own end'. Sometimes the desire to return to an allegedly better past is accompanied by a feeling that we have in the present lost something of value. Thus Glasser (1973) deplores 'the erosion of the great religions in the maintenance of a frame of reference for conduct', but later (1975) observes that the practitioners of the marketing process of leisure 'now exercise the leadership function of the high priesthood of old'.

The reactionist view of the work–leisure relationship is that we have lost the earlier integration of the two spheres and so we should seek to restore the seemingly more harmonious conditions of the past. There was no dividing line between work and leisure in primitive communism, for example, but many would argue that to give up the conveniences and comforts of civilization is too high a price to pay for 'integration'. Even today the 'work parties' still common in many parts of Africa which feature a blurring of work and leisure may be said to point only to the *principle* of integration, a principle that will require a different set of practices if it is to be implemented in the future.

REFORMISM

When we come to the reformist approach to work, we are faced with a plethora of proposals to improve its future. These proposals are reformist rather than revolutionary because they assume the continuation of some form of capitalist (free-market or 'mixed economy') system of employment. Such proposals are concerned with improving the conditions, distribution and consequences of employment, not with its abolition. They fall roughly into three groups: (1) reduce time in employment, coupled with spreading job opportunities to reduce unemployment; (2) provide everyone with a minimum income that does not depend on their being employed; and (3) change (improve) the character of employment.

Handy (1984) suggests that there are five ways of reducing time in employment: (1) reduce daily or weekly hours; (2) increase annual holidays; (3) lower the age of retirement; (4) raise the age of leaving full-time education; and (5) introduce sabbaticals for all workers. These reforms of time spent in employment have met with varying degrees of success at different times, in different industries and in different countries. Employers will normally concede these reforms if no loss of productivity is negotiated as part of the deal.

The provision of a guaranteed wage for all employees, and especially the further stage of a guaranteed annual income for all citizens, may appear to border on revolution, but in fact it depends on the continuation of the present system where most people are employed for much of their adult lives. A guaranteed annual *wage* is the annualized equivalent of a minimum hourly wage rate, a reform that has been pursued by trade unions with some success in the past but very little success in the last two decades. A guaranteed annual *income* seeks to narrow the gap between those who are in employment and those who are not: Reid (1995) believes that it would provide 'a basic, yet acceptable, standard of living to everyone in society'. But he admits the danger that 'a few transnational corporations operate outside the laws of the community or nation and simply bid down wages to the lowest common denominator, resulting in a subsistence wage for all'. In practice, this is only a trend that is reversible rather than inevitable, because if wages are too low people cannot afford to buy back the goods and services they collectively produce.

The third type of employment reform is that of seeking to change its character for the better. The suggestions for improvement include accelerating the change from unskilled or semi-skilled goods-producing jobs to skilled knowledge-intensive jobs, promoting self-service activities and enabling individuals to have a variety of paid work in their lifetime. The growth of the self-service economy is particularly notable: Gershuny (1978) has been prominent among those who point out that the diminishing manufacturing sector increasingly provides us with the means to do things for ourselves – having washing machines, filling our own petrol tanks, preserving food in domestic freezers. This is part of the domestic economy, which is estimated to be as large as 40 per cent of the formal economy. As Veal (1987) observes,

> It is possible to envisage a future scenario in which people's engagement in the formal economy is minimal – either people would work very few hours per week or per year, or for just a few years in their lives – but this minimal involvement would produce all of society's needs from the formal economy.

Sherman (1984) would like us to 'abandon our total dependence on employment and at the same time upgrade the importance of free time'. It is, of course, an exaggeration to say that we are totally dependent on employment to produce goods and services, but Sherman is right to point out that the work ethic is deeply ingrained in our society. Writing more than a decade ago, he was pessimistic about the prospects for reducing unemployment, a situation that has since worsened. His proposed reforms are to 'have all sorts of combinations of part time work and community work' and that 'leisure activities, especially hobbies, can be turned into sources of income'. Research on the income-producing activities of the unemployed points to this being a triumph of hope over experience. Stonier (1989), whose views on the destructive effect of technology on jobs are similar to those of Sherman, would like us to become 'an education-oriented society', eventually having 50 per cent of the workforce employed in education. A laudable aim, but not likely to be seriously pursued by any political party seeking to run capitalism in the short term.

Some interesting ideas about the future of work are put forward by writers in a recent publication *Demos*. Zeldin (1995) raises the potentially revolutionary questions of the different ways we have of spending our time and what kinds of experiences we should ideally fill our lives with. But his actual proposals are somewhat less than revolutionary and concern alternative forms of study, employment and leisure:

> If people are to choose between a variety of occupations, they need to have a full menu of the possibilities, and of the side effects which indulgence causes, and to plan a whole life as a ten or twenty course meal, not just as one career heading for retirement and death.

Having a full 'menu' of the possibilities and planning a twenty-course meal are fine if the food is available in sufficient amount, quality and variety. It contrasts with the present situation where 'four fifths of British nurses are dissatisfied because the institutional arrangements of hospitals prevent them from giving patients the quality of care they would like to give' and over half of British diplomats are dissatisfied with their work, despite their prestige and high salaries. Zeldin believes that 'in work and leisure, we have to be catalysts to each other, or we shall never be able to enjoy our freedom' and he advocates 'mentors' to help the underprivileged. But it is difficult to see how people can be expected to help each other when dozens, and sometimes hundreds, of applicants are chasing one job vacancy.

The reformist approach to the future of leisure has not received as much attention as work *per se*. More time for leisure is a popular demand and the quality of leisure is a subject for debate. The demand and the debate often centre around the leisure needs of particular groups in the community, who are seen to have special problems or to be exceptionally deprived – for example, young people, the elderly, women and ethnic groups.

After a period of mainly public investment in new sports and leisure centres in the 1960s and 1970s, notably as a means of reducing juvenile delinquency, such investment has tailed off in the 1980s and 1990s and been replaced by commercial enterprises offering facilities not affordable by low-income groups. Measures to improve the leisure lives of the elderly are seen to be needed, but have low priority in relation to more basic needs such as for health, housing and nutrition. As Abrams (1980) shows, opportunities for leisure outside the home are severely restricted for the elderly, and most indoor 'leisure' is confined to watching television.

Some progress has been made in reducing the gap between women's leisure opportunities and those of men, and more is proposed. Green *et al.* (1990) note that the commercial sector is the major provider of adult leisure and that 'many women will simply not be able to buy into ever more commodified leisure'. They do not view the future prospects as encouraging, but point to what some women have been able to do to claim time for themselves and make 'real inroads into the male bastions of leisure'. They look forward to building on those achievements.

In a multi-racial society such as Britain, the aim of community recreational strategies is to provide for cultural differences (Haywood *et al.*, 1989). But there is plenty of evidence of inequality in leisure activity related to ethnic identity. Reforms to improve ethnic leisure opportunities consequently take two directions: to encourage participation in indigenous cultural forms (music, dance, film, sport, etc.) and to remove obstacles to all forms of leisure participation regardless of ethnic identity.

Taking a more ambitious view of how leisure can or should be reformed in the future we may turn to the use of Delphi predictions, the nature of which consists of several rounds of questioning experts about what they think has at least a 50–50 chance of happening in the future. Veal (1987) quotes from the results of one such exercise carried out in the US in 1975: it was predicted that by the year 2000 small recreational submarines would be common, the average age of retirement would be 50 and 'weekends' would be distributed throughout the week. As Veal drily remarks, experts may or may not be gifted with Delphic vision.

The work–leisure relationship may be reformed as a result of changes in work, in leisure or in both. If it is only work that will be changed, while leisure remains more or less as it is, then the consequences for the relationship will depend on what kind of changes in work take place. If work expands its role in our lives, for example by embracing serious leisure (Stebbins, 1992) as well as employment activities, then we may expect a narrowing of the gap between the two spheres. But if work 'collapses' or is much reduced, then presumably leisure will be the main beneficiary. Machines will do all or nearly all the work hitherto done by people and the question of what relationship there will be between this emasculated work sphere and the virtually all-embracing leisure sphere will be answered by declaring the latter the winner. Neulinger (1990) has argued for such a leisure society, but Stormann (1989) and I (Parker, 1991) have maintained that, though employment may cease to exist in the future, work will not.

It is possible that substantial changes will be made in the leisure sphere while work (meaning the present combination of employment and non-employment work) will remain. What kind of changes in leisure? If market-provided leisure ousts non-market leisure – that is to say, if we all become dominated by mostly passive, consumerist, spectator leisure – then opposition, or at least neutrality, between the spheres will remain. But again this seems extremely unlikely. Market forces may still have further to go in conquering the world, but that part of leisure which is not for sale will surely not disappear, encircled by the cash nexus though it may be.

More or less simultaneous and perhaps complementary changes in both work and leisure may be expected to lead to a change in the relationship between the two. Martin and Mason (1982) outline four scenarios depending on polarized values of economic growth and social attitudes. Above I noted that what they called the 'frustration' scenario (low economic growth and no change in attitudes to work and leisure) is essentially conservative. Their other three scenarios are reformist – not revolutionary because they envisage the continuation of capitalist employment. The first is 'conventional success': an affluent world, work hard, play hard, a minority left out. The second is 'self-restraint': low economic growth, more informal work, blurring of work and leisure. The third is 'transformed growth': full use of new technologies, redistribution of work, leisure and incomes, greater flexibility in time use.

Martin and Mason clearly favour this last scenario. They put their faith in 'a general acceptance that work and leisure should be more fairly shared'. But they admit that 'where we are now' is largely frustration with some conventional success, but very little transformed growth.

REVOLUTIONISM

The line between a far-reaching reform and a somewhat hesitant and certainly bloodless revolution is not easy to draw. I propose to call 'revolutionary' any change in work, leisure or the relationship between the two that is post-capitalist, or at least seriously tending in the direction of a system of post-capitalism. Such a system may be called socialism (in the original Marxist sense, indistinguishable from communism), communism, anarchism or even Utopianism (except that this last term is commonly used by opponents of revolutionary change to denote its impossibility).

The meaning and experience of work have undergone revolutionary change in the past, and will no doubt again do so at some point in the future. In primitive communism – and in surviving simpler societies today – work was and is done on a cooperative, non-market basis. In slavery work was done by slaves who were owned by masters; feudalism saw workers freed from owners but tied to lords through land tenure. Only with capitalism did employment – the system of buying and selling labour – become the dominant form of work.

Although Utopian socialists such as Fourier were among the first to envisage the ending of employment and its replacement by communes in which labour would be cooperative and without a master class, those ideas gained wide currency only with the extensive critique of capitalism by Marx and Engels. Even to outline this critique would take us too far from our subject here, but Marx and Engels' (1846) views on the consequences for work of their revolutionary proposals are epitomized in this often-quoted passage:

> In the communist society, where nobody has one exclusive sphere of activity but each can become accomplished in any branch he wishes, society regulates the general production and thus makes it possible for me to do one thing today and another tomorrow, to hunt in the morning, fish in the afternoon, rear cattle in the evening, criticise after dinner, just as I have a mind, without ever becoming a hunter, fisherman, shepherd or critic.

Today we might say we would work with our computer in the morning, discuss our problems with others in the afternoon, plan a family holiday in the evening, do a little storytelling after dinner, without ever becoming a computer programmer, social worker, tourist guide or media hack.

William Morris, in his visionary *News from Nowhere* (originally published in 1890 but with several later editions) had much to say about work in a genuinely socialist future society, but he did so in the form of a Utopian romance rather than a polemical treatise. In his classless, moneyless, stateless society, work would be done not for money but because of the usefulness of its products or services: hence the well-dressed dustman and the boatman puzzled at being offered coins in return for his rowing the narrator-passenger. Socialists still refer to the *principles* of post-capitalist work illustrated in Morris' writings, but the details, particularly relating to technological developments in the last hundred years, have been overtaken by events, in some ways giving *News from Nowhere* a more reactionary than revolutionary flavour.

In the twentieth century revolutionary writing about work has been thin on the ground. As noted earlier, there have been plenty of proposals for reforming work within the existing, or a modified, capitalist framework. But getting rid of the idea that at least some of us will have to continue to work for money has found few advocates.

In my *The Future of Work and Leisure* (Parker, 1972) I looked forward to a time when work and leisure would become more integrated and when we should all have 'opportunities for rewarding work and for the various kinds of leisure that complement rewarding work'. Ivar Berg, in a Foreword to the American edition of that book, correctly perceived that my proposals for 'a fusion of leisure and work are related to revolutionary changes in society'. A quarter of a century later, during which time capitalism has strengthened its hold on the world economy and on received wisdom, the revolutionary changes look further away than ever.

Macpherson (1979) rejects the idea that democracy cannot exist without the market system. He argues that

> the ethical principle, or, if you prefer, the appetite for individual freedom, has outgrown its capitalist market envelope and can now live as well or better without it, just as man's productive powers, which grew so enormously with competitive capitalism, are not lost when capitalism abandons free competition or is replaced by some form of socialism.

Another critic, Stormann (1989), believes that 'industrial society is full of meaningless work and purposeless leisure'. To claim that leisure is 'purposeless' is surely to misunderstand its value in its own right, as a part of life that does not need a purpose because it is an end itself, not a means to something else. Stormann does indeed call for a revolution in work: 'Labour must be seen as the avenue by which people discover their true identity, and not as a means of earning the money that allows them to search for this identity in all the wrong places'. But he sees work as in effect subsuming leisure; he answers the question in his article title 'Work: true leisure's home?' in the affirmative.

Although many writers have speculated about the direction leisure may take in the future, very few have made forecasts that deserve the appellation 'revolutionary'. Veal's (1987) book is entirely devoted to leisure and the future: it is fascinating to read about the forecasts that have been made in the past and how few of them have come true. As if to avoid the fate of those forecasters, Veal restricts himself to modest forecast of the 'if . . . then . . .' variety. If economic policies 'eventually bring about an end to recession and a return to full employment . . . leisure time would increase'. If unemployment continues high 'then the argument in favour of policies to share paid work more equitably is surely unassailable', including a consequent better sharing of leisure opportunities and a better distribution of leisure time during the lifespan of individuals through 'flexible life scheduling' (Best, 1980).

Haywood and his colleagues (1989) devote a chapter to 'leisure futures'. They discuss 'leisure fictions', both of the Utopian or socialist variety and the dystopian or authoritarian variety. They look at what three traditions in theories of society and of social change have to offer on the future of leisure. And they are even handed when it comes to choosing optimistic, realistic or pessimistic futures, the choice of which 'depends on a variety of factors including one's personal biography and not least one's understanding of leisure and the nature of society'.

It is left to Kelly (1982) to envisage leisure futures which he believes are revolutionary (he uses the term three times – and the associated adjective 'revolutionary' four times – in his chapter on leisure and the future). Kelly outlines what he takes to be the direction of change in the revolutionary model: 'Conditions of internal conflict recognized → Organization of the powerless → Revolutionary struggle → Replacement of old power structure → Reorganization of social institutions'. Although he allows that the revolutionary model of social change is 'always a possibility', he thinks that 'such change would be so radical and pervasive that predicting the consequences for leisure roles and resources would be an exercise in imaginative construction – intriguing but imprecise'. So he regales us instead with tales of consumerist leisure in a 'technological tomorrow': wall-sized telesensing, satellite vertical-lift stations connecting the major long-distance terminals, 'the home a leisure center and every community a full-service resort'. Technological revolution it may be, but social revolution it is not. Kelly does, however, make one rather wistful comment on what sophisticated machines will not do for us: 'only satisfying relationships with other people will be outside the call of the electronic consoles in every "recreation room"'.

CONCLUSION

We have considered possible work and leisure futures according to whether they are seen to be extensions of the present, returns to the past, to involve small, surface changes or large, fundamental changes. There is no line of demarcation between these approaches: they simply enable us to see where the emphases lie and to help us sort out what kind of work and leisure futures we would like for ourselves, for others and for the shape of the society and world in which we live.

Table 12.1 summarizes the four approaches to the future of work, leisure and the work–leisure relationship that have been discussed in this chapter.

The conservative, or stay-more-or-less-as-we-are, future is the most likely in the short run. It can include some straight-line extrapolations of existing trends: more cars, more service jobs, more computerized leisure, more privatization, a growing gap between rich and poor individuals and nations. But some of those trends cannot continue indefinitely, at least not on a world scale: we would come up against environmental limits and morally repulsive consequences. So we may go either backwards or forwards. If backwards, how far back and how selectively? If forwards, at what pace: slowly and hesitantly or rapidly and decisively?

A close inspection of the futures envisaged to date in the three spheres of work, leisure and the work–leisure relationship leaves me with the conviction that the engine of change is most likely to be first in work, then the work–leisure relationship and only consequentially in leisure. Although recent trends in work have been mostly in the direction of seeking to make labour more productive in its employment relationship with capital, a number of reforms – particularly those directed to workers' roles as consumers of new products and services – may be expected in the short to medium term. In the longer term, the wider question of whether the labour/capital, employment/unemployment system should go on indefinitely may well be raised, if only because it treats people as marketable commodities. Any proposal for revolutionizing work is likely to

Table 12.1 Approaches to the future of work, leisure and the work–leisure relationship

	Conservative	*Reactionary*	*Reformist*	*Revolutionary*
Work	Mostly employment	Pre-industrial arts/crafts	Shorter hours/ better conditions	Production for need, not market
Leisure	Mostly consumerist	Simple pleasures	More choice, more provision	Promotion of communal forms
Work–leisure relationship	Mostly in different worlds[1]	No strong dividing line[2]	Mostly in different worlds[1]	No strong dividing line[2]

Notes
1 Reformists tend to be more imaginative than conservatives about the future of the two worlds.
2 Reactionaries look back to a supposed golden age of integration, revolutionaries look forward to a new age.

contain an element of going back to the past, when individuals were without the sophisticated modern means of exploiting each other and the environment.

In 1976 I wrote that there is a widely held belief that a 'society of leisure' is coming. Two decades later, there is little evidence of that happening. There is scope for change in the way we experience leisure, but most of the projected changes are in the details rather than the fundamentals, the surface rather than the substance. The predictions are for more leisure time, more leisure goods and services – what might be called the expanding market/technological scenario.

Although there are voices in support of a workless future, they are generally not taken seriously, neither should they be. Only by defining leisure in terms of an ingredient in a life and society in which effort and enjoyment, means and ends, contributions given and received, are balanced in a harmonious whole can we rescue leisure from the category of second-class concerns. To paraphrase Seabrook (1988), we should not worry if we miss an episode of *Dallas* when millions in the world are starving.

My remarks should not be taken as dismissive of the importance of leisure. Along with work itself, the work–leisure relationship should be at the centre of our concerns. In the short to medium term we need to insist that leisure is not the means to any work end, but that each interpenetrates the other. Furthermore, both play their part, hopefully a positive one, in other spheres of life and society such as education and the family. The long-term challenge is that the best kind of work should meet and merge with the best kind of leisure.

REFERENCES

Abrams, M. (1980) 'Leisure time use by the elderly and leisure provision for the elderly', in A. Tomlinson (ed.), *Leisure and the Quality of Life*, Eastbourne: Leisure Studies Association.

Applebaum, H. (1992) *The Concept of Work*, Albany: State University of New York Press.

Best, F. (1980) *Flexible Life Scheduling*, New York: Praeger.

De Grazia, S. (1962) *Of Time, Work and Leisure*, Garden City, NY: Anchor Books.

De Man, H. (1929) *Joy in Work*, London: Allen and Unwin.

Dubin, M. (1990) *Futurehype*, Markham, Ontario: Penguin.

Gershuny, J. (1978) *After Industrial Society? The Emerging Self-service Economy*, London: Macmillan.

Glasser, R. (1973) 'Leisure and the search for a satisfying identity', in M. Smith *et al.* (eds), *Leisure and Society in Britain*, London: Allen Lane.

Glasser, R. (1975) 'Leisure policy, identity and work', in J. Haworth and M. Smith (eds), *Work and Leisure*, London: Lepus Books.

Green, E., Hebron, S. and Woodward, D. (1990), *Leisure, What Leisure?*, London: Macmillan.

Handy, C. (1984) *The Future of Work*, Oxford: Basil Blackwell.

Haywood, L., Kew, F. and Bamham, P. (1989) *Understanding Leisure*, London: Hutchinson.

Kelly, J. (1982) *Leisure*, Englewood Cliffs, NJ: Prentice-Hall.

Macpherson, C. (1979) *The Life and Times of Liberal Democracy*, Oxford: Oxford University Press.

Martin, B. and Mason, S. (1982) 'Leisure and work: the choices for 1991 and 2001', in T. Veal *et al.* (eds), *Work and Leisure*, Eastbourne: Leisure Studies Association.

Marx, K. and Engels, F. (1846) *The German Ideology*, Moscow: Progress Publishers (1976 edn).

Morris, W. (1890) *News from Nowhere*, Boston: Roberts Bros.

Neulinger, J. (1990) *The Road to Eden, After All*, Culemborg: Bruno.

Parker, S. (1972) *The Future of Work and Leisure*, London: Paladin.

Parker, S. (1976) *The Sociology of Leisure*, London: Allen and Unwin.

Parker, S. (1983) *Leisure and Work*, London: Allen and Unwin.

Parker, S. (1991) 'A society of work and leisure', *World Leisure and Recreation Journal* 38, 4.

Reid, D. (1995) *Work and Leisure in the 21st Century*, Toronto: Wall and Emerson.

Seabrook J. (1988) *The Leisure Society*, Oxford: Basil Blackwell.

Sherman, B. (1984) 'Leisure versus work', in A. Tomlinson (ed.), *Leisure: Politics, Planning and People*, Eastbourne: Leisure Studies Association.

Stebbins, R. (1992) *Amateurs, Professionals and Serious Leisure*, Montreal: McGill-Queen's University Press.

Stonier, T. (1989) 'Technological change and the future', in F. Coalter (ed.), *Freedom and Constraint: The Paradoxes of Leisure*, London: Routledge.

Stormann, W. (1989) 'Work: true leisure's home?', *Leisure Studies* 8: 1, 25–33.

Veal, A. (1987) *Leisure and the Future*, London: Allen and Unwin.

Zeldin, T. (1995) 'An intimate future of time', *Demos* 5, 35–6.

Appendices

APPENDIX 1: ACCESS TO CATEGORIES OF EXPERIENCE QUESTIONNAIRE

Respondent No: ____

INSTRUCTIONS: We'd like to ask you how you use your time and relate to people. We'd like you to answer some specific questions: they have 'seven point scales' beside them. Please tell us how far you agree or disagree with each statement by checking one of the numbers. The more strongly you disagree the further left your tick should be, the more you agree the further right. If you neither agree or disagree with the statement then your tick will be in the middle.

USE OF TIME

These questions ask about how busy and committed your time is.

Completely disagree						Completely agree

How far do you agree that:

Statement	1	2	3	4	5	6	7	Type
My time is filled with things to do	1	2	3	4	5	6	7	Activity item (+ve)
I very rarely ever need to be punctual	1	2	3	4	5	6	7	Time structure item (−ve)
Much of the day I've got things to do at regular times	1	2	3	4	5	6	7	Time structure item (+ve)
Things I have to do keep me busy most of the day	1	2	3	4	5	6	7	Activity item (+ve)
Time often lies heavy on my hands	1	2	3	4	5	6	7	Activity item (−ve)

SOCIAL CONTACTS

This set of questions asks about
your everyday social contacts

| Completely disagree | | | | | | Completely agree |

How far do you agree that:

Question	1	2	3	4	5	6	7	Item
Most days I meet quite a range of people	1	2	3	4	5	6	7	Social contacts item (+ve)
I sometimes feel that people are looking down on me	1	2	3	4	5	6	7	Status item (−ve)
Society in general respects people like me	1	2	3	4	5	6	7	Status item (+ve)
I don't get to meet many people regularly	1	2	3	4	5	6	7	Social contacts item (−ve)
I see a lot of my friends or workmates	1	2	3	4	5	6	7	Social contacts item (+ve)
People often rely on me to turn up at the right time	1	2	3	4	5	6	7	Time structure item (+ve)

THE WIDER SOCIETY

This last set of questions asks about
your relations with the wider society.

| Completely disagree | | | | | | Completely agree |

How far do you agree that:

Question	1	2	3	4	5	6	7	Item
I'm doing things that need doing by someone	1	2	3	4	5	6	7	Collective purpose item (+ve)
Sometimes I feel like I'm on the scrapheap	1	2	3	4	5	6	7	Status item (−ve)
At this time in my life I feel I'm making a positive contribution to society at large	1	2	3	4	5	6	7	Collective purpose item (+ve)
Nothing I'm involved in has much value for many other people	1	2	3	4	5	6	7	Collective purpose item (−ve)

APPENDIX 2: LIFE SATISFACTION AND AFFECTIVE WELL-BEING QUESTIONNAIRES

A Life Satisfaction Questionnaire

Based on Warr, Cook and Wall (1979), this is a twelve-item measure scored on a seven-point scale (1 = extremely dissatisfied, 7 = extremely satisfied). A combination of the first 11 questions gives a measure of Total Life Satisfaction; question 12 gives a measure of Overall Life Satisfaction.

SATISFACTION

Instructions: Please consider the following aspects of your life as they seem to you at the moment. Please indicate for each one how satisfied you feel about them by putting a tick in the appropriate box.

	Extremely dissatisfied	Very dissatisfied	Moderately dissatisfied	Not sure	Moderately satisfied	Very satisfied	Extremely satisfied
How satisfied do you feel about:							
1. The house or flat in which you live.							
2. The local district in which you live.							
3. Your standard of living: the things you can do or buy.							
4. The way you spend your leisure time.							
5. Your present state of health.							
6. The education that you have received.							
7. What you are accomplishing in life.							
8. What the future seems to hold for you.							
9. Your social life.							
10. Your family life.							
11. The present government.							
12. Taking everything together your life as a whole these days.							

B Affective Well-being Questionnaire

This questionnaire, developed by Warr (1989, 1990a, 1990b), measures three axes of mental health proposed by Warr (1987). The three axes are 'pleasure', 'anxiety–contentment' and 'depression–enthusiasm'. The questionnaire can be administered separately for work and leisure.

Axis 1 (Pleasure)   measured by Question 1A–C on a five-point scale (e.g. 1 = I do not enjoy, 5 = I really enjoy). Question 1 measures enjoyment, satisfaction and happiness and these are scored both separately and as an overall mean score of pleasure.

Axis 2 (Anxiety–contentment) and Axis 3 (Depression–enthusiasm)   measured by Question 2A–L. Each axis is measured by three positive and three negative (reverse scored) mood states on a six-point scale (1 = never, 6 = all of the time). A mean score for each axis is obtained.

The mood states are categorized in the following way:

Axis 2 (Anxiety–contentment)

Positive	–	2C	Calm
		2I	Contented
		2K	Relaxed
Negative	–	2A	Tense (R)
		2E	Worried (R)
		2H	Uneasy (R)

Axis 3 (Depression–enthusiasm)

Positive	–	2D	Cheerful
		2G	Enthusiastic
		2L	Optimistic
Negative	–	2B	Depressed (R)
		2F	Gloomy (R)
		2J	Miserable (R)

AFFECTIVE WELL-BEING: WORK LIFE

These questions ask about the way you feel about your work life. Think about how your work life has been in the past few weeks and tick the most appropriate statements.

1. Taking all things together, how do you feel about your work life?

A. I really enjoy my work life and could not enjoy it more. _____
   I enjoy it very much. _____
   I enjoy it quite a lot. _____
   I just about enjoy it. _____
   I do not enjoy it. _____

B. I am extremely satisfied with my work life and could not be more satisfied. _____
   I am very satisfied. _____
   I am quite satisfied. _____
   I am just about satisfied. _____
   I am not at all satisfied. _____

C. I am extremely happy in my work life and could not be happier. _____
   I am very happy. _____
   I am quite happy. _____
   I am just about happy. _____
   I am not at all happy. _____

2. Please indicate how often during the past few weeks you have felt each of the following emotional states while you have been at work. Place a tick in the appropriate box for each of the emotional states.

	Never	Occasionally	Some of the time	Much of the time	Most of the time	All of the time
A. Tense						
B. Depressed						
C. Calm						
D. Cheerful						
E. Worried						
F. Gloomy						
G. Enthusiastic						
H. Uneasy						
I. Contented						
J. Miserable						
K. Relaxed						
L. Optimistic						

APPENDIX 3: PRINCIPAL ENVIRONMENTAL INFLUENCE (PEI) QUESTIONNAIRE

The nine principal environmental influences (PEIs) proposed by Warr (1987) as important for mental health can be divided into two 'context-free' PEIs ('money' and 'physical security') and seven PEIs which can be measured for specific contexts, such as work and leisure.

The PEI 'money' is measured by three context-free questions concerning the person's feelings about their financial situation. Q1 is scored 'Very easy = 5, to 'Very difficult' = 1; Q2 is scored 'Very often' = 1, to 'Never' = 5; Q3 is scored 'Very often' = 1, to 'Never' = 5. A high mean score of the three questions represents a lack of immediate problems with money and a low score indicates immediate problems.

YOUR FINANCE

How easy or difficult it is to manage on the money that you receive? (Please tick one.)

Very easy	☐
Fairly easy	☐
Uncertain	☐
Fairly difficult	☐
Very difficult	☐

Do you find that a shortage of money stops you engaging in activities? (Please tick one.)

Very often	☐
Quite often	☐
Uncertain	☐
Very rarely	☐
Never	☐

Do you ever feel that you have to refuse invitations from your friends through not having enough money? (Please tick one).

Very often	☐
Quite often	☐
Uncertain	☐
Very occasionally	☐
Never	☐

The PEI 'physical security' is measured by three context-free questions concerning the person's feelings about their environment. A high mean score indicates lack of problems. Q1 is concerned with three physical features which may cause difficulties in concentrating. A mean is calculated from the three components and reverse scored for analysis. For example, if the mean was 3, then it would be scored as 5. Q2 concerned with 'threats' is also reverse scored. Q3 concerned with 'safety' is not reverse scored. An overall mean is calculated from the three questions.

YOUR ENVIRONMENT

Do you ever experience difficulty in concentrating (e.g. when doing a task) due to any of the following? (Please circle the appropriate number from 1 to 7.)

	Never				*Very often*		
Discomfort of temperature	1	2	3	4	5	6	7
Too much noise	1	2	3	4	5	6	7
Poor lighting	1	2	3	4	5	6	7

Do you ever feel threatened in some way? (Please circle the appropriate number from 1 to 7.)

Never   *All the time*

1   2   3   4   5   6   7

What sorts of things cause you to feel threatened?

_____

Would you say that the world is, in general, a safe place to live? (Please circle the appropriate number from 1 to 7.)

Extremely unsafe   *Very safe*

1   2   3   4   5   6   7

Context-specific PEIs

A questionnaire concerned with 'use of time', 'social contacts', and 'wider society' is used to measure the seven context-specific PEIs for either time at work or time not at work. Thirty-five questions are concerned with the PEIs. Each question is measured on a seven-point scale (1 = 'Completely disagree', 7 = 'Completely agree'). Some questions are reverse scored, indicated by (R). For example, if the respondent circled 2 then they would score 5. A mean is calculated for each PEI from the component questions. A high score represents access to that PEI. Each PEI can also be divided into sub-components, which can be analysed separately.

The breakdown of the questionnaire is as follows:

Externally generated goals
Intrinsic demands: Q1, Q19 (R), Q20, Q21
Extrinsic demands: Q4, Q8 (R), Q30

Environmental clarity
Intrinsic environmental clarity: Q3, Q38 (R)
Extrinsic environmental clarity: Q31, Q39 (R)

Opportunity for control
Intrinsic control: Q2, Q5
Extrinsic control: Q16 (R), Q29 (R)

Opportunity for skill use
Use of new skills: Q6, Q17 (R)
Use of existing skills: Q7 (R), Q18

Variety
Intrinsic variety: Q9, Q22
Extrinsic variety: Q10, Q23

Opportunity for interpersonal contact
Quantity of contact: Q27 (R), Q24
Quality of contact: Q28, Q32

Valued social position
Personal meaning: Q33, Q35 (R)
Cultural evaluation: Q26, Q36
Sub-cultural evaluation: Q25 (R), Q37 (R)

Instructions

We'd like to ask you how you use your time and relate to people. Please tell us how far you agree or disagree with each statement by circling one of the numbers. The more strongly you disagree the further left your circle should be, the more you agree, the further right. If you neither agree or disagree with the statement then your circle will be in the middle. Please answer the following questions with reference to *when you are at work*.

Use of time

How far do you agree that:

		Completely disagree						Completely agree
1.	My time is filled with things to do.	1	2	3	4	5	6	7
2.	Much of the day, I can choose the way in which I carry out my tasks.	1	2	3	4	5	6	7
3.	In the things I do, I usually know the kind of results I will get.	1	2	3	4	5	6	7
4.	Much of the day I have things to do at regular times.	1	2	3	4	5	6	7
5.	I usually like to plan and organise the way I spend my time.	1	2	3	4	5	6	7
6.	I feel as though I am learning a great deal.	1	2	3	4	5	6	7
7.	I don't really feel that I am 'stretched' in my everyday life.	1	2	3	4	5	6	7
8.	Time often lies heavily on my hands.	1	2	3	4	5	6	7
9.	My life varies greatly from day to day.	1	2	3	4	5	6	7
10.	I am always doing new things and visiting different places.	1	2	3	4	5	6	7
11.	Most things I do, I do well.	1	2	3	4	5	6	7
12.	I sometimes think I am not very competent.	1	2	3	4	5	6	7
13.	I like to set myself challenging targets.	1	2	3	4	5	6	7
14.	Things I have to do keep me busy most of the day.	1	2	3	4	5	6	7
15.	I very rarely need to be punctual.	1	2	3	4	5	6	7
16.	I don't feel I can personally influence aspects of my job, such as wages, hours or company policy.	1	2	3	4	5	6	7
17.	I rarely get the chance to develop new skills at work.	1	2	3	4	5	6	7
18.	I think that I am able to respond to tasks effectively.	1	2	3	4	5	6	7
19.	I rarely have to deal with conflicting demands.	1	2	3	4	5	6	7
20.	My work provides me with many targets/goals which I have to try and achieve.	1	2	3	4	5	6	7
21.	I often have to undertake difficult tasks.	1	2	3	4	5	6	7
22.	I carry out a wide range of duties in an average day.	1	2	3	4	5	6	7
23.	I am able to experience pleasant changes in my work environment during the day.	1	2	3	4	5	6	7

Social contacts

This set of questions asks about your everyday social contacts. How far do you agree that:

		Completely disagree						Completely agree
24.	Most days I meet quite a range of people.	1	2	3	4	5	6	7
25.	I sometimes feel that people are looking down on me.	1	2	3	4	5	6	7
26.	Society in general respects people like me.	1	2	3	4	5	6	7
27.	I don't get to meet many people regularly.	1	2	3	4	5	6	7
28.	I see a lot of my workmates.	1	2	3	4	5	6	7
29.	I have to do what other people want a lot of the time.	1	2	3	4	5	6	7
30.	People often rely on me to turn up at the right time.	1	2	3	4	5	6	7
31.	People often talk things over with me.	1	2	3	4	5	6	7
32.	I have one or more friends who I am close to and share a lot with.	1	2	3	4	5	6	7

The wider society

This last set of questions asks about your relations with the wider society.

How far do you agree that:

		Completely disagree						Completely agree
33.	I am doing things that need doing by somebody.	1	2	3	4	5	6	7
34.	I am not very interested in the world around me.	1	2	3	4	5	6	7
35.	Sometimes I feel like I am on the scrap-heap.	1	2	3	4	5	6	7
36.	At this time in my life I feel that I am making a positive contribution to society at large.	1	2	3	4	5	6	7
37.	Nothing I'm involved in has much value for many people.	1	2	3	4	5	6	7
38.	Sometimes I just can't see where to go next in my life.	1	2	3	4	5	6	7
39.	Sometimes I feel I don't really know what people expect of me.	1	2	3	4	5	6	7
40.	The most important things that happen to me are as much due to luck as to planning.	1	2	3	4	5	6	7
41.	I feel I am pressurized into participating in many of the activities I do.	1	2	3	4	5	6	7

REFERENCES

Warr, P., Cook, J. and Wall, T. (1979) 'Scales for the measurement of some work attitudes and aspects of psychological well-being', *Journal of Occupational Psychology* 52, 129–48.

Warr, P. (1987) *Work, Unemployment and Mental Health*, Oxford: Clarendon Press.

Warr, P. (1989) *The Measurement of Well-being and Other Aspects of Mental Health*, MRC/ESRC Social and Applied Psychology Unit, Memo, Sheffield: University of Sheffield.

Warr, P. (1990a) 'The measurement of well-being and other aspects of mental health', *Journal of Occupational Psychology* 63, 193–210.

Warr, P. (1990b) 'Decision latitude, job demands and employee well-being', *Work and Stress* 4: 4, 285–94.

Index